The Early Danish-Muscovite Treaties, 1493-1523
Texts, Contexts, Diplomacy

The Early Danish-Muscovite Treaties, 1493-1523
Texts, Contexts, Diplomacy

Carsten Pape

AARHUS UNIVERSITY PRESS |

The Early Danish-Muscovite Treaties, 1493-1523
© The Author and Aarhus University Press 2022
Cover: Jørgen Sparre
Layout and typesetting: Ryevad Grafisk
This book is typeset in Minion Pro and printed on 130 g Arctic Volume White
Printed by Narayana Press, Denmark

Printed in Denmark 2022

ISBN 978 87 7219 405 9

Aarhus University Press
aarhusuniversitypress.dk

Published with the financial support of
Aage og Johanne Louis-Hansens Fond

All rights reserved. Except for the quotation of short passages for the purpose of criticism and review, no part of this publication may be reproduced, stored in a retrieval system, or transmitted, in any form or by any means, without the prior permission of the publisher.

International distributors
Oxbow Books Ltd., oxbowbooks.com
ISD, isdistribution.com

/ In accordance with requirements of the Danish Ministry of Higher Education and Science, the certification means that a PhD level peer has made a written assessment justifying this book's scientific quality.

Cover illustration: The first Danish envoy arriving in Moscow in June 1493. The envoy, Hans Claussen, Doctor of Canon Law and Provost of Roskilde Cathedral, is depicted entering the Kremlin with his entourage (right) and appearing before Grand Prince Ivan III in the throne hall (left). In the background, King Hans sends off Claussen. Miniature from the Russian so-called "Illustrated Chronicle Compilation" (Licevoj letopisnyj svod) dating from the third quarter of the 16th century.
Copyright: AKTEON Publishing House, Moscow.

Contents

Acknowledgements   7

Introduction   9
   A Late-Medieval Danish-Muscovite Alliance   9
   Historiography of the Alliance   12
   Purpose and Structure of the Book   14
   Transliteration and Dates   16

1. Acts Constituting the Treaties   19
   European Treaty-making Procedures   19
   Treating with Muscovy   22
   Differences in Intellectual Form   29
   Surviving and Missing Acts   31
   Traces of the Missing Acts   33
   Referencing the Surviving Documents   36

2. The Treaties in Context   39
   East Meets West   39
   A. The Treaty of 1493   46
   First Mission to Moscow   49
   Finalizing the Treaty   54
   The Treaty in Brief   57
   B. The Treaty of 1506   58
   C. The Treaty of 1516   67
   First Step: The Treaty of 1514   67
   The Treaty Annulled   75
   The Treaty Completed   85

3. The Texts   89
   Publication Principles   89
   Note on Translations   90
   A. The Preserved Danish Text of the Treaty of 1493   91
   B. The Preserved Danish Text of the Treaty of 1506   102
   C. The Original Russian Text of the Treaty of 1516   108

4. Reconstructing the Lost Originals — 123
The Uses of Reconstructions — 123
The Feasibility of Reconstruction — 127
The Sources Assessed — 130
A. The Danish Texts — 134
1. King Hans to Ivan III, 1493 — 135
2. King Hans to Vasilij III, 1506 — 138
3. Christian II to Vasilij III, 1514 and 1516 — 142
B. The Russian Texts — 145
1. Ivan III to King Hans, 1493 — 145
2. Vasilij III to King Hans, 1506 — 150
3. Vasilij III to Christian II, 1514 — 153

Epilogue — 155

Appendix: Text Matrix — 159

Bibliography — 171

Index — 185

Acknowledgements

I owe many people my gratitude for their encouragement, comments and advice during the writing of this book on the dry delights of medieval diplomacy. My thanks go first and foremost to my wife Marie, who has been vying with King Hans for my attention ever since we met and never wavered for a moment in her support of the enterprise. Her good-humored spirit and keen intellect were and are a constant source of inspiration and joy.

Prof. Michail Krom, St Petersburg, patiently answered what must have seemed an endless number of questions about the fine details of Russian and Lithuanian history and the status and location of important sources. Michael von Cotta-Schønberg gave generous amounts of time improving my reading of the Latin-language sources, while Markus Hedemann readily supplemented my knowledge of Low German; both helped decipher particularly difficult documents and individual passages in the handwritten sources. It has been a distinct pleasure to make the acquaintance of all three in the course of the project.

Friends and former colleagues from Denmark's Russian Studies community kindly read and commented the book at various stages of its drafting: John H. Lind, Helen Krag, Niels Erik Rosenfeldt, Nils Bjervig and Niels Gottlieb. I am indebted to them and other Slavist friends for their sustained interest in the project and for a friendship that for most reaches back over forty years.

Further, I wish to thank the staffs of the Danish Royal Library, not least Ole Henrik Sørensen for his gentle stewardship of the research reading room, and the Danish National Archives, both in Copenhagen.

Finally, I extend my gratitude to Aage og Johanne Louis-Hansens Fond for its generous support, without which the book would not have seen the light of day.

Naturally, all errors of fact and interpretation are mine.

Hellerup, September 10, 2021.
Carsten Pape

Introduction

A Late-Medieval Danish-Muscovite Alliance

In 1493, King Hans of Denmark and Norway concluded a treaty of alliance and cooperation with Grand Prince Ivan III of Moscow. The agreement united the signatories against Sweden and Lithuania and established a framework for further cooperation in areas such as border regulation, legal protection of each other's subjects, diplomacy and trade. From a historical perspective, the treaty was significant not only for being the founding act of a diplomatic relationship that was to be a lasting feature of the foreign policies of Denmark and Russia for centuries,[1] but, in particular, for belonging to the earliest pacts concluded between the Catholic West and the rising Orthodox state of Ivan III. Only two alliances of a similar kind, one between Ivan and King Matthias Corvinus of Hungary in 1482 and one with the designated German-Roman Emperor Maximilian I of Habsburg in 1490, preceded the treaty of 1493.[2] As these were purely military alliances directed against the Central European Jagiellonian dynasty, the Danish-Muscovite accord was the earliest treaty of alliance *and* cooperation

---

[1] For a collection of articles about the relationship over time, see Christensen and Gottlieb, Danmark og Rusland = Christensen and Gottlieb, Danija i Rossija.

[2] I exclude Catholic Lithuania from the list as the longstanding diplomatic relationship between Vilnius and Moscow did not entail an alliance proper. For the Hungarian alliance, see Karge, Ungarisch-Russische Allianz; Bazilevič, Vnešnjaja politika, pp. 220-5 (2001 ed.). The main sources are in PDS I, cols. 159-73; SIRIO 41, 11, 13, 19, 20. For the alliance with Maximilian, see, e.g., Bazilevič, Vnešnjaja politika, pp. 225-48; Biskup, Rivalität, passim; Fennell, Ivan the Great, pp. 117-31; Forstreuter, Preussen und Russland, passim; Karge, Kaiser Friedrich's III, pp. 259-87; Sach, Hochmeister und Grossfürst, passim; Uebersberger, Österreich, Ch. 1; Wiesflecker, Kaiser Maximilian, Vol. 1, pp. 303-17; Wimmer, Livland, passim. The main sources are in PDS I, cols. 1-115.

concluded between a Muscovite grand prince and a Western monarch.³ By the same token, the making of the treaty, including the negotiated formulation of its text and the diplomatic missions between Copenhagen and Moscow that ensued, belongs to the earliest formative experiences of Muscovite diplomacy vis-à-vis the West and Danish diplomacy vis-à-vis Muscovy.⁴

Apart from the military gains promised by his new European alliances, Ivan III was highly conscious of their symbolic value to his political stature. Dispatching an embassy to Grand Prince Alexander of Lithuania in 1498 to compel the latter to accept his title "Sovereign of all Russia" (*Gospodar' vsea Rusi*), he buttressed his demand by instructing his envoys to "state that emperors and kings write to our sovereign as Sovereign of all Russia; and that [the envoys] have copies of letters written to our sovereign by the Roman Emperor Frederic [III] and his son Maximilian, King of the Romans, and Matthias [Corvinus], King of Hungary, and Hans, King of Denmark. And they shall present the letters. And the title of our sovereign is written in the same manner in the letters of treaty of Maximilian and Matthias and the King of Denmark."⁵

The statement is ironic on two counts. First, Ivan's list of prestigious foreign partners was not particularly impressive and rather served to demonstrate the relative isolation of Muscovy on the European political scene at this stage in its history. Second, of the three alliances claimed by the grand prince, two had foundered long before 1498. Matthias Corvinus had died in 1490, after which

---

3   It is true that the Muscovite-Habsburg treaty of 1490 contained a paragraph on free travel by diplomats and merchants (PDS I, col. 38, and Appendix, items 24 and 25, in this book). The clause, however, is divided in two in the Danish-Muscovite treaties, in which the one on free trade is far more detailed than the 1490 paragraph.

4   It should be stressed that "the West" is not a modern term as used here. Medieval Russians perceived the Catholic world as *Zapad*, the West, in contradistinction to the East of the Orthodox world, with Eden, Jerusalem, etc. (Černaja, Evropa kak Zapad, pp. 5 ff.).

5   SIRIO 35, p. 257. Ivan used the argument again in 1503 (SIRIO 35, p. 381). "King of the Romans" (*Rex Romanorum* was Maximilian's official title as heir apparent to the Imperial throne. He was never officially crowned Emperor but was granted the title "Emperor-elect of the Romans" (*Electus Romanorum Imperator*) by the Pope following an attempt to reach Rome in 1508. There is possibly a reference to some of the Danish letters shown to Alexander or his successor in an inventory of the tsars' archive produced in 1614 which mentions that "a bundle of Danish letters, written using the title tsar [emperor], were brought to Lithuania with Afanasij Vlasev for the [discussion of the] title tsar" (Opisi, p. 83).

the crown of St Stephen had passed to a member of the Jagiellonian dynasty with whom Ivan III had been at war since the mid-1480s.[6] A year later, Maximilian, who had established his Moscow alliance to secure the crown of Hungary for himself, negotiated a favorable settlement of the Hungarian succession and immediately lost interest in his Russian connection.[7] Not until 1514 would he enter into a new treaty with Muscovy, and then only because his envoy to Moscow exceeded his mandate.[8]

By contrast, the Danish-Muscovite treaty of 1493 established an intense diplomatic relationship between the two sovereigns and their immediate successors that was to last for three decades before ebbing out following the deposal of King Christian II of Denmark and Norway – the son and heir of King Hans – in 1523.[9] In the course of these thirty years the parties renewed the treaty twice, in 1506 and 1514-6, and dispatched an astounding fifty-plus diplomatic missions and courier runs between Copenhagen and Moscow.[10] There followed a lull of forty years before contacts were resumed and a new treaty concluded between King Frederik II and Tsar Ivan IV in 1562.[11] In consequence, the early Danish-Muscovite treaties and the diplomacy they engendered constitute a distinct episode in the history of diplomatic relations between the two states, and not only in chronological terms. With one exception in 1514-6, the treaties were practically identical in form and content, not least because their renewals were prompted by the successive deaths of their original signatories rather than by political circumstance. Taken together, they reflect an inner coherence of the episode.

---

6   For the Jagiellonian dynasty, see p. 43 n. 14
7   Bazilevič, Vnešnjaja politika, pp. 225-48; Biskup, Rivalität, passim; Fennell, Ivan the Great, pp. 117-31; Forstreuter, Preussen und Russland, passim; Karge, Kaiser Friedrich's III, pp. 259-87; Sach, Hochmeister und Grossfürst, passim; Uebersberger, Österreich, Ch. 1; Wiesflecker, Kaiser Maximilian, Vol. 1, pp. 303-17; Wimmer, Livland, passim.
8   The Grand Prince had even invited Maximilian to enter an anti-Polish alliance in 1508 (SGGD V, 52). For the 1514 treaty, see pp. 67-83 in this book.
9   True, the correspondence between Vasilij III and Christian II continued until 1528 (Vasilij's last known letter is in Russkie akty, 12), but by then it no longer reflected an ongoing Danish-Muscovite political relationship.
10 See Pape, Comprehensive Register, for a complete list of documented missions.
11 Venge, Københavnertraktaten, pp. 21-27 = Venge, Kopengagenskij traktat, pp. 21-27. The treaty is printed in Russkie akty, 20, and SGGD V, 119.

Historiography of the Alliance

The political and diplomatic rapprochement between Denmark and Muscovy in the closing decades of the Middle Ages is obviously relevant to the study of late-medieval Danish, Russian, Nordic, and Baltic history as well as medieval diplomatic history in general. As stated by Dieter Klose, even if the community of interests between the treaty partners was not always pronounced and frequently absent, the treaty of 1493 was important in the sense that it formed a permanent backdrop for the ever-changing power constellations in the Baltic space. "Through the possibility of jointly influencing and reacting in this play of forces and counterforces, the relationship of the two states acquires historical significance."[12] Klaus Zernack expanded the notion by writing, without specifically referring to the Danish connection, that the rising Muscovite state to a certain degree acted as an "internal crystallization point" of the political thinking and acting in this peripheral region of Europe.[13] Sweden, in particular, is testimony to the validity of these observations, as its late-medieval foreign and domestic policies cannot be properly understood without reference to the Danish-Muscovite alliance of 1493. Choroškevič, for one, spoke about a Danish-Swedish-Russian triangular relationship of which the Danish-Swedish and Swedish-Russian edges were both antagonistic.[14]

Yet the alliance is surprisingly under-illuminated and under-appreciated in the historiography of the region. The treaty of 1493 is referred to in many, but far from all, standard national and foreign policy histories of Denmark, Sweden, Russia and other Baltic actors, though only in passing and mostly without

---

12 "Durch die Möglichkeit gemeinsames Einwirkens und Reagierens in diesem Spiel der Kräfte und Gegenkräfte erhält das Verhältnis dieser beiden Staaten zueinander eine historische Bedeutung" (Klose, Dänemark, p. 1).
13 "[…] dass das eben gefestigte und aufstrebende Moskauer Zartum die politischen Energien der anderen Ostseeanlieger besonders intensiv auf sich zog und dadurch zum gewissermassen internen Kristallisationspunkt des politischen Denkens und Handelns in dieser Randzone Europas wurde" (Zernack, Handelsbeziehungen, p. 118).
14 Choroškevič, Russkoe gosudarstvo, p. 139.

proper contextualization.¹⁵ Works focusing on the late-medieval history of the region or more narrowly on the Danish-Muscovite relationship may elaborate somewhat on the contents and context of the treaty, but not very extensively.¹⁶ The preserved text of the Danish treaty diploma has been published fairly widely (pp. 100–1), but the subsequent treaties have received only scant attention and mostly been treated independently of one another, if referred to at all.¹⁷ Only three historians have to my knowledge been aware that there was a botched treaty-making process in 1514-6, a fact which confused others.¹⁸ In general,

---

15   See, e.g., Huitfeldt, Kong Hans, pp. 109-10; Olaus Petri, p. 328; Heise, Danmarks Riges Historie, p. 50; Schultz Danmarkshistorie, II, pp. 317-8; Arup, II, 1932, p. 290; Albrechtsen, Danmark Norge, I, p. 264; Christensen and Rasmussen, Politikens Ruslandshistorie, p. 116; Danstrup, Politikens Danmarkshistorie, V, p. 101; Andersen, Den danske kirkes historie, III, pp. 65-6; Karamzin, VI, pp. 228 ff.; Solov'ev, Istorija, Vol. 1, col. 1485; Bazilevič, Vnešnjaja politika, pp. 334-5; Borisov, Ivan III, pp. 480-81; Alekseev, Istorija, p. 699; Ignat'ev, Istorija vnešnej politiki, pp. 119-20; Nitsche, Mongolenzeit, p. 656, et al.

16   See, e.g. Paludan-Müller, De første konger, p. 158-9; Jahn, Danmarks politisk-militaere historie, pp. 358-61; Klose, Dänemark, pp. 1-35; Pape, In fraternitate; Venge, Københavner-traktaten, pp. 10-15 = Venge, Kopengagenskij, pp. 10-17; Rasmussen, Historie og diplomati, pp. 11-2; Westergaard, Denmark, Russia, pp. 131-4; Kraft, Sveriges Historia III/2, p. 241; Hagnell, Sturekrönikan, pp. 319 f.; Tiberg, Moscow, Livonia and the Hanseatic League, pp. 67 f.; Grey, Ivan III, pp. 96-9; Fennell, Ivan the Great, pp. 166-9; Šaskol'skij, Ėkonomičeskie svjazi, pp. 16-7; Kazakova, Russko-datskie torgovye otnošenija, pp. 89-92, 102; Kazakova, Danija, Rossija i Livonija, pp. 108-12; Choroškevič, Russkoe gosudarstvo, pp. 139-41; Forsten, Bor'ba, pp. 153-55; Zimin, Rossija na rubeže, pp. 101, 105.

17   Exceptions include Kazakova (Russko-datskie torgovye otnošenija, passim, and Danija, Rossija i Livonija, passim) and Šaskol'skij (Ėkonomičeskie svjazi, pp. 17-20), both of which include all three treaties in their studies of the economic relations between Denmark and Muscovy in the period under consideration. Choroškevič mentions the treaties in the chronological context of her general narrative but does not catch the continuity between them. Her treatment of the making of the treaty of 1516 in particular is quite flawed (Russkoe gosudarstvo, pp. 140-2, 150-51, 155-57). The same is true of Ignat'ev, Istorija vnešnej politiki, p. 120. Tiberg briefly mentions the three accords (Moscow, Livonia and the Hanseatic League, p. 18) and discusses the treaty-making of 1514-16 in some depth (pp. 154-60).

18   Uebersberger, Österreich, pp. 89-90; Selnes, König Christian II, p. 307; Tiberg, Moscow, Livonia and Hanseatic League, pp. 156-57. Among those who were confused by the chronological gap between the Danish draft of 1514 and the Russian original of 1516 (see pp. 67–85) were Grönblad (Grönblad, Nya källor, pp. 618, 651) and Allen (Allen II, pp. 153-54).

no scholar has offered a comprehensive study of any of the treaties concerning their substantive content and the contexts in which they came into being. Nor has anyone examined the number, form and legal status of the acts constituting the treaties, the languages in which they were written, their conformity or lack of conformity with typical European diplomatic acts, the relationship between perished and preserved treaty texts, or any other relevant topics. In short, the treaties have been used only sparingly as the potential sources they are for the study of early Danish-Muscovite relations and their wider Baltic and European contexts and consequences.

There are surely multiple reasons for this curious lacuna. One will be the state of the source base. As will be detailed in the following chapters, only three documents containing the texts of the three treaties with some level of authenticity have survived to the present day. Of these, two are secondary, though contemporaneous, copies of the Danish acts of 1493 and 1506, both in Latin, while the third is the original Russian letter of treaty of 1516. Furthermore, the three documents have been published unsystematically – no volume includes them all – and in dated editions not quite living up to modern publication standards. To give just one example, the only existing publication of the Russian diploma of 1516 leaves out the titles of the signatories, presumably to save space or because the publisher deemed them unimportant (obviously, they are not).[19]

Another reason will be language. The treaties and the variety of surviving historical sources relevant for their study are written in late-medieval Latin, Russian, High and Low German, Danish, Swedish, English and French, and this naturally limits the access of many historians to the full documentary record.

Purpose and Structure of the Book

The present volume is intended to remedy this deplorable state of affairs by providing a solid and accessible textual base for further study of the treaties in tandem with an introduction to the political and diplomatic contexts in which they came into existence.

---

19   Russkie akty, 8.

I begin, in Chapter 1, by analyzing the material form of the original treaties in order to establish the exact number and types of acts which together constituted them. This is a prerequisite for detailing the full treaty-making process and relating the surviving documents to it. In addition, I survey the traces left by the missing treaty acts in extant sources of the period.

In Chapter 2 I place the treaties, treaty-making processes and surviving documents in their proper historical context by detailing the course of events leading to the conclusion of each of the accords in 1493, 1506 and 1514-6. As this is largely *terra incognita* in the historiography of the region, the narrative provides a certain amount of minute information – the dates and routes of individual diplomatic missions, the names and status of participating envoys, etc. – that would normally be left out in a study of this kind. I include the details to provide "hooks" for integrating the history of the early Danish-Muscovite relationship with the full historical record of the time. Also, I am writing with a Danish-, Russian-, general- and diplomatic-history readership in mind, and these will not necessarily be interested in identical types of information. What is excessive or redundant to one set of readers may be of prime value to another.

In Chapter 3 I publish the surviving texts in a new, critical reading, adding English translations and accompanying commentary.

Further, in Chapter 4 I restore or reconstruct the lost original treaty texts as fully as possible based on the surviving documents and some related evidence. This is doubtlessly controversial, though not entirely unprecedented in modern historiography,[20] but I shall argue in detail that the endeavor is not only relevant for the further study of the treaties, but also feasible in this particular case.

Finally, following a short Epilogue, the Appendix presents a horizontally aligned matrix of the three surviving texts serving as a quick reference point for the comparative analyses developed throughout the book. For reasons explained in Chapter 4, the matrix includes certain sections of Ivan III's treaty of 1490 with the future emperor Maximilian.

I stress that the book is a reasoned presentation of the surviving texts, not an interpretation of them. Likewise, its narrative parts focus on the treaty-making processes *per se*, not on the effects of the treaties on actors and events in

---

20   For a recent example, see Lobin, Poslanie gosudarja. Lobin reconstructs the lost Russian version of an extant document written in Latin, which is taking reconstruction much farther than in the present book.

the periods between their making. These topics will have to be addressed in a different context.

Transliteration and Dates

I use the term "Muscovy" instead of "Russia" to stress that the book is about Denmark's treaties with the late-medieval Moscow-based Russian political entity ruled by Ivan III and his descendants, not about treaties concluded by earlier Danish kings with individual Russian princes.[21] Incidentally, contemporaneous Europeans used both terms about the early Moscow state.[22]

Whenever I quote sources and literature in Russian, Latin, German or other languages, I provide translations in English. When citing or publishing Russian text at length, I use the Cyrillic alphabet, but when integrating Russian words, formulae and shorter snippets of text into the main narrative, and when listing Russian works in the bibliography, I transliterate the Cyrillic letters into Latin script using the following equivalents:[23]

ж = ž	х = ch	ш = š	ю = ju	ь = ʼ
з = z	ц = c	щ = šč	я = ja	ъ = ʺ
й = j	ч = č	э = è	ы = y	

All other letters are transliterated using their direct Latin equivalents, e.g. и = i, п = p, etc. This system appears to me to transmit the Russian originals more precisely than the standard English transliterations.

---

21 See, e.g., Lind, Den dansk-russiske traktat 1302, passim (in particular note 5); Lind, De russiske ægteskaber, passim.

22 For example, Italian writers of the period would refer to the Muscovite grand prince as both "re di le Russia" and "il ducha di Moscovia" (Kudrjavcev, Kayser vnnd herscher, p. 46).

23 This transliteration is known as the Scando-Slavica system after the eponymous Scandinavian journal. The only non-intuitive transliteration (unless one knows Polish) is ц = c. To English language speakers, the й = j will appear unusual in the final position of words, for instance in the name Vasilij III.

Medieval Russia used the Byzantine calendar, which was identical to the Julian calendar in terms of dates and months, including the names of the months,[24] but different in two important respects. Byzantium measured time from the creation of the world (*ab origine mundi*, in Russian *ot sotvorenija mira*), which was thought to have taken place 5508 years before the birth of Christ; and the Byzantine year began on September 1, meaning that it was offset in relation to the Julian calendar year which in itself began on different dates in Europe according to region and time period.[25] In Denmark, the year had begun on January 1 since the early 14th century.[26] This means, to give an example, that the year 7000 AM (Anno Mundi) in Russia corresponded to the period September 1, 1491, through August 31, 1492 AD (Anno Domini) in Denmark.

---

24 The Gregorian calendar was not introduced in the West until 1582, and then only gradually.
25 Čerepnin, Russkaja chronologija, pp. 24-9; Bauer, Calender, pp. 103-11. The old Russian calendar year could also begin in March, but from 1492 at the latest September became standard in Russia (Čerepnin, p. 27). In Europe, the most typical dates would be December 25 and March 25.
26 Bauer, Calender, p. 105.

Они же пришеше попиноу, и приидоша от великаго князя Александра ли то писка и целованию на докончалны грамотах, и разоимаша грамоты докончалные про ме
жи се
бя

1. Acts Constituting the Treaties

In a purely material sense, treaties are made up of several physical instruments negotiated, issued, validated, and exchanged in accordance with diplomatic custom and mutually recognized diplomatic procedures and legal norms. The exact number and types of acts have varied over time and across regions as a reflection of historically determined fluctuations in the political, religious and diplomatic cultures of the signatories. Consequently, to properly analyze, contextualize and restore the early Danish-Muscovite treaties, we must first determine their specific material form.

European Treaty-making Procedures

European treaties of the high and late Middle Ages were normally concluded in a two-stage process referred to as the "indirect" or "composite" treaty-making procedure in much of the legal-historical and diplomatic literature.[1] In the first

◄ **Finalizing a treaty with Muscovy**
The image illustrates the final stages of the making of a Muscovite-Lithuanian treaty (see pp. 25–9). In the foreground, Russian envoys present Grand Prince Alexander of Lithuania with Grand Prince Ivan III of Moscow's original letter of treaty issued at the conclusion of the preceding negotiations in Moscow. Alexander is about to validate the treaty by "kissing the cross" on Ivan's letter and his own corresponding diploma, both placed on a shrouded vessel with a cross on top. In the background, the diplomas are exchanged beween Alexander (seated left) and the Russian envoys (right).
Miniature from the "Illustrated Chronicle Compilation" (*Licevoj Letopisnyj Svod*). Copyright: AKTEON Publishing House, Moscow.

---

[1] Bittner, Lehre, p. 6 ("zusammengesetzte [mittelbare] Beurkundungsverfahren"); Neitmann, Staatsverträge, pp. 148 ff. ("Zusammengesetztes Vertragsschliessungsverfahren"); Lesaffer, Medieval Canon Law, p. 192; Lesaffer, Three Peace Treaties, p. 47.

stage, representatives of the treaty competent parties – for convenience labelled princes in the following – convened, negotiated and concluded an agreement which was subsequently codified in two basically identical reciprocal acts, one for each party to the other.[2] The envoys issued the acts on behalf of their princes, but in their own names and under their own seals and signatures, meaning that they were legal subjects in the treaty-making process.[3] Apart from their formulaic and substantive content, the acts included a statement promising subsequent ratification of the agreement by the princes. The latter had provided their negotiators in advance with full powers (*plena potestas*) to work out the given treaty and were bound to comply with its substantive provisions unless the envoys exceeded their mandates in the negotiations.[4]

In the second stage of the process, the princes issued letters of ratification to each other. The letters typically cited the agreement reached by the negotiators either verbatim or in summary before concluding with a ratification formula.[5] Consequently, the full documentary assembly of a standard medieval treaty consisted of four fully validated documents, or two sets of basically identical

---

2   Of course, many treaties also included different obligations of the signatories to each other. Bittner names these documents "Unterhändlerurkunden" (negotiators' diplomas: Bittner, Lehre, p. 6), Gasiorowski and others "Vorurkunden" or "Präliminärurkunden" (preliminary diplomas: Gasiorowski, Friedensvertragsurkunden, p. 161). The reason the negotiators' agreements were issued in this formal form was a need to nail down their terms early on due to the time it would often take rulers to ratify them (Neitmann, Staatsverträge, p. 228).

3   Neitmann, Staatsverträge, p. 148; Picard, Gesandschaftswesen, p. 71-2; According to Queller, "*Plena potestas* [full powers, see below] transformed the medieval diplomat who received it from a mere messenger into an agent with authority to bind his principal" (Office of Ambassador, p. ix). Certain authors maintain the opposite point of view or take up a middling position. Mattingly, for example, claims that "full powers" were only conferred in less important diplomatic matters, not in the case of "really major treaties" where the prince wished to see the result of the negotiations before accepting or rejecting it (Renaissance Diplomacy, p. 40). Few authors will agree with this point of view, however.

4   Neitmann, Staatsverträge, pp. 148, 244, 249; Nicholson, Evolution, pp. 40-1. Queller asserts that ratification was not mandatory if the negotiators were fully empowered, but his point of view seems not to be commonly accepted, as he himself acknowledges (Office of Ambassador, pp. 212-13).

5   Lesaffer, Peace Treaties from Lodi, p. 22; Meron, Authority, pp. 6-7. The ratifications are sometimes called "Haupturkunden" (main diplomas) in the literature (Gasiorowski, Friedensvertragsurkunden, p. 162).

acts, viz. those of the negotiators and those of the princes. The treaty formally took effect the moment the letters of ratification were exchanged.[6]

It should be noted in passing that the chanceries of the treaty-making princes normally made copies of their outgoing diplomas for filing in their own archives before transmitting them to the receiving princes. In this book I label such transcripts *chancery copies*. Further, the chanceries could well make additional transcripts of the chancery copies for a variety of purposes, including the drafting of subsequent treaties. This is important for correctly interpreting the status of the surviving documents of the Danish-Muscovite treaties.

In addition to the acts mentioned above, several scholars include the negotiators' mandates or powers as issued by their princes in the full treaty complex.[7] It seems to me, though, that even if these acts were an indispensable part of the treaty-making *process* they need not be considered part of its *product*, i.e. legal instruments on a par with those constituting the treaty in a narrow juridical sense.

In the real world of diplomacy, the standard procedure outlined above could be modified in a variety of ways and generate fewer or further legally binding acts.[8] If, for instance, negotiations were conducted in the presence of one of the contracting princes, treaties could consist of the foreign envoys' initial letter and the present prince's original act, plus the absent prince's subsequent letter of ratification. Additionally, a variety of domestic and foreign dignitaries,

---

6   Bittner, Lehre, p. 6; Neitmann, Staatsverträge, pp. 221, 244, 249; Metzig, Kommunikation, p. 96. For Muscovy, this point can be inferred from the account of the 1494 peace and marriage negotiations with Lithuania described below pp. 25–9 (SIRIO 35, 24, p. 134, section XVIII).

7   Bittner, Lehre, p. 6; Neitmann, Staatsverträge, p. 148; Jørgensen, Traktatformalia, p. 20; Lesaffer, Medieval Canon Law, p. 192. The argument is supported by modern practice. According to the UN's *Vienna Convention of the Law of Treaties* (1969), Article 77, 1 (a), the functions of a depositary of treaties comprise "keeping custody of the original text of the treaty and of any full powers delivered to the depositary" (https://legal.un-.org/ilc/texts/instruments/english/conventions/1_1_1969.pdf. Accessed 09.08.2021).

8   Neitmann, Staatsverträge, pp. 219-26.

up to and including emperor and pope, could issue letters of accession to or approbation of a treaty.[9]

The alternative to the "indirect" or "composite" approach was the so-called "immediate" or "simple" treaty-making procedure,[10] which would largely have been abandoned by the later Middle Ages, at least among the greater powers.[11] According to this model, the princes met and negotiated the agreement in person and subsequently issued reciprocal letters of treaty to each other, i.e. two acts in total.[12] More rarely, a joint letter of treaty was issued.[13] This ideal kind of direct diplomacy would frequently be substituted by a procedure whereby one prince negotiated the terms of treaty with representatives of the other and transmitted his validated act to the addressee, who would then issue and return his corresponding act; or the treaty was concluded by envoys of both princes, this process eventually sliding into the indirect procedure described above. The importance of the method lay not so much in the type of diplomatic process leading to the agreement as in the fact that the final treaty complex consisted of the acts of the two princes to each other and nothing else.[14] For this reason, the procedure did not entail ratification.

Treating with Muscovy

When diplomatic relations were first established between the Catholic West and Muscovy in the final quarter of the 15th century, Grand Princes Ivan III

---

9   See Neitmann, Staatsverträge, pp. 220 ff. for details. A good example of this kind of process is the Danish-English treaty of 1490, which was negotiated in Copenhagen. At the conclusion of the negotiations, King Hans issued his final letter to Henry VII while the English diplomats issued their act under their own names, promising subsequent ratification by their sovereign. King Hans' letter is printed in Rymer XII, pp. 381-7, the English envoys', issued on the same day, in Repertorium Diplomaticum II/4, 6667, and Henry VII's ratification in Repertorium Diplomaticum II/4, 6719.

10 Bittner, Lehre, p. 5 ("einfache, unmittelbare Beurkundung"); Neitmann, Staatsverträge, pp. 137-9, 219 ("Unmittelbares Vertragsschliessungsverfahren"); Lesaffer, Medieval Canon Law, p. 192.

11 Nicholson, Evolution of Diplomatic Method, pp. 42-43, offers some of the reasons why.

12 Lesaffer, Peace Treaties from Lodi, p. 22; Neitmann, Staatsverträge, p. 139.

13 Bittner, Lehre, pp. 4-5; Gasiorowski, Friedensvertragsurkunden, p. 161.

14 Neitmann, Staatsverträge, pp. 139-40.

(1462-1505) and Vasilij III (1505-33) would dictate a treaty-making procedure to their would-be partners resembling the direct or simple process described above, specifically the version in which the sovereign of one side – in this case the Muscovite grand prince – negotiated the terms of treaty with empowered envoys of the other. Negotiations would always take place in Moscow, not at the court of the prospective partner, and the resulting treaties would consist of only two acts, viz. the treaty diploma issued by each of the princes to the other.

In contrast to European diplomatic practice, according to which all treaty acts were normally formulated in one and the same language, be it Latin, German, French, Danish, English, etc., the grand princes would insist on issuing their letters of treaty in Russian while at the same time accepting corresponding letters written in the preferred language of their treaty partners, *in casu* Latin in the Danish case and German in the treaties with Maximilian.[15] In consequence, whenever historians refer to a given treaty with Muscovy, it should be kept in mind that it consisted of two differently worded texts purporting to express the same content and that, strictly speaking, there was no such thing as "the" treaty text. This, too, is important to the analyses following below.

Furthermore, the Muscovite rulers insisted on following a specific procedure of issuing and validating the relevant diplomas. Once an agreement had been reached in Moscow, the grand prince would draw up his original *dokončal'naja gramota*,[16] or *letter of treaty*, as I label this particular act throughout the book, written on parchment and sealed with his pendant golden bull. Simultaneously,

---

15 In time, the Russians would also attach translations into Latin of their letters. The Danish National Archives holds three examples from 1514 and 1515 (TKUA, Rusland: Akter og dokumenter vedrørende det politiske forhold til Rusland, l.nr. 73-13, 1493-1578).

16 *Dokončal'naja gramota* was the standard Russian technical term for the diploma issued by either treaty partner to the other when concluding a treaty. It derives from the verb *končat'*, literally "to finish" or "to end" like in modern German "schliessen", Medieval Low German "endigen" (Hanserecesse III/2, p. 118) and Danish "(af)slutte" when used about treaties, agreements and contracts. For the same reason, an "agreement" was sometimes called a *konec* (e.g. SIRIO 35, pp. 120, 121, 122). In treaties with the West (e.g. PDS I, col. 38), the Russians at times used the term *gramota utverženaja* instead, i.e. a "confirmed letter" (from *tverdyj*, hard or firm), a term they would later translate into *litterae roboratae* or *litterae fortificatae* in Latin when referring to their own letters of treaty (e.g. Kopengagenskie akty, p. 9; Grönblad, Nya källor, 149).

the foreign envoy would have a reciprocal version of the agreement written out in his language of choice and seal it with his own seal. Both documents would then be read aloud, placed on a shrouded silver vessel with a cross on top, and validated by the grand prince and the envoy each kissing the cross.[17] No signing of the documents would take place. The envoy would subsequently return home carrying the original grand princely letter of treaty to his sovereign accompanied by a Russian embassy bringing his, the envoy's, act with them. Having received the documents, the foreign prince would produce his own original letter by copying the text of his envoy's act word for word, seal it, cross-kiss both originals in the presence of the Muscovite delegation, and exchange them. Following this, the Russians would bring the foreign prince's diploma back to the grand prince in Moscow.[18]

Although this procedure generated three fully validated acts, the treaty complex *per se*, as perceived by contemporaries, consisted of only two, viz. the letters of treaty issued by the rulers to one another. The act issued by the oreign envoy in Moscow was understood as a preliminary incarnation of his sovereign's subsequently transmitted diploma and consequently had no legal existence in and of itself. I label it the envoy's *preliminary letter of treaty*. As this point is not well understood by most historians, but important to a cor-

---

17 For a concrete example, see the Moscow chancery's account of the Muscovite-Lithuanian peace negotiations in early 1494 in SIRIO 35, 24, pp. 124-5 (described below). On this occasion, Grand Prince Ivan III made a short speech announcing his intention to observe the treaty ("and we kiss the cross to him [Alexander] on these letters and wish to observe vis-à-vis him what is written in them") without actually swearing an oath on it. His treaty partner, Grand Prince Alexander of Lithuania, having received Ivan's original diploma in Vilnius and issued his own corresponding letter, swore a formal oath on the treaty in connection with the cross-kissing: "I swear to God and God's Mother on this holy cross" [to observe the treaty] (SIRIO 35, 25, p. 142). The difference in approach reflected a cultural difference: Russian grand princes never swore oaths on treaties – the cross-kissing sufficed in terms of binding the issuer to keeping the terms – whereas Catholic rulers did (Juzefovič, Kak v posol'skich, p. 178). In the Russian context, the kissing of the cross, *krestocelovanie*, was a particularly powerful oath. On its origins and meaning, see Mikhailova and Prestel, Cross Kissing, passim, and Juzefovič, Kak v posol'skich, pp. 172-80.

18 SIRIO 35, 25, pp. 140–1.

Grand Princes Ivan III and Vasilij III
No contemporaneous portraits of Ivan III and Vasilij III exist, nor were any most likely made. The images shown here, reflecting Western curiosity about Muscovy in the Age of Discovery, are the most frequently used in the literature. The likeness of Ivan (left) appeared in the Frenchman André Thevet's La Cosmographie Universelle published in Paris in 1575, while the image of Vasilij was first used in the 1556 Basel edition of Sigismund von Herberstein's famous account of Muscovy, Rerum Moscoviticarum Commentarii.

rect understanding of the documents involved in the process of treating with Muscovy, I shall substantiate it in some detail.[19]

The accounts of the Russian-Lithuanian peace negotiations in Moscow in 1494 and truce negotiations in 1503 entered into a Muscovite "embassy book"

---

19   The sources referred to in the following are summarized and discussed in Croskey, Muscovite Diplomatic Practice, Ch. 4.

concerning relations with Lithuania are particularly instructive in this respect.[20] According to its own wording, the act drawn up by the Lithuanian envoys at the conclusion of the negotiations in 1494 was issued by Grand Prince Alexander of Lithuania, not the envoys, as would have been the case under the typical Western treaty-making regime.[21] Indeed, the act is described in the accounts as "Grand Prince Alexander's word" (*velikogo knjazja Aleksandrovo slovo*),[22] paralleling the description of Ivan III's original letter of treaty to Alexander as "the Grand Prince's letter of treaty, his word" (*se gramota velikogo knjazja dokončal'naja, ego slovo*).[23] In a parallel example from the Danish-Muscovite relationship, when the treaty of 1493 was renewed for a second time in 1514 (pp. 67–85), Grand Prince Vasilij III in the oration of his ambassadors to King Christian II in Copenhagen referred to the preliminary letter issued, sealed and cross-kissed by the Danish envoy in Moscow as "*your* [Christian's] letter" and "the letter of *yours* which shall be with us," i.e. as the original letter of the Danish king which would *eventually* be received and filed in Moscow.[24]

---

20 SIRIO 35, 24. In brief, the embassy books constituted the foreign policy archive of the grand princely administration. They were chronologically organized collections of written accounts detailing individual diplomatic proceedings, e.g. negotiations carried out in Moscow, interspersed with copies of relevant original documents – instructions, letters of credence, missives to foreign authorities, reports from envoys abroad, ambassadorial orations, full treaty texts, etc. – pertaining to Muscovite diplomatic relations with a particular country or Tatar horde over a certain period of time. The materials were stitched into "quartos" (*tetradi*, four folios each folded once) which were subsequently, but not systematically, stitched and sometimes bound into books (*knigi*). See Rogožin, Posol'skie knigi, pp. 121, 147-8, 170-1. In my translation of the term, I take for granted that the adjective *posol'skaja* derives not from *posol* (envoy, ambassador), but from *posol'stvo* (embassy, in the sense of a separate diplomatic mission, not a permanent residence).

21 SIRIO 35, 24, pp. 129-33. The diploma issued by Alexander's envoys in 1503 was left out of the account by the editor of the publication (except for a procedural postscript), but it would have mirrored Ivan III's letter and thus been issued by Alexander (ibid., 75, pp. 398-403). In 1503, Alexander was King of Poland in addition to Grand Prince of Lithuania, a fact which was reflected in the diplomatic proceedings and resulting diplomas.

22 SIRIO 35, 24, pp. 124-5, 129; 76, 419.

23 SIRIO 35, 24, p. 125; 75, p. 405 (*svoe slovo* vs *korolevo slovo*).

24 "Da i *gramotu tvoju* posol gerald" Davyd velel napisati latyn'skim pismom, kakove gramote prigož u nas tvoej byti" (Russkie akty, 2, col. 4, conferred with the original in the Danish National Archives. Emphasis added).

All King Christian had to do, said the Russian ambassadors, was to copy his envoy's preliminary letter verbatim to draw up his own original diploma, seal and cross-kiss it, and transmit it to the grand prince.

In addenda to their diplomas of 1494 and 1503 the Lithuanian envoys stated that they cross-kissed and sealed the documents on behalf of their sovereign. This may look similar to the procedure used in the West, but it was not. The addendum of 1494 stipulated that once the document arrived in Vilnius, the envoys' seals were to be "cut off" and replaced by Alexander's own seal. In the event, Alexander disregarded the instruction and issued an original letter of treaty to Ivan III by copying his envoys' diploma "word for word."[25] This in turn led to a new set of Russian instructions in 1503. This time, Alexander was supposed to issue an original letter of treaty based on the wording of the diploma his envoys had previously issued in Moscow. However, should he insist on sealing this particular document, the Russian ambassadors should cut off the seals of the envoys and bring them back to Moscow together with the letter.[26]

This obsession with obliterating any evidence of the existence of a separate diploma not issued by Alexander in person further impacted the diplomatic procedures prescribed by Ivan III. The Russian embassy transmitting the treaty diplomas from Moscow to Vilnius brought with it not only the sealed letter of the Lithuanian envoys, but also a copy of it. They were to bring the original to their audiences with the Lithuanian court, but not to show it.[27] For producing Alexander's corresponding letter of treaty, the Polish-Lithuanian scribes were to use the copy, not the original. Only if they insisted should they be shown, but not given, the original, and Russian envoys were to be present during the actual copying. Finally, the boyars were instructed to bring back the Polish-Lithuanian envoys' letter to Moscow.[28]

---

25 According to the embassy book, Alexander's original letter of treaty was written out by "Fëdor the [Russian] secretary" and "Fedka the [Lithuanian] scribe" (SIRIO 35, 25, p. 142). Also, in a change of procedure, Ivan instructed the boyars he sent to Vilnius with his diploma in the spring of 1494 to see to it that Alexander *copied* the letter issued by his envoys (SIRIO 35, 25, p. 140).

26 SIRIO 35, 76, pp. 419-420.

27 The point is repeated in the account of a Russian embassy to the Grand Master of the Teutonic Order in 1517, in which the Russian envoy is instructed to *show* the Prussian envoy's preliminary letter, but not to hand it over (SIRIO 53, 3, p. 28).

28 SIRIO 35, 25, p. 140; SIRIO 35, 76, p. 419.

The information cited above is testimony to two points important for our understanding of the minutiae of treating with Moscow. First, the preliminary acts issued in Moscow by foreign envoys were brought to their sovereigns by Muscovite embassies for copying, not left in Moscow as surety that the forthcoming letters of treaty of the foreign rulers conformed to the agreement concluded with their envoys.[29] Second, having been copied, the letters were returned to Moscow by the Russian embassies, not left with the foreign courts or thrown out.[30] The reasons for both points seem obvious. The grand princes needed to be able to demonstrate to their foreign counterparts the exact terms their envoys had agreed to *under their seals*; and the sequestering of the letters – which were in fact redundant once the foreign princes had issued and exchanged their original acts, copying them word for word – as well as the cutting-off of the seals of the envoys was Moscow's way of rendering the letters legally non-existent.

In summary, it may safely be concluded that in formal and legal terms Muscovite treaties with Western sovereigns consisted of only two acts, the letters of treaty issued by each prince to the other.[31] The envoys' preliminary act was part of the diplomatic process as a legal fiction, not of the resulting treaty complex, and the envoys were not subjects in the treaty-making process. Grand Prince Alexander was.[32] For this reason, the envoys' act does not mention or mandate subsequent ratification.

---

29   For a Danish example, the oration of Vasilij III's ambassadors to Copenhagen in 1514 at one point recounts how the Danish envoy to Moscow issued and cross-kissed his preliminary letter of treaty, then continues: "and when, God willing, our [Vasilij's] envoys come to you [Christian II] *with this letter* [...]" (Russkie akty, 2, col. 4. Emphasis added).

30   This explains the fact that an inventory of the tsars' archive from the 1570s refers to the presence in the Moscow archive of several such acts in various document files (Opisi, pp. 17-18, boxes 1-5, 8, p. 27, box 87, p. 34, box 173).

31   Interestingly, Russian inter-princely treaties differed from this format. In their most developed form, each prince (A and B) would issue two acts (*protivni*) which were subsequently stitched together in pairs (AB/AB) and each pair sealed by both princes. There was no ratification involved in the process (Čerepnin, Russkie feodal'nye archivy 1, pp. 94, 231, 235-6).

32   In the Middle Ages, diplomatic representation could roughly be exercised by envoys speaking and issuing binding acts *for* their sovereign or *as* their sovereign, as his incarnation. Brigitte Bedos-Rezak writes about "a symbiotic relationship between human presence and representation, one in which representation matches real pres-

One advantage of this procedure was the absence of sequencing. The two princely letters of treaty were fictively issued and validated at the same time, even though the "real" letters were by necessity issued at *various* times.

All this is not as trivial as it may sound. Few scholars are aware of the process outlined above, and historian after historian has incorrectly labeled the letter chronologically issued last a "ratification" of the one issued first,[33] despite the fact that in the perception of contemporaries the two princely letters of treaty were fully identical in terms of legal status and chronology. They and only they constituted the treaty in the material sense. For clarity, I label the letter chronologically issued last the *corresponding letter of treaty*.

Differences in Intellectual Form

Without going into detail, it should be added that Muscovite treaties with the West differed significantly from standard European treaties not only in terms of diplomatic process and material form, but also intellectual form.[34] Western texts were conventionally organized in a tripartite structure comprising a formal opening section, the *protocol*, a formal closing section, the *eschatocol*, and a

---

ence" (When Ego Was Imago, pp. 109-10). Oliver Daldrup writes in the same vein: "Darüber hinaus kann jedoch auch von Stellvertretung gesprochen werden, wenn der Gesandte während der Ausübung seiner Tätigkeit keine erkennbare bzw. relevante eigene Identität mehr besitzt, sondern vollständig die Identität des Absenders annimmt. […] In dieser Betrachtungsweise erscheint der Gesandte als Verkörperung des Absenders, er ist im Moment der Gesandtschaft der Absender" (Further, it is also possible to speak of representation when the envoy during the execution of his duties no longer possesses an identifiable or relevant personal identity but assumes the identity of the sender. […] In this view the envoy appears as an incarnation of the sender, he *is* the sender at the moment of the embassy) (Daldrup, Zwischen König und Reich, p. 39).

33 Some examples: Allen II, p. 153; Jahn, Danmarks politisk-militaire historie, p. 360; Fennell, Ivan the Great, p. 168; Kraft, Sveriges Historia III/2, p. 241; Venge, Københavnhavner-traktaten, pp. 10 and 15 = Venge, Kopengagenskij, pp. 10 og 15; Selnes, König Christian II, p. 307; Klose, Dänemark, p. 7; Bazilevič, Vnešnjaja politika, p. 334; Wiesflecker, Das älteste, p. 149; Choroškevič, Russkoe gosudarstvo, p. 141. Croskey seems to use "ratification" for "validation" (Croskey, Muscovite Diplomatic Practice, e.g. pp. 141-2, 147-8).

34 The following after Bresslau, Handbuch I, pp. 45 ff; Leist, Urkundenlehre, pp. 115 ff.; Gasiorowski, Friedensvertragsurkunden, pp. 163 ff.

middle section labeled the *text* or *context* in the legal-historical literature.³⁵ The same was true of Muscovite treaties with the West, but where the opening and closing sections were roughly though not fully identical in the two diplomatic cultures (and will conditionally be named protocol and eschatocol in this book when referring to Russian treaties), the middle section differed considerably between them.³⁶ In Western diplomatic practice, a standard context included several well-defined subsections, such as the *arenga*, pronouncing the deliberations of the signatories on the moral or religious imperatives and benefits of entering into the particular treaty; the *narratio*, detailing the steps taken so far to make the agreement happen, naming, among others, the negotiators and citing their mandates; the *dispositio*, containing the dispositive provisions of the treaty, its "content;" the *corroboratio*, validating the treaty; and the *publicatio* or *promulgatio*, making it public and turning its constituent acts into open letters, or letters-patent *(litterae apertae, litterae patentes)*. Western treaties, though essentially private-law contracts, belonged in the public domain and in principle perceived the public as their audience because they implicitly bound the political communities of the signatory princes.³⁷ The texts occasionally included additional formulae (e.g. *exordium, prooemium, praescriptio, prologus* or *praeambula, notificatio, apprecatio* etc.), and the list of elements given above is schematic in the sense that not all treaties necessarily included all components.

Muscovite treaties with the West had none of this. If, following Bresslau, the *corroboratio* is moved from the context to the eschatocol,³⁸ their middle section consisted solely of the *dispositio*, the section containing the "real" or

---

35   Kaštanov, Očerki, p. 27, uses the terms *protokol* or *načal'nyj protokol*, *eskatokol* or *konečnyj protokol*, and *tekst* in Russian.
36   Kaštanov, Očerki, p. 28.
37   Fisch, Krieg und Frieden, p. 337; Schreiner, Gerechtigkeit und Frieden, p. 63; Steiger, Vorsprüche, p. 8: "Friedensverträge mußten – jedenfalls nach der Ratifikation – allgemein publiziert werden, da dadurch der Friedenszustand wirksam und die Einzelregelungen vollziehbar wurden" (Peace treaties must – at any rate after their ratification – be generally published as this rendered the condition of peace effectual and their individual clauses enforceable).
38   "Die Korroboration wird in nachstaufischer Zeit vielfach aufs engste mit der Datierung verbunden und kann dann geradezu als ein Teil des [Schluß]Protokolls aufgefaßt werden" (In the post-Staufen era the *corroboratio* is frequently linked to the *datum* and can then be perceived directly as a part of the [concluding] protocol). See Bresslau, Handbuch I, p. 48, n. 5. Other authors likewise place the *corroboratio* in the eschatocol, e.g. Gleixner, Sprachrohr, p. 10.

substantive provisions of the treaty. As a reflection of Muscovite political culture, in which ultimate power was the patrimony – the paternal inheritance, or *otčina* – of the incumbent grand prince and power-sharing with an entrenched aristocracy non-existent, there was no *arenga, narratio,* or *publicatio*; that is, none of the components that in the West addressed the public. Russian treaties were not open letters designed for a wider audience, and Western rulers had to accept a treaty form which was alien to their own norms and practices in order to obtain their coveted alliances with the Moscow grand princes.[39] They also had to unconditionally accept the Russian form of validation, the kissing of the cross.

Surviving and Missing Acts

As the early Danish-Muscovite accords were each constituted by two diplomas, the treaties of 1493, 1506 and 1516 consisted of altogether six letters of treaty, three Danish in Latin and three Muscovite in Russian, to which should be added two letters constituting a treaty which was concluded but abrogated in 1514-5 (pp. 67–85).

Of these eight diplomas, Grand Prince Vasilij III's letter of treaty to King Christian II of 1516 is the only one to have survived in the original, while the texts of the Danish letters of 1493 and 1506 have been preserved more or less accurately in secondary copies made by the royal chancery in 1506 and 1514, respectively (see the following chapter). The copies were produced to serve as drafts of new treaties concluded in those two years and therefore contain revisions to the copied texts. The remaining original diplomas and the variety of copies that may have existed have all been lost.

The following diagram illustrates the "paperwork dynamics" of the treaty-making processes of 1493-1516, indicating the position of the surviving documents in these:

---

[39] Little occasional slips demonstrate how unnatural the Muscovite format appeared to Western chanceries. For instance, Maximilian's 1491 letter of treaty to Ivan III contained the *publicatio* "bekennen offennlich mit diesem briefe" (announce publicly with this letter) (Lichnowsky, Part C, No. X, pp. DCCLIII–DCCLV), and King Hans' letter of treaty of 1493 referred to itself in the *corroboratio* as a letter-patent: "cum nostris presentibus literis patentibus" (with our present letter-patent) (pp. 95 and Appendix, item 38).

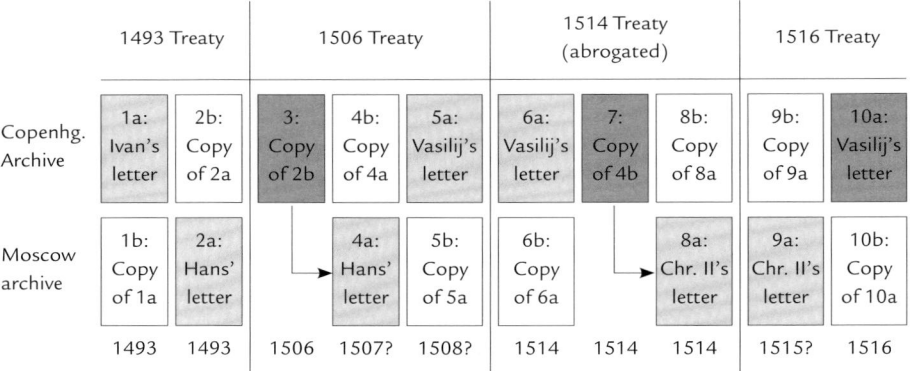

Light grey boxes represent the original letters of treaty, white boxes the chancery copies taken of them before transmission to the treaty partner,[40] and dark grey boxes the surviving documents, of which nos. 3 and 7 are copies of the Danish texts and no. 10a Vasilij III's original letter to King Christian II. Note that the term "archive" in the left-hand column refers to the Copenhagen and Moscow chancery archives at the time, not to their modern successors; that the light grey boxes denoting the original letters of treaty are placed in the sequence in which they were issued in each particular case, as explained in Chapter 2; and that the preliminary letters of treaty issued by the Danish envoys at the conclusion of the negotiations in Moscow in 1493 and 1514, but not in 1506, are not included in the diagram.

The figure illustrates how Ivan III's and Vasilij III's original letters of treaty were transmitted to and filed in Copenhagen (nos. 1a, 5a, 6a and 10a) while chancery copies of them remained in Moscow (1b, 5b, 6b, and 10b), and vice versa. It also illustrates how the surviving Danish copies (nos. 3 and 7) were made from the chancery copies of the originals (2b and 4b) and how they serve as sources for both the documents they copy and the documents they are drafts of (4a and 8a).

---

40   In truth, there is no proof that such copies were taken by the royal chancery, as they are not preserved in the Danish National Archives. However, chancery copies are mentioned quite frequently in the surviving Russian inventories of the tsars' and "foreign office" archives of the 16th and 17th centuries. See, e.g., Opis' I, p. 182, 183, and Opisi, pp. 18 (box 7), 25 (box 62: a copy of Vasilij III's letter of treaty to King Hans, see pp. 58–67).

All three surviving documents are held in the Danish National Archives in Copenhagen.[41]

Traces of the Missing Acts

With one exception, there are no references to any of the documents listed in the diagram above in the extant inventories of the late-medieval Danish chancery archives[42] or the state documents brought into exile by King Christian II in 1523.[43] The exception is a reference to Vasilij III's original letter of 1516 (no. 10a in the diagram) in the inventory of a chancery archive set up in the reign of King Frederik I (1524-33).[44] The closest hint at the existence of the missing Russian documents in the Copenhagen archives may possibly be "an inventory of all letters deposited in the little desk standing in the chancery at Copenhagen [Castle]" produced by King Hans' chancellor Ove Bille, in which a box under Litra M is said to contain "some letters of alliance and negotiation between my lord grace [King Hans] and foreign lords and princes."[45] It can only be deplored that Bille was not a bit more specific when drawing up the list.

No documents containing the treaty texts, be they Muscovite chancery copies of the grand princes' original letters of treaty or preliminary and original Danish treaty acts, have been discovered in Russian archives to the present day. However, traces of these documents appear in some surviving early Muscovite archival inventories.

---

41 The Danish documents (nos. 3 and 7 in the diagram above): TKUA, Rusland: Akter og dokumenter vedrørende det politiske forhold til Rusland, l.nr. 73-13, 1493-1578; the Russian original (no. 10a): Udenrigsministeriet, Forholdet til udlandet (traktater): E 1 Forholdet til udlandet. Pergamentsbreve (1454-1751) a-83: Rusland 1516 8 2.

42 ÆDA IV and V/1, passim.

43 The question of whether Christian II had brought the Russian original of the 1493 treaty with him into exile was raised by Jahn in his Danmarks politisk-militaire historie, p. 361, n. 1. No Russian documents, however, are mentioned in the inventory of the so-called Munich Archive (München-Samlingen, passim).

44 ÆDA IV, p. 398, item 3.

45 "nogre forbu[n]dzbreff oc forhandlingzbreff mellom myn herres nade [: King Hans] oc vdlensk herrer oc försther" (ÆDA V/1, p. 32). The publisher of the inventory suggests that it may have been produced by Ove Bille during the lifetime of King Hans (p. 20). Bille was appointed chancellor in 1506 or 1507.

An inventory of the tsar's archive drawn up in around 1570 states that "Box No. 10" contains "letters [*gramoty*] of Danish Kings Hans and Christian [II] with Grand Princes Ivan [III] and Vasilij [III] – six letters of treaty [*gramot dokončal'nych*] and six missives [*gramot posyl'nych*]."[46] In view of the fact that only three valid treaties were concluded between the parties in the reigns of the rulers in question, it is a safe guess that three of the six letters of treaty were the Danish originals. The remaining three could be either Muscovite chancery copies of the outgoing grand princely letters of treaty, Russian translations of the Danish letters, or the preliminary letters of treaty issued by the Danish envoys. The latter option is less likely, though, as no such letter was issued in 1506 (p. 63). One letter might even be the abrogated treaty of 1514. Several entries in the inventory concerning Muscovite relations with other foreign powers mention all of these possibilities.[47] On the other hand, "Box No. 62" contained a (chancery) copy of Vasilij III's letter of treaty to King Hans,[48] but whether this

---

46   Opisi, p. 18; Zimin, Gosudarstvennyj archiv, p. 37. According to Slovar' russkogo jazyka XI–XVII vv., Vol. 17, *Posyl'naja gramota* means letter or missive (*pis'mo, poslanie*), but S. O. Šmidt understands the term as referring to a missive issued by the ruler himself to, *inter alia*, foreign sovereigns (Šmidt, Carskij archiv, p. 272-3, 275 as well as Juzefovič, Kak v posol'lskich, p. 158). Incidentally, the term *posyl'naja gramota* was known in Danish at the time in the direct translation "sendebrev" (ÆDA V/1, p. 24). Both were probably calques of the Latin "missivus".

47   Examples: Box No. 7 held the original letter of treaty of 1482 by Matthias Corvinus, a copy (*spisok*), i.e. a chancery copy, of Ivan III's original act, and two missives from Matthias, probably examples of the abovementioned *posyl'nye gramoty* (Opisi, p. 18; Zimin, Gosudarstvennyj archiv, pp. 36-37). Box No. 1 held Grand Prince Alexander of Lithuania's letter of treaty of 1494, the preliminary diploma issued by his envoys, and a special act concerning his marriage to the daughter of Ivan III (Opisi, p. 17). Box No. 3 held "King Sigismund of Poland's letter of treaty to Grand Prince Vasilij [III] Ivanovič of all Russia; and the letter which his [Sigismund's] envoys Stanislav Glebov and entourage issued in Moscow, with their seals [appended]" (ibid.). From a different source we know that the Moscow chancery translated Maximilian's 1491 letter of treaty to Ivan III (PDS I, cols. 66-69) and King Frederik II's 1562 letter of treaty to Ivan IV (Opis' I, p. 183) into Russian. Another chancery copy is listed in Opis' I, pp. 153-4. That the Moscow chancery generally took copies of outgoing letters of treaty is evident from the fact that part of the Russian inter-princely diplomas published by Čerepnin in DDG are such copies, as the originals have been lost. See for example DDG, 9, the text of which concludes with the words "And this is a copy of the sworn letter to Tver" (A sii spisok s gramoty s kr[e]stnoj, s tfer'skoj).

48   Opisi, p. 25; Zimin, Gosudarstvennyj archiv, p. 54. Zimin apparently does not know about the abrogated treaty of 1514.

was the only copy taken by the Muscovite chancery is unknown. A. A. Zimin opines that "Box No. 10" contained only the three Danish originals and that the remaining nine documents were copies of ordinary communications, but that, too, is conjecture.[49]

The tsar's archive was reorganized sometime after the 1570s and a new inventory drawn up in 1614.[50] According to the latter, an "iron-clad coffer containing records from various states" held, among other things, "a letter from King Hans of Denmark to Grand Prince Vasilij [III] Ivanovič, but in which year it was written cannot be ascertained, it has faded." This could possibly be King Hans' original letter of treaty to Vasilij III issued in 1506 or 1507 (pp. 64–6). Further, the coffer contained "a letter [*gramota*] from the Danish King Ivan [Hans] to Grand Prince Ivan [III] Vasilevič of all Russia, transmitted in the year 7002, without indication of whom it was transmitted by [*sc.* who was the Russian envoy bringing it to Moscow], with a seal appended."[51] The year 7002 AM corresponds to the period from September 1, 1493 to August 31, 1494, in which Russian envoys brought Ivan III's letter of treaty to Copenhagen and subsequently returned to Moscow with King Hans' corresponding letter (pp. 54–7). The word *gramota* lacks the qualifying adjective *dokončal'naja* which would indisputably define it as a letter of treaty, but as the seal is appended and not simply applied to the document there is little doubt that the reference is to King Hans' original letter of treaty of 1493. Indeed, the text of the letter, as conveyed by the extant copy, states that the king has appended his seal to it (*appendens hiis nostris fortibus literis sigillum nostrum*).

Additionally, there is frequent reference to the letters of treaty of both sides in the preserved diplomatic communications between Denmark and Muscovy as well as in the Russian chronicles, as will become apparent throughout this book.

---

49 Zimin, Gosudarstvennyj arhiv, pp. 116-7.
50 Zimin, Gosudarstvennyj arhiv, p. 12.
51 Opisi, p. 84.

Referencing the Surviving Documents

To avoid repetitive and cumbersome language when referring to the three surviving documents, I use the following shorthand designations:

*1493: The extant copy of the chancery copy of King Hans' letter of treaty of 1493 to Grand Prince Ivan III, produced in 1506 or 1507 in preparation of the king's letter of treaty to Grand Prince Vasilij III. The treaty is referred to as "the 1506 treaty" throughout the book, as it was negotiated and agreed in that year, whereas the pertinent letters were probably issued and exchanged in 1507 (Hans) and 1508 (Vasilij). See pp. 64–7. In Latin. No. 3 in the diagram above.

*1506: The extant copy of the chancery copy of King Hans' letter of treaty of 1506 or 1507 to Grand Prince Vasilij III, produced in 1514 in preparation of King Christian II's letter of treaty to Vasilij III of that year (pp. 74–5). In Latin. No. 7 in the diagram above.

*1516: The original letter of treaty of 1516 from Grand Prince Vasilij III to King Christian II. In Russian. No. 10a in the diagram above.

It is worth keeping in mind when reading the following chapters that in the case of the two Danish copies the date of issue of the original letters of treaty differs from the date of their being copied, and that the copies in both cases were prepared to serve as drafts of the ensuing treaty. This tends be somewhat confusing. Therefore: The Danish text of the 1493 treaty was copied in 1506 or 1507 in preparation of the Danish letter of the treaty of 1506, while the Danish text of the 1506 treaty was copied in 1514 in preparation of what eventually became the treaty of 1516.

The Kremlin of Ivan III

There are no contemporaneus depictions of Moscow at the turn of the 15th and 16th centuries, the period in which Danish diplomats first began arriving in the Muscovite capital. But what did the city look like? What did the envoys see? A. M. Vasnetsov (1856-1933) imagined this scene in which Ivan III inspects the construction of the Cathedral of the Archangel in Cathedral Square in the Kremlin.

Most of the buildings in the watercolor owe their construction to Ivan and are still standing: right to left, they include the Cathedral of the Dormition, later the coronation church of the Russian tsars; the Palace of Facets, the main reception hall of the greater grand princely palace seen in the center and today replaced by the Grand Kremlin Palace of the 19th century; the Cathedral of the Assumption and, in the foreground, the Cathedral of the Archangel, the sepulchre of all Russian grand princes and tsars from Ivan III to the end of the 17th century.

The Palace of Facets was finished in 1491 and may well have been the venue where the Danish envoys were received by Ivan III and Vasilij III. With its diamond-shaped stone blocks it has a striking similarity to the Palazzo dei Diamanti in Ferrara, giving away the fact that it was constructed by Italian master builders inspired by early Renaissance Italian architecture. The same is true of the Archangel Cathedral as demonstrated by the large coquillages (shell-shaped moldings) being entered along the roof-line.

There are many inaccuracies and some conjecture in the image, including the fact that the grand prince had died when construction of the cathedral reached the level depicted here. But it does convey a general sense of the city of Moscow and the bustling building activity in the Kremlin at the time of Ivan III witnessed by the Danish and other foreign diplomats often spending long periods of time in the city.
Wikipedia

о приходе великаго князя послов к нѣмецкому и к датцкому послѣ. Того же лѣта приидоша на Москву послы великаго князя из Нѣмець, Дмитрей Ралевъ да Дмитрей Зайцевъ, что посылалъ их князь великий к Максимьяну цесарю и к датцкому королю и пану Шатбри и к братье. А ко князю щетиньскому рождь целованию приидоша до конца. А ныне грамоты и грамоты разорвалъ до

2. The Treaties in Context

East Meets West

A treaty of alliance between a Danish king and a Muscovite grand prince was an unlikely proposition in the late Middle Ages.[1] The religious chasm between Catholicism and Orthodoxy was profound, and Catholic rulers entering diplomatic relations with their religious adversaries, be they Ottoman Turks or Orthodox Christians, risked immediate opprobrium from their co-religionists, especially if these were the projected targets of the resulting alliances. The Russians were vilified in Western discourse as dangerous schismatics and heretics bent on invading and destroying Christendom, often in verbiage originally developed

◄ **Completing the treaty of 1493**
Background: Upon the return from Moscow of his envoy Hans Claussen together with Ivan III's ambassadors, King Hans is brought to kiss the cross on Ivan III's and his own treaty diplomas. Following the ceremony, the acts are exchanged.
Foreground: The King's diploma is transmitted to Ivan III by his returning ambassadors accompanied by the Danish envoy David Cochran. The company is first seen entering the Kremlin, then presenting the act to Ivan seated on his throne.
Miniature from the "Illustrated Chronicle Compilation". Copyright: AKTEON Publishing House, Moscow.

---

1   According to John Lind, up to the end of the 13th century "Scandinavians and Russians […] had felt that they still belonged to the same undivided religious community despite the schism between the Eastern Orthodox and Western Catholic Churches," forming a "Russian-Scandinavian cultural symbiosis". Scandinavian participation in the Baltic crusades changed that situation (Lind, Scandinavian Nemtsy, p. 481).

in reference to the Turks;[2] and the West was castigated in no less acrimonious terms by the Muscovite hierarchy and the Orthodox world at large.

More to the point – religious antagonism could be ignored when commercially or politically expedient – the parties were widely ignorant of one another. When Ivan III acceded to the Moscow grand princely throne in 1462, northeastern Russia had been separated from the West (and vice versa) by more than two centuries of Tatar domination and was still divided into a number of principalities with varying degrees of formal and real autonomy. The ascendancy of Moscow had begun in the second quarter of the 14th century, but it took until the middle of Ivan's long reign before the Russian lands were amalgamated into a unified, centralized, and autocratically ruled polity significant enough for the Catholic world to notice.[3] To the rulers and merchants of northern Europe, "Russia" had until then been more or less synonymous with Novgorod and Pskov due to the extensive trade of the Hanse with the two republics.[4] Novgorod in particular had shielded interior Russia from interaction with the West for the simple geographical reason that her enormous territories in northern

---

2   Compare, for instance, "contra perfidos Turchos christiani nominis hostes" (against the perfidious Turks, enemies of the name of Christ: DN VI, 640) with "[ab] eisdem Ruthenis christiani nominis inimicis" ([from] the same Russians, enemies of the name of Christ: Acta Pontificum IV, 3108); or "wedir die Tattern und Turken" with "contra Ruthenos […] ac Tartaros infideles" (against the Tatars and Turks / against the infidel Russians and Tatars: FMU VI, 4700, and DN III, 1036). Turks and Russians were lumped together in a statement like "wedir die ungloubigen Rewszen, Tattern und Turken" (against the infidel Russians, Tatars, and Turks: LUB II/1, 629, p. 459). See the excellent treatment of the subject by Madis Maasing in his Infidel Turks, passim.

3   Non-Russian readers not conversant with the history of Russia in the Middle Ages are recommended to consult Martin, Medieval Russia; Crummey, Formation of Muscovy; or Nitsche, Mongolenzeit. For a novel Russian approach to the formation of Muscovy as compared to the teleological conception inherent in Soviet historiography, see Krom, Roždenie gosudarstva, Chapters 1-3.

4   Novgorod was the eastern terminus of the enormous trading network of the Hanse which had one of its four trade yards, later called *Kontore*, in the city (the others were in Bergen, London and Bruges). Bessudnova calls Novgorod a "buffer zone of sorts, located at the junction of Orthodox (Russian) and Catholic (Western European) cultural-historical spaces". Consequently, "the Western understanding of politics was foreign to the Moscow rulers of the 15th and 16th centuries, in particular Grand Prince Ivan III" (Bessudnova, Prevratnost' sud'by, pp. 172-3). "Republic" is conventional shorthand for Novgorod's and Pskov's rather more complex political systems.

and northwestern Russia had formed a buffer between the two worlds (see the map on p. 45).

True, the Russian principalities had long interacted politically and diplomatically with the grand principality of Lithuania – a Catholic power since joining Poland in a dynastic union in 1385[5] – but these were essentially Russian-Russian, not Russian-Western relations. Lithuania had conquered much of the early medieval Kievan State, or Kiev Rus', in the 14th and early 15th centuries,[6] for which reason the bulk of its population were Orthodox, Slavic-speaking Ruthenians whose parishes and bishoprics were subordinate to the Moscow metropolitanate. Hence, military, diplomatic and matrimonial relations between Lithuania, Moscow, Novgorod and other Russian lands essentially concerned the distribution of power within this common Russian space, in particular because Lithuania would often intervene, or be asked to intervene, in the struggles among the principalities for supremacy or survival.[7] So "Russian" was this Russo-Lithuanian space that its internal diplomatic affairs were conducted in Russian, not Latin as was the case with Lithuania's relations with the West.[8] As a consequence, Western influence on Muscovy resulting from these diplomatic encounters was limited, as was the knowledge about Russia disseminated through Lithuania to the wider Catholic world. What did come across was the standard enemy image of ferocious heretics mentioned above.

Apart from his Lithuanian diplomacy, Ivan III maintained certain ties to the Vatican and other Italian states following his marriage in 1472 to a niece of the last Byzantine emperor on the initiative of the Papacy.[9] The ties, which included Milan, Naples and Venice and amounted to five diplomatic missions to Italy during the reign of Ivan, were of a non-political nature, focusing almost

---

5 The exact character of the union is disputed, but Lithuania was for long periods *de facto* independent from, but in some form of ill-defined union with, Poland held together by the Jagiellonian house (Jablonowski, Westrussland, pp. 23 ff.).
6 Jablonowski, Westrussland, pp. 11 ff.
7 The observant Austrian envoy Sigismund von Herberstein, who visited Moscow in 1517 and 1526, wrote that Russia consisted of three parts belonging to the grand prince of Moscow, the grand prince of Lithuania and the king of Poland, respectively (Filjuškin, Tituly, p. 157).
8 The Lithuanian court even had two chanceries: one for Russian and one for Western affairs.
9 Pierling, Rossija i papskij prestol, pp. 147 ff.; Bazilevič, Vnešnjaja politika, pp. 67-73.

entirely, and quite successfully, on attracting Italian master artisans to Moscow.[10] Beyond these relations, the Muscovite court had precious little knowledge of the wider European political scene – and no perceived interest in entering it.[11] Well into the reign of Ivan III, the Moscow grand princes were preoccupied with establishing their fledgling state in the geopolitical space surrounding it, focusing their energies almost exclusively on the Tatars, the Lithuanians, the Moldavians and eventually the Ottomans, to say nothing of the variety of Russian princes and outlying areas they were striving to bring under their rule.[12] It is telling in this respect that not only were the three early alliances referred to in the Introduction – with Hungary in 1482, the German-Roman Empire in 1490 and Denmark in 1493 – Muscovy's sole West European partnerships for decades to come; they were established on the initiative of the Catholic sovereigns, not of Ivan III, though once approached he readily agreed to the proposed initiatives.

The interest of the Papacy in providing Ivan III with a prestigious wife had rested on the hope of involving Muscovy in the common crusade against the Turk and of converting the Russians to Catholicism or, as a minimum, of bringing the Russian Orthodox church into what was left of the Florentine Union of 1439.[13] In contrast, the interest of Matthias Corvinus of Hungary

---

10 Bazilevič, Vnešnjaja politika, pp. 75-76. It may not be commonly known, but the Kremlin of the late 15th and early 16th centuries, including the existing walls and towers, churches of the Dormition and the Archangel, Palace of Facets and belltower "Ivan the Great," was largely built by Italian architects.

11 Bessudnova, Prevratnost' sud'by, p. 174; Wimmer, Livland, p. 57. Rogožin points out that the reports of the returning Russian envoys on the general political situation in Europe concerned only the countries they had visited and were factual, not analytical at all (Posol'skie knigi, p. 101); Pochlebkin sees one reason for the relative isolation of Muscovy at the time in the simple lack of language skills among the servitors of the grand princes, which in itself was the reason for the prominence of expatriate Greeks in the Muscovite foreign service of the late 15th century (Pochlebkin, Vnešnjaja politika, p. 154).

12 See, e.g. Pochlebkin, Vnešnjaja politika, p. 152; Hösch, Die Stellung Moskoviens, pp. 323 ff.

13 Bazilevič, Vnešnjaja politika, pp. 69-71; Halecki, From Florence to Brest, pp. 49-51; Pierling, Rossija i papskij prestol, pp. 147 ff. The union was functioning to a degree in parts of Lithuania's orthodox dioceses and was high on the Vatican agenda at the time: Halecki, pp. 56-61, 84 ff.; Ljubavskij, Očerk, pp. 187 ff.; Jablonowski, Westrussland, pp. 85 ff. For an interesting example of the papal agenda dating from as late as 1503, see SIRIO 35, p. 407.

and Emperor Frederic III and his son and designated heir Maximilian in their Russian alliances had everything to do with territory and dominance. The creation of the Polish-Lithuanian union in 1385 had established a new powerful dynasty in East Central Europe, the Jagiellonians, who in time were to rule not only Lithuania and Poland, but also Bohemia and Hungary.[14] The crown of the latter in particular became a bone of contention in the growing rivalry between the Jagiellonians and the Habsburgs over control of central Europe, eventually causing Frederic and Maximilian to seek the support of Ivan III against their adversaries.[15] The reason the Muscovite grand prince so willingly accepted the proposed anti-Jagiellonian alliances was a strong aspiration on his own part to recover the lands of Kiev Rus' conquered by Lithuania during the preceding centuries.[16] To achieve this goal he had launched a protracted low-intensive war on Lithuania in the mid-1480s which would obviously benefit significantly from allied attacks on the Jagiellonians from the West.[17]

Muscovy had entered the European political stage by default, as it were. In 1478 Ivan III annexed Novgorod to his growing unitary state by force – Pskov was effectively under his sway by then – and in the act inherited two borders facing Catholic Europe: one with Livonia, the peculiar confederation of mini-states

---

14 The Jagiellonians were named after Grand Prince Jogaila of Lithuania who was crowned King of Poland as Wladyslaw II Jagiello in 1386 after marrying the heiress to the last Angevin king of the country, thereby uniting the two realms in a personal union. Both were ruled by Kazimir IV between 1447 and 1492. Between 1492 and 1501, they were divided between his sons Alexander as Grand Prince of Lithuania and Jan Olbracht as King of Poland. Following the death of the latter, the two realms were reunited under first Alexander and then, from 1506-1548, Kazimir's youngest son, Sigismund I. The oldest son, Vladislav, ruled Bohemia from 1471-1516 and Hungary from 1490-1516.

15 PDS I, col. 28.

16 His argument was that God had placed his forefathers – the grand princes who had preceded him since the earliest days – in possession of all Rus' (SIRIO 35, 22, p. 107), the implication being that any part of "Russia" that had ever been ruled by a grand prince of his lineage was his *otčina*, or paternal inheritance (SIRIO 35, 73, p. 354). This was an expansionist political program of sorts. See Filjuškin, Tituly, pp. 170 ff.

17 Zimin, Rossija na rubeže, pp. 93 ff.

located in the area of present-day Estonia and Latvia,[18] and one with Sweden in Finland. He also inherited Novgorod's age-old commercial relationship with the Hanse, including the treaty regime regulating it. The new cross-border relations proved confrontational from the beginning and remained so, with ebbs and flows, for centuries. In 1492 Ivan founded the fortress and walled town Ivangorod on the Russian side of the border river with Livonia, directly opposite the Livonian town of Narva, to strengthen his forward defenses and possibly establish a merchant port designed to attract a share of the profitable East-West trade of the Livonian towns.[19] Ivangorod would become a point of transfer of several of the embassies traveling between Copenhagen and Moscow in the future.

Novgorod's boundary with Sweden in Finland had been established and delimited by the Swedish-Novgorodian Treaty of Nöteborg (*Orechov*) of 1323. It ran from present-day Sestroretsk in the Gulf of Finland to a point on the north-eastern shore of the Bothnian Bay, or so most scholars believe.[20] Over

---

18 Livonia was ruled by five *Landesherren*, viz. the Master of the Livonian Order (Livonian branch of the Teutonic Order), the archbishop of Riga and the bishops of Ösel-Wieck, Kurland and Dorpat. State-wide political decisions were made by a common Diet (*Landtag*) seating representatives of the rulers, the church, the towns and the landowning aristocracy ("vassals"). Towns and corporations had a variety of medieval freedoms as well. For instance, the Hanseatic towns of Riga, Reval (Tallinn), Pernau and others had internal self-government and largely conducted their own foreign commercial policy.

19 The river Narva still functions as the state border between Russia and modern-day Estonia. See, e.g., Vozgrin and Terjukov, Ešče raz o naznačenii Ivangoroda, pp. 312 ff. and Tiberg, Moscow, Livonia and the Hanseatic League, pp. 141-42) for a discussion of the intentions of Ivan III in establishing Ivangorod.

20 In an alternative view, the border according to the Nöteborg Treaty was a double boundary running partly to the Bothnian Bay, partly to the White Sea. The former would mark the western extension of Novgorodian rights, the latter the eastern extension of Swedish rights in the area between them which had the status of a great commons. See Gallén-Lind, Nöteborgsfreden, pp. 302-29 (by John Lind) and Lind, Russian-Swedish Border. Most of the considerable literature on the Nöteborg border is in Finnish and Swedish, with a sprinkling of Danish, Russian and, lately, some English. A good résumé of the historiography of the topic is available in Gallén, Nöteborgsfreden, pp. 1-38 (in Swedish) and Gallén-Lind, Nöteborgsfreden, pp. 366-413 (by John Lind, in Danish). For discussions of the various issues as well as the concept of "border" as applied to Karelia, English-speaking readers are recommended to consult John Lind's English summary of the full discussion in Gallén-Lind, pp. 482-96. The most authoritative Russian treatment of the topic is Šaskol'skij, Bor'ba Rusi, Ch. 3. For recent works in English, see Korpela, Finland's Eastern Border; Ylimaunu, Borderlands as Spaces; Katajala, Drawing Borders; Katajala, Origins of the Border; Tolstikov, From Mezha and Rån.

Scandinavia, East Central Europe, and Russia about 1500

All cities and countries (or political entities) referred to in the book are entered on the map. Borders are approximate, and feudal subdivisions of territories are left out. Note that (1) northern Fennoscandia and Russia was sparsely inhabited and effectively lacked boundaries; (2) the line crossing Finland is the Swedish-Novgorodian boundary established by the Nöteborg Treaty of 1323 (p. 44, esp. n. 20). The character and actual trace of the border are disputed in modern research, and the line shown here is merely indicative. By 1500, Swedish settlement had circled the entire coastline of the Bothnian Bay; (3) the border of Lithuania is that of c. 1500, with Muscovite gains in the war of 1500-1503 indicated by the red line; (4) "Prussia" is shorthand for the lands ruled by the main branch of the Teutonic Order; (5) the island of Gotland belonged to Denmark.

time, however, the central section of the boundary in the Finnish lake district was pushed eastwards by Swedish colonization of the wilderness. As long as

Novgorod was an independent republic it made only feeble attempts to reverse the process, but Ivan III took a more assertive stand. Following the incorporation of Novgorod in 1478, he began to specifically demand a restitution of his lost Novgorodian patrimony in the short-term border truces he had his lieutenants in Novgorod conclude at regular intervals with the governors at Sweden's Karelian stronghold Viborg (present-day Vyborg in Russian Karelia).[21]

The procedure was characteristic of the way Ivan decided to handle Novgorod's age-old relations with her Baltic commercial and diplomatic partners after the annexation: he let the city continue to manage this branch of what was now Muscovite foreign affairs, only henceforth decisions would be made by Ivan's lieutenants and in his name, not by Novgorod's now defunct own authorities.[22] Incidentally, this would give Denmark a significant advantage over Sweden when King Hans succeeded in bypassing Novgorod and establishing direct diplomatic relations with Ivan III in Moscow.

This happened in 1493.

A. The Treaty of 1493

The establishment of diplomatic relations between Copenhagen and Moscow was accomplished on the initiative of King Hans (1481-1513) without previous contacts or prior consultations between the future treaty partners.[23] Hans had

---

21 The making of short-term truces securing border stability will probably have been a regular feature of Swedish-Novgorodian relations over time, but only five texts have been preserved up to the death of Ivan III in 1505. They exhibit a marked increase in the level of demands for a border restitution after Ivan's annexation of Novgorod in 1478. See ST III, 512 (1468), 517 (1473), 525 (1482), 535 (1487), 549 (1497) and 568 (1504). Technically, the truces were confirmations of the Nöteborg treaty.

22 Scholars debate whether this happened for purely practical reasons – Novgorod's foreign relations archive was not moved to Moscow until the reign of Ivan IV, if ever (e.g. Šaskol'skij, Sud'ba, pp. 214 ff.) – or because Ivan III wished to signal that Novgorod's Baltic relations – the Hanse, the Livonians, the Teutonic Order, even Sweden as a member of the Danish-dominated Kalmar Union – were inferior, non-sovereign political entities, and that the Moscow grand princes only dealt directly with other sovereign rulers (e.g. Borisov, Ivan III, p. 478; Wimmer, Livland, p. 61).

23 See my argumentation below. Karamzin (Karamzin IV, pp. 228-9) and Bazilevič (Vnešnjaja politika, p. 334) both agreed with this point of view, but most Russian and Soviet historians have been averse to the notion that the treaty was *not* initiated by

been elected heir to the throne of Sweden in 1458 during the short Swedish reign (1457-1464) of his father, Christian I of Denmark and Norway, and even though the validity of the election was questionable in view of the ousting of Christian shortly afterwards, the Swedish Council of the Realm formally accepted Hans as king in 1483, provided that he acknowledge a number of limitations to his rule and settle certain Swedish grievances from the reign of his father.[24] Negotiations over the terms were obstructed, however, by the Swedish regent Sten Sture, who had been ruling the country in the absence of a king since 1470 and had no interest in relinquishing his considerable powers to a foreign monarch.[25] After a decade of talks and recriminations, King Hans lost patience with the Swedes and began considering ways to obtain his crown by force, or threat of force.

At this juncture, someone or something must have drawn the king's attention to and changed his mind about the distant Muscovite ruler as a potential ally – and a potent one, at that. Muscovy's location on Sweden's eastern frontier made a military pincer operation against Sten Sture a strategic option, and Ivan III might, to the knowledge of the well-informed Danish court,[26] have a positive interest in entering an anti-Swedish alliance in view of his border conflict with the Swedes.

Ivan III. Choroškevič states it directly: "It was Russia that took the initiative to the Danish-Russian relationship" (Russkoe gosudarstvo, p. 140), but normally the approach is more subtle. Ju. G. Alekseev, for instance, writes: "For his fight against the Hanse Ivan needed an ally with a relatively strong navy. Such an ally was the king of Denmark, the old enemy of the Hanse. For the first time, negotiations *are opened* with Denmark, envoys *are exchanged*, and a treaty of fraternity and union *is concluded* in 1493" (Alekseev, Istorija Rossii, p. 699. Emphasis added). The apparently neutral statement that Ivan "needed" an ally and that one was readily at hand leaves the impression that it was Moscow that took the initiative, while the passive verbal forms "are opened", "are exchanged" and "is concluded" mask the fact that the diplomatic process was unilaterally initiated by King Hans.

24 The act accepting King Hans is known as "Kalmar recess" after the Swedish city in which it was negotiated and issued. Technically, it was not a treaty, but a unilateral declaration by the Swedes. The recess is published, with an introduction in Swedish on its status in late-medieval Scandinavian politics, in ST III, 529.

25 Incidentally, King Hans himself may initially have rejected the terms. For the best treatment of the topic, see Carlsson, Kalmer Reces. For Sten Sture the Elder in general and the Danish-Swedish conflict in particular, see Palme, Sten Sture, passim.

26 King Hans had strong supporters in the Swedish Council of the Realm who kept him in the know of Swedish affairs.

Kings Hans and Christian II

While Christian II had his portrait painted several times – e. g. by Michel Sittow in 1515 (top right) – the features of King Hans are known only vaguely from a few hewn or carved portraits made in his lifetime or shortly after his death. They show him broadfaced, with a forceful chin and wearing his hair long. The figure top left was made by Adam van Düren in 1503, while the figures below of both kings were carved by Claus Berg c. 1515-25 for the main altar of the Cathedral of St Canute in Odense.
Wikimedia Commons

That "something" was undoubtedly the alliance of 1490 between Maximilian and Ivan III. The embassies traveling between the Habsburgs and Russia in the years 1489-93 were no secret in the Baltic region, as will become apparent below. What will have interested King Hans in particular was that the alliance was directed against the Jagiellonian rulers of Poland, Lithuania and Bohemia (Hungary was yet to come), i.e. rulers whose lands were more or less sandwiched between those of the alliance partners. The analogy with Sweden-Finland being situated between Denmark and Muscovy was obvious.

Additionally, the fact that the German-Roman emperor had engaged in diplomacy and treaty-making with the Russian schismatics would mitigate the odium that would befall the king for allying himself with an Orthodox ruler against a Catholic neighbor (a point the Swedes were quick to raise in their subsequent verbal warfare against him).[27] Hans was well aware that treating with Muscovy made him politically vulnerable. He therefore took steps on more than one occasion to counteract real or potential criticism by asserting that the ultimate aim of his Russian alliance was to convert the "enemies of the name of Christ" to Catholicism.[28]

First Mission to Moscow

As relations with Sweden soured in the early 1490s and other pretenders to the Swedish throne appeared on the horizon,[29] King Hans decided to move. In spring 1493 he dispatched the provost of Roskilde Cathedral, Hans Claussen,

---

27   It was a particularly strong argument against King Hans in the international propaganda war following his ousting from Sweden in 1501 (p. 58), in which his treaty with Ivan III was called, *inter alia*, "yn vorbunth vnd broderschop myt den affgesneden Ruyssen tho ewigh tidh teghen vnss Cristen luyden" (an eternal fraternal alliance with the cut-off [*sc.* schismatic] Russians against us Christian people) (BSH IV, 220; see also BSH IV, 191).

28   Allen I, pp. 611-617; Bazilevič, Vnešnjaja politika, p. 341, citing Forsten, Bor'ba, p. 153. For a concrete example, see p. 65 below.

29   By 1493, King Hans' mother had officially promoted her younger son Frederik (later King Frederik I), while the future emperor Maximilian had promoted either himself or his son Philip (Lundholm, Sten Sture, p. 146; Kellerman, Jakob Ulvsson, p. 165).

to Moscow with full powers to propose, negotiate and conclude a treaty of alliance and cooperation with Ivan III.[30]

Claussen was the quintessential medieval diplomat. Like so many of his European colleagues he was doctor of canon law (probably from Cologne), held high clerical office, presumably spoke fluent Latin and was conversant with law in the broadest sense. Canon law, it should be remembered, applied not only to the internal justice of the church, but to anything the pope in Rome considered an ecclesiastical matter, a field that would often include international relations.[31] As Claussen would later be promoted to the post of royal chancellor, i.e. head of the royal chancery, he was most likely in possession of administrative skills as well.[32] Whether he was also the brain behind the king's overture to Moscow as claimed by Henry Bruun cannot be verified.[33]

---

30   Strictly speaking, his instructions have not been preserved, but several identically worded Russian chronicles state that he arrived petitioning for "friendship and brotherhood" (*ljubov' i bratstvo*) which was a Russian metaphor for close, treaty-based relations (PSRL VI/2, col. 337, PSRL VIII, p. 226, PSRL XII, p. 236, PSRL XX, p. 359, PSRL XXIV, p. 211).

31   Ullman, Law and Politics, Ch. 4; Mattingly, Renaissance Diplomacy, pp. 19-20. As an example, the fact that treaties were validated by oath made canon law competent in judging whether a treaty had been broken or discontinued by a prince breaking his oath (Lesaffer, Medieval Canon Law, pp. 182 ff., esp. pp. 193 and 195; Lesaffer, Peace Treaties and the Formation of International Law, p. 74).

32   The Danish envoy is identified as "the provost of Roskilde" in two contemporaneous foreign sources (FMU V, 4518, and Sturekrönikan, vv. 3412-8). The prelature was held by Claussen in 1490-1501 (Repertorium diplomaticum II:4, 6776 conferred with Danmarks gilde- og lavsskraaer, p. 370 [*docther Hanss prepositi*] and Løffler, p. 97, no. 24). Claussen entered the University of Cologne in 1481 (Jørgensen, Danske og norske studerende, p. 92) and graduated as *bacchalaureus decretorum* (bachelor of canon law) in 1484 (Pinborg, Danish students, p. 107 [*Johannes Nicolai de D[acie]*], both conferred with Repertorium Diplomaticum II:4, 7377). Two years later he appears as doctor and canon at Roskilde (Danmarks gilde- og lavsskraaer, p. 369 [*docther Hanss Clawssøn, canick*]), probably having obtained his doctorate in Cologne as well. He was royal chancellor from 1495 (Repertorium Diplomaticum II:4, 7973) to sometime in 1496 or 1497. Claussen Latinized his name Johannes Nicolai, which was in turn Russianized as Ivan Mikolaj in one Russian source (Opisi, p. 116). His proficiency in Latin is documented in an account of a meeting of the Nordic councils of the realm in Kalmar in 1495 which he wrote in his capacity as notary public (Aarsberetninger IV, p. 277, 9).

33   Bruun, Poul Laxmand, p. 38.

The Danish envoy travelled to Moscow by way of Gotland, "Livonia's shore" (probably Reval, perhaps Narva) and Novgorod,[34] from where the Muscovite governor (*namestnik*) announced his arrival to Ivan III.[35] The grand prince's return message leaves no doubt that the Danish diplomatic mission had not been prepared or signaled in advance. Was the envoy really the king's man, he asked, and were the letters he carried with him genuine or forged? The reason he asked, he continued, was that he had recently turned away an imposter claiming to be a representative of the pope.[36] Ivan would not have posed these questions if he and his Novgorod lieutenants had been expecting an envoy from King Hans following a prior agreement.[37]

In fact, he probably posed them because he had good reasons to doubt the sincerity of a Danish envoy suddenly appearing on his doorstep proposing a treaty of alliance. Two years earlier, in 1491, his ambassadors traveling to Maximilian had informed him in a letter from Lübeck that King Hans and "the local dukes" – probably the Dukes of Mecklenburg – had gotten news of their mission and planned to abduct them as soon as they left the town on their further journey.[38] We shall never know if an ambush on the envoys was actually planned, but the Russians may well have had a point in suspecting some form of foul play. While waiting in Lübeck, they wrote, they had been approached by an envoy of the Polish king, the Greek Antonis Lascaris (*Antonej Laskar'*), who had recently been with the King of Denmark and Duke Bogislaw

---

34 Sturekrönikan, vv. 3412-8. Claussen returned home with a Russian embassy via Reval, so the city was probably his entry point as well (Sturekrönikan, vv. 3420-3).
35 SIRIO 35, p. 87. The Muscovite governor names Claussen *Ivan Magistr*.
36 SIRIO 35, pp. 88-89.
37 That the initiative belonged to King Hans was confirmed by Ivan III much later, in 1501. Following the Russian invasion of Finland in 1495-6, King Hans asked him to release the Swedes who had been taken prisoner by his troops. Ivan answered that the king ought not have asked this favor because it was on his, the king's, initiative that they had both become enemies of Sweden: "vobis autem, fratri nostro, pro istis captiuis nos non licebat postulare, propterea, quia tunc terra Suecorum *secundum vestram commissionem* ambobus nobis erat inimica" (BSH IV, 180, p. 264. Emphasis added).
38 PDS I, cols. 62-63. Since "dukes" is in the plural, the phrase most likely refers to the co-rulers of Mecklenburg, the brothers Magnus II and Balthasar, with whom King Hans was on good terms. Mecklenburg bordered on the free imperial city of Lübeck.

X of Pomerania.³⁹ Lascaris had inquired about their mission, but they had said nothing.⁴⁰

The episode is revealing. Considering that the leader of Ivan III's mission to Maximilian was Jurij Trachaniot (*Jurij Grek*), the senior Byzantine-Greek expatriate in the service of Ivan III,⁴¹ it may safely be assumed that a sudden meeting between two Greek-speaking diplomats in the town of Lübeck was no chance encounter. More likely, King Hans and Duke Bogislaw had purposely sent Lascaris to the Hanse town to approach and question the Russians. In all likelihood, the affair took place on the initiative of Kazimir IV, the father-in-law of Bogislaw, who as Jagiellonian Grand Prince of Lithuania and King of Poland was conscious of being the obvious target of the Imperial-Muscovite negotiations. The Russians must later have convinced Maximilian of the truth of their allegations, for in the oration of his ambassador to Moscow later in 1491 the emperor-elect referred to the joint efforts of the kings of Denmark and Poland to block the Muscovite missions and even ordered the dukes of Mecklenburg to provide future Russian envoys with safe-conducts through their lands.⁴²

Hans Claussen arrived in Moscow sometime in June 1493.⁴³ Suspicions notwithstanding, Ivan III welcomed the Danish envoy, opened negotiations (through Latin-speaking interpreters from his staff) and eventually con-

---

39   The duke is referred to in the Russian letter merely as the "son-in-law" of King Kazimir IV of Poland, but this suffices to identify him via e.g. Schleinert, Pommerns Herzöge, pp. 66-69, and Allgemeine Deutsche Biographie III, pp. 48-55. The rulers in question probably acted in close accordance with each other. Bogislaw X was a brother-in-law of the Mecklenburg dukes, and his ties with King Hans were close. A later Danish archival inventory lists a treaty of alliance – *ett confederatz breff* – between the two (ÆDA IV, p. 398, with no date), probably from 1511 (Huitfeldt, Kong Hans, p. 279), and when in 1496 the duke went on a pilgrimage to the Holy Land, he placed Pomerania under the protection of King Hans, King Kazimir and the Mecklenburg brothers.

40   "tot posol […] s nami sja videl, da nas, gosudar', i o dorose nas sprašival, koli nam echati i kotoroju dorogoju, i my emu ne skazali" (and that envoy met with us; and he asked us, Sovereign, about our journey, where we were going and by what route, and we did not tell him) (PDS I, col. 63).

41   See the works listed p. 54 n. 48 for detailed information about the envoy.

42   PDS I, cols. 75-76. Ivan later thanked the dukes for actually having done so (ibid., cols. 88-89).

43   PSRL VI/2, col. 337, PSRL VIII, p. 226, PSRL XII, p. 236, PSRL XX, p. 359, PSRL XXIV, p. 211, except that PSRL VIII by mistake has both June and July (pp. 226 and 227, respectively).

cluded what became the treaty of 1493. We know for certain that Ivan followed Muscovite custom and issued, sealed and cross-kissed his letter of treaty to King Hans on the occasion, as the letter was subsequently brought to Copenhagen by the returning Danish envoy and an accompanying Russian embassy.[44] Claussen most likely responded by issuing and validating a preliminary royal letter (for this type of document, see pp. 22–29), though there is no evidence of the fact in the extant sources.

Few details of the negotiations or Hans Claussen's stay in Moscow in general are provided by surviving documents, be they Danish or Russian, not least because the "Danish" embassy books (*posol'skie knigi*) initiated by the Moscow chancery upon the arrival of the envoy have been lost.[45] A little can be gauged, though. First, those of the Russian chronicles that relate the arrival of the Danish envoy in Moscow continue to state that the grand prince "honored" him before taking leave of him.[46] This particular term is a standard phrase in the chronicles indicating that a foreign envoy was invited to dine in the presence of Ivan III himself or with some of his boyars to celebrate the conclusion of a treaty.[47] Second, as will be argued in Chapter 4, the wording of the formal opening and closing sections, as well as major parts of the "alliance" section of the treaty text, were dictated to Claussen by the Russian negotiators, who copied them verbatim from the text of the 1490 treaty with Maximilian (though obviously changing the names, titles and epithets of the signatories and their common adversaries). On the other hand, the nine "cooperation" clauses of the text had no precedent in earlier Russian treaties and were therefore formulated in Rus-

---

44   PSRL VI/2, col. 341, PSRL VIII, p. 228, PSRL XII, p. 238, PSRL XX, p. 361.
45   The early "Danish" books are mentioned in Opisi, p. 25 (box 62) and p. 116 ("Danish books from 7001 to 7009," i.e. 1493-1501). On "embassy books," see p. 26 n. 20.
46   "Knjaz' veliki *počtiv ego posla*, otpusti ego v svoju zemlju" (The Grand Prince, *having honored his* [*sc.* the king's] *envoy*, dismissed him to his own land. Emphasis added). See PSRL VI/2, col. 337, PSRL VIII, p. 226, PSRL XII, p. 236, PSRL XX, p. 359, PSRL XXIV, p. 211.
47   A month before the arrival of Hans Claussen in Moscow, Ivan III had been visited by an envoy of the Polish Duke Konrad of Mazovia (Konrad Mazowiecki) asking, among other things, for the hand of Ivan's daughter. No agreement was reached, and the chronicles registering the event do not mention an "honoring" of the envoy when he was dismissed (e.g. PSRL XII, p. 236). For an example of the meal as a ceremonial feature, see the detailed account of the Muscovite-Lithuanian negotiations in early 1494 in SIRIO 35, 24, p. 123.

sian and Latin in a genuine piece of negotiation and communication between the parties. Finally, as further explained in Chapter 4, the fact that the letters of treaty were written in two different languages reflecting two widely different political cultures resulted in a variety of greater or lesser incongruities between them, offering historians the possibility of closing in on and drawing certain conclusions about the negotiation process itself.

Finalizing the Treaty

Hans Claussen returned to Copenhagen by way of Reval sometime in the fall of 1493 accompanied by a Russian embassy headed by Dmitrij Ralev, another Byzantine expatriate in the service of Ivan III, and Dmitrij Zajcev, a secretary (*d'jak*) in the grand princely chancery, plus their entourage of eighteen servitors.[48] If the normally well-informed Swedish rhymed chronicle is correct in stating that the parties "talked for two weeks or three" after reaching Copenhagen,[49] the envoys will have arrived by mid-October. On November 8, 1493, King Hans issued, sealed and cross-kissed his corresponding letter of treaty and exchanged it with the act of Ivan III, at which point the accord officially went into effect.[50]

---

48 The names of the two Russian envoys are given in PSRL VI/2, col. 337, PSRL VIII, p. 226, PSRL XII, p. 236, PSRL XX, p. 359, PSRL XXIV, p. 211 and in the abovementioned archival inventory from the 1570s (Opisi, p. 116, though only Ralev). The route as well as the number of Russians appear in Sturekrönikan, vv. 3420-2. Ivan III's small group of Greek expatriate servitors is surveyed in several works, the authors of which do not necessarily agree on their identification and provenance. See, e.g., Alef, Diaspora Greeks; Croskey, Byzantine Greeks; Harris, Greek Emigres; Hösch, Die Stellung Moskoviens, pp. 328-336; Skržinskaja, Kto byli Ralevy; Choroškevič, Russkoe gosudarstvo, pp. 176-96.

49 Sturekrönikan, v. 3426.

50 The place, date and cross-kissing appear in the treaty text itself, items 34 and 40. The exchange of letters in Copenhagen is reported by several Russian chronicles: the Muscovite envoys "korolja k celovan'ju privedoša i gramoty rozoimaša dokončalnye" (led the king to the [cross-]kissing and exchanged the letters of treaty) (PSRL VI/2, col. 341, PSRL VIII, p. 228, PSRL XII, p. 238, PSRL XX, p. 361). That *rozoimaša* means "exchanged" in this context is evident from the nearly identical chronicle accounts of the cross-kissing by Grand Prince Alexander of Lithuania of his 1494 peace treaty with Ivan III: the Russian envoys "privedoša velikago knjazja Aleksandra Litovskogo k celovaniju na dokončalnych gramotach i *rozoimaša* gramoty dokončalnye *promež sebja*" (led [Alexander] to kissing [the cross] on the letters of treaty and *exchanged* the letters of treaty *between them*" (PSRL XII, p. 238. Emphasis added).

Emperor Maximilian receiving a Russian embassy

The embassy brought Grand Prince Vasilij III's letter of treaty of 1514 to Emperor Maximilian in Austria. The image shows the moment the letter is exchanged with the Emperor's corresponding diploma. Both letters are sealed with pendant bulls, as is Vasilij's extant original letter of treaty of 1516 to King Christian II (see p. 84). The Russian ambassadors are Dmitrij Laskirev and Elizar Sukov, both of whom went on diplomatic missions to Denmark (pp. 66 and 67). Note the interpreter in the center. As King Hans wore his hair long like Maximilian, the image conveys a good impression of the receptions of Russian embassies at Copenhagen Castle in 1493 and 1506.

The image, a woodcut, was prepared for Weisskunig [the White King], a chivalric novel-cum-biography of Maximilian which remained unpublished, however. Copyright: Alamy Stock Photos.

The Russians remained in Copenhagen during the winter and returned to Moscow in two separate groups the following spring. One party took the direct route across the Baltic Sea, while the other circumnavigated northern Norway and the Kola Peninsula, crossed the White Sea and reached Moscow by way of the north Russian rivers, passing the town of Ustjug.[51] The latter party was obviously the most important as it included the two leaders of the Russian embassy, Ralev and Zajcev, and the new Danish envoy to Russia, David Cochran.[52]

Cochran was a Scotsman in the service of King Hans who would in time become the most frequently used Danish envoy to Muscovy in this early period of Danish-Russian relations.[53] In fact, he was probably the European diplomat outside Lithuania who visited Moscow the most in the closing decades of the Middle Ages. Cochran frequently appears as *magister* in the sources,[54] indicating that he had a university master's degree and consequently spoke Latin. His field of study is unknown. From 1490 at the latest he was the ranking Danish herald, known as Denmark King of Arms, *Danmark Rex Armorum*.[55] His last known journey to Russia took place in 1521.[56]

---

51   Sturekrönikan, vv. 3436-41; Huitfeldt, Kong Hans, p. 110; Olaus Petri, p. 283; ULS, p. 100 (the passage of the diplomatic party through Ustjug is entered under 7005, i.e. 1496-7, but it is immediately followed by an entry about the Muscovite-Lithuanian peace settlement of February 1494); RK 1977, p. 58 (with incorrect dating as well); FMU V, 4574 conferred with FMU VI, 4946. I have discussed the reasons for taking this cumbersome route in Pape, Rethinking the Medieval Russian-Norwegian Border, pp. 171-4, and, in a briefer version, Pape, Three Forgotten Border Treaties, pp. 33-34.

52   PSRL VI/2, col. 341, PSRL VIII, p. 228, PSRL XII, p. 238, PSRL XX, p. 361 plus ULS, p. 100.

53   Cochran's Scottish origins are stated by Herberstein in his *Rerum Moscoviticarum Commentarii*: "cum magistro David natione Scoto, regis Daniae tunc Oratore" (with Master David, a Scotsman by nation, at that time an envoy of the King of Denmark) (1556 edition, in Herberstein, Synoptische, p. 374). The imperial envoy met Cochran and the Russian diplomat Grigorij Istoma, whom we shall encounter below, during his visit to Moscow in 1517 and therefore has the information first-hand.

54   E.g. Herberstein, op. cit.; Opisi, pp. 116-7; Kopengagenskie akty, pp. 9, 16; LUB II/3, 230.

55   E.g. Grönblad, Nya källor, 320, 344; LUB II/3, 444; Kopengagenskie akty, 15, 16; Russisch-Livländische Urkunden, CCCLIII. Note that in Russian-language sources, herald (*haraldus* in Latin) is rendered *gerald* or *gerlad*, e.g. Russkie Akty, cols. 3-4, 9; PSRL VI/2, sp. 396.

56   Russkie akty, 10. For further biographical information, see Verwohlt, Kongelige danske herolder, pp. 210-3; Breve og aktstykker, p. 483, note 1; Grosjean, A time when

The diplomats reached Moscow sometime between May 29 and August 31, 1494,[57] and conveyed King Hans' letter of treaty to Ivan III.

None of the letters has come down to us in the original, but a copy of the Latin text of the Danish letter has, as previously stated, been preserved in the document labeled *1493 in this book.

The Treaty in Brief

The treaty of 1493 established a fully fledged, mutually binding political relationship between two sovereigns of equal standing,[58] as evidenced by the inclusion in the protocol and initial clauses of the *dispositio* (items 03 and 06) of the vintage political relationship-building terms *fraternitas*, *amicitia* and *confoederatio*, or *bratstvo*, *ljubov'* and *dokončanie* (brotherhood, friendship and union).[59] More specifically, it created the offensive military alliance against Sten Sture desired by King Hans, albeit at the cost to the latter of also entering an alliance against Ivan III's chief enemy and future son-in-law, Grand Prince Alexander of Lithuania

---

fools, pp. 178 ff. None of these biographers is aware of the substantial number of journeys made to Russia by Cochran. In my catalog of missions I have registered 16 confirmed and two possible journeys (Pape, Comprehensive Register, passim).

57   PSRL VI/2, col. 341, PSRL VIII, p. 228, PSRL XII, p. 238, PSRL XX, p. 361. The previous entry is dated May 29, and the arrival is the last entry under 7002, which ended on August 31.

58   It should be noted that medieval treaties were not concluded between states or other abstract political entities, but by the ruling princes as individuals. This is the reason that treaties expired at the death of one of their signatories. To avoid this situation, the latter typically added their heirs as co-signatories and included "barons and prelates", subjects and subject lands among those bound by the treaty provisions. See Bittner, Lehre, p. 17; Lesaffer, Three Peace Treaties, p. 44-47; Lesaffer, Peace Treaties from Lodi, pp. 17-21; Fisch, Krieg und Frieden, p. 337; Mitteis, Politische Verträge, p. 572. The Danish-Muscovite and Imperial-Muscovite treaties had none of this.

59   For this core medieval treaty terminology, see, e.g., Wielers, Zwischenstaatliche, passim; Lesaffer, Amicitia, passim; Roschin, Friendship, passim; Roschin, Supplanting love, passim; Filjuškin, Tituly, Chapter 10. Strictly speaking, European treaties would normally use *pax* (peace) instead of *fraternitas* (brotherhood). As the latter was a staple of Russian domestic treaties, it may safely be assumed that it was entered into the text on the insistence of the Muscovite side.

(1492-1506).⁶⁰ Unlike the anti-Swedish clauses, however, the anti-Lithuanian paragraph did not stipulate the use of military force by the signatories; it was primarily designed by Ivan to isolate Alexander diplomatically.

Further, as stated in the Introduction, the parties agreed to enter certain areas of future cooperation, formulated in nine reciprocal clauses concerning issues such as border regulation, mutual legal protection, unrestricted trade and free diplomatic travel. The free trade provision points to an additional, though secondary, motive of the alliance: a strong anti-Hanseatic bent characteristic of both King Hans and Grand Prince Ivan III.⁶¹

B. The Treaty of 1506

Ivan III died on October 27, 1505 and was succeeded on the Moscow throne by his son and heir Vasilij III (1505-33). As medieval compacts were normally thought to expire at the death of their signatories,⁶² the treaty of 1493 would have to be renewed to remain in force. By coincidence, David Cochran – the Danish envoy of 1494 – happened either to be in Moscow at the time of Ivan's death or to arrive in the city shortly afterwards.⁶³

His was an urgent mission. King Hans had forced his way onto the Swedish throne by military means in 1497, but four years later, in 1501, he had been ousted by an insurgency initiated by members of the Swedish Council of the Realm, among them Sten Sture. Three years of verbal warfare ensued before the parties agreed in May 1504 to hold a joint Scandinavian council meeting in Kalmar the following midsummer to settle certain contentious issues.⁶⁴ The Swedes, however, failed to appear at the meeting. In response, the king initiated

---

60 Alexander married Elena Ivanovna, the daughter of Ivan III, in 1495 in the hope of appeasing the aggressiveness of the Muscovite grand prince towards Lithuania – in vain, as it turned out.

61 Choroškevic, Russkoe gosudarstvo, pp. 139-40; Borisov, Ivan III, p. 481; Šaskol'skij, Èkonomičeskie svjazi, pp. 16-17.

62 See p. 57 n. 58.

63 A Swedish source of September 9 refers to him as being in Ivangorod (FMU VI, 5142). From here he could easily have reached Moscow by October 27. A Russian source places his arrival in 7014 AM, i.e. after September 1, 1505 (SIRIO 35, 84, p. 480).

64 The agreement is printed in ST III, 567.

a case of *lèse-majesté* (crime of injured majesty, or high treason) against the insurgents and had them convicted by the councils of Denmark and Norway.[65] In November, the verdict was confirmed by Emperor Maximilian and applied to "totum Imperium Romanum,"[66] and a year later the Imperial Chamber Court (*Reichskammergericht*) outlawed the insurgents – placed them under the imperial ban, or *Reichsacht* – for failing to appear at the court to redeem themselves.[67] The rebellion was clearly seen by the Imperial jurists as an illegitimate uprising against a legitimately constituted ruler.[68] Not surprisingly, King Hans shared the view and would reclaim his throne and retain his Swedish royal title to the end of his days.

The Kalmar debacle was the immediate reason for David Cochran's mission to Moscow in the late summer of 1505. (He probably set out from Kalmar rather than Copenhagen.) His commission will have been twofold. On the one hand, he was to announce the verdict to Ivan III and persuade him to put diplomatic and perhaps military pressure on the rebellious Swedes in support of King Hans, as intimated by the description of the Swedish adversaries in the renewed treaty[69] and the king's covering missive to Vasilij III in 1507.[70] On the other, he

---

[65] ST III, 569a; Aarsberetninger I, p. 8, no. 11. The verdict also restored the kingdom of Sweden as well as the property of the insurgents, including a significant amount located in Denmark and Norway that could easily be confiscated, to King Hans. For this and the following events, see Allen I, pp. 355-60; Bisgaard, Christian 2, pp. 107-12. The king in fact began selling off the Swedish properties of some insurgents in Denmark (Repertorium Diplomaticum II/5, 10685, 10751).

[66] Aarsberetninger I, p. 8, no. 11.

[67] ST III, 569c, 569d, 569e, 569f. The act was actually disseminated in the North (Repertorium Diplomaticum II/5, 10765, 10800).

[68] Enemark, fra Kalmarbrev, p. 120.

[69] Appendix, item 10.

[70] In his letter, an answer to Vasilij III's first missive of 1506 (see below), King Hans went out of his way to castigate the Swedish insurgents, writing, *inter alia*, "O princeps, frater noster, Suecie occupatores [et] rebelles adhuc totum nostrum regnum Suecie occupant et detinent contra Deum, contra omnem iusticiam et iuratam fidelitatem, nobis prestitam" (Oh prince, our brother, the usurpers of Sweden [and] rebels occupy and hold the whole of our kingdom Sweden to this day, against God, against all justice and the fealty they have sworn us). Less modestly he went on to complain that the Swedes had opposed him "in effectu faciendj nobiscum sicut Judej fecerunt contra Christum" (in effect doing to us what the Jews had done to Christ). He therefore asked the grand prince to have the iniquity of the rebels in mind: "Vnde ex corde mouemur rogare fratrem et confederatum nostrum, ut jniquitatem rebellium nostrorum menti

was most likely charged with trying to counter the disturbing fact that the status of Sweden at the Muscovite court had recently changed significantly for the better. Ivan III had fought a war with a Lithuanian-Livonian alliance in 1500-3 in which his forces had prevailed against the former – though not taking Smolensk as intended – but performed less convincingly against the latter.[71] At the outset of the conflict, King Hans had been a guarantor of Swedish neutrality,[72] but his ousting in 1501 nullified that role and turned Sweden with its Finnish possessions into a potential threat to Muscovy's northern flank.[73] Peace was restored in 1503, but conflict with Livonia and especially Lithuania remained probable – it flared up again in 1507 – so Ivan must have felt a need to permanently neutralize his northern neighbor. In 1504, he concluded yet another of his recurring border truces with the Swedes, only this time the duration was extended to an unprecedented twenty years.[74] The treaty retained his demand for a return of his lost Novgorodian lands, but the timeframe of the agreement belied the seriousness of the claim. The real intention with the agreement was revealed by the addition of a new paragraph forbidding Sweden to aid Livonia in case the latter should wage war on Novgorod and Pskov.[75] Furthermore, the grand prince broke long-standing Muscovite diplomatic custom by sending a Russian embassy all the way to Stockholm to have the treaty confirmed not by King Hans, but by the effective ruler of the country, Svante Nilsson, who had succeeded Sten Sture as regent in 1504.[76] Previously, all border truces had been concluded between the Swedish *capitaneus* at Viborg and the Novgorodian leadership, from 1478 Ivan III's *namestniki* in the city. King Hans was being

---

      sue habeat" (Grönblad, Nya källor, 162; Kopengagenskie akty, 6; FMU VI, 5202; Aarsberetninger I, p. 54, 5; SGGD V, 112 (incorrectly listed under 1505).

71 Bazilevic, Vnešnjaja politika, Ch. 8; Borisov, Ivan III, pp. 455 ff., 492 ff.
72 Bazilevič, Vnešnjaja politika, p. 385.
73 One significant evidence of this is offered by Borisov (Ivan III, pp. 498-9). After the ousting of King Hans and return to power of Sten Sture in 1501, Ivan III worried so much about the safety of Ivangorod (which had been sacked by the Swedes in a raid across the Gulf of Finland during the war of 1495-6) that he diverted one of his armies otherwise fighting the coalition to the area to protect the town and fortress.
74 ST III, 568.
75 ST III, 568, p. 505.
76 Sten Sture the Elder had died in 1503. The improved status of Sweden did not gain the Swedes direct access to the grand princes in Moscow for decades to come. For the Russian embassy to Stockholm, see FMU VI, 5125, 5135, 5136; Opis' I, p. 244.

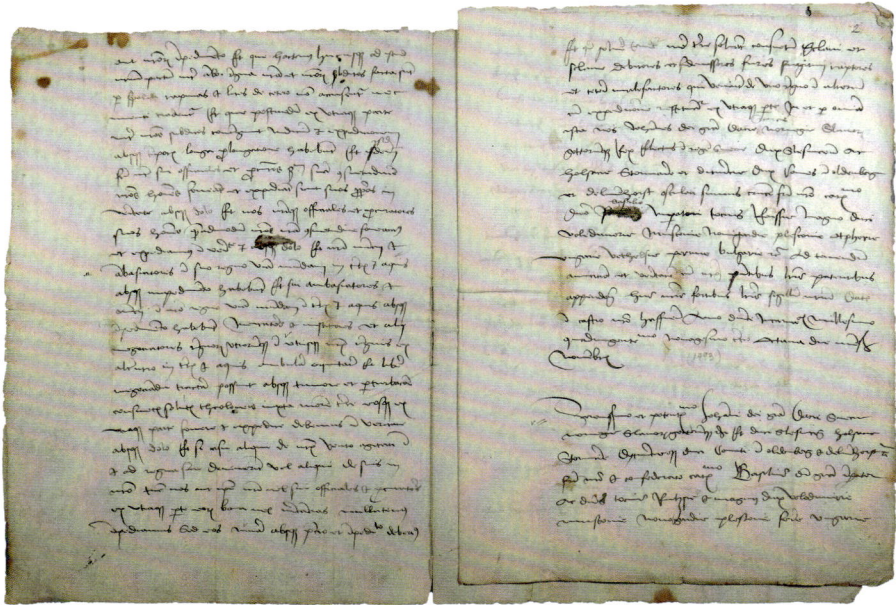

First missive from Vasilij III, 1506
The image shows pages 2-3 of the folios containing the copies of the treaty of 1493 (King Hans' letter) and Grand Prince Vasilij III's earliest letter to King Hans in 1506. The latter begins on the same sheet as the closing section of the former (page 3) and written in the same hand. Danish National Archives. Photo: Carsten Pape.

sidetracked by this piece of Russian *Realpolitik*,[77] but he was not quite written off by Ivan, who continued to acknowledge him as legitimate King of Sweden and prime treaty partner.[78]

---

77   This was noticed by the Swedes. In the letter in which the governor at Viborg, Erik Turesson, announced the new treaty to the Swedish Council in Stockholm, he also mentioned that the friendship between King Hans and the Russians was not as close as it had been (FMU VI, 5075).

78   As late as early 1503 Ivan had rejected a plea by Alexander of Poland-Lithuania to conclude a six-year truce with Sten Sture, motivating the rejection by his alliance with King Hans. The plea had originated with the Pope in Rome who wished to enroll Sweden in the battle of Christendom against the Turk, and Sten Sture had shrewdly responded that he would be happy to join the crusade but was unable to do so due to "a certain enmity" with "neighbors of his realm" (SIRIO 35, 75, pp. 397-8). For another example of Ivan's continued adherence to King Hans as King of Sweden in 1504, see ibid., 80, p. 468.

Having gained access to the new grand prince, David Cochran expressed the desire of his sovereign to renew the expired treaty.[79] Since he was not empowered to do so – the Danish chancery could not have foreseen the death of Ivan III when issuing his instructions – he had to dispatch a courier back to Copenhagen for a new royal mandate, letter of credence, ambassadorial oration and, possibly, a personal missive from King Hans to Vasilij III.[80] Once the courier returned to Moscow with the required documents in the summer of 1506,[81] the grand prince consented to renewing the treaty.

Two decisions stand out in this connection. First, it was agreed that the new compact would be a word-for-word copy of the previous one.[82] This was far from atypical in European diplomatic practice, which often led to verbatim renewals of treaties or parts thereof, but there is reason to believe that in this case it was an easy way out of the dilemma caused by Ivan III recently having made peace with the very Swedes he was supposed to combat according to the expired treaty with King Hans. In this particular policy area, Vasilij III would retain his father's objective of keeping Sweden out of future conflicts on his western border. In consequence, rather than Cochran and the Muscovite boyars renegotiating the 1493 alliance based on the new realities, it probably seemed easier to simply repeat the wording of the previous treaty and thus confirm the general *amicitia* between the two sovereigns while at the same time keeping the Danish king happy and future options open. Also, having just assumed power,

---

79 The course of events described in the following can be deduced from Vasilij III's first missive to King Hans dated July 17, 1506 and transmitted to the king with the returning Cochran (Grönblad, Nya källor, 149; Kopengagenskie akty, 5; Forsten, Bor'ba, p. 155, n. 1). A copy of the letter made by the Royal Archivist Grimur Thorkelin (see p. 100) is printed, with a translation into 19th-century Russian, in SGGD V, 111; it is incorrectly dated 1507.

80 According to Vasilij III's 1506 missive (p. 64), the courier brought back the king's letter of credence (for Cochran) and "words", i.e. a missive or new oration for the envoy to deliver. Russian sources name the courier either Johannes Plagh (the missive) or Hans Plug (Opisi, p. 116). The sending of supposedly low-ranking couriers back and forth between Moscow and Copenhagen demonstrates the degree to which the diplomatic missions had become commonplace.

81 Opisi, p. 116.

82 According to Vasilij III's 1506 missive, King Hans' letter of treaty should be "quales apud genitorem nostrum vestre litere fuerunt" (the same as the letter of yours which was with our father [Ivan III]).

Vasilij had more pressing issues on his agenda than redefining the terms of treaty with the King of Denmark.[83]

Secondly, it was decided that King Hans would be the first among the two rulers to issue, seal, cross-kiss and transmit his letter of treaty, upon receipt of which Vasilij would draw up *his* letter, repeating the king's act "de verbo ad verbum", and transmit it to Copenhagen.[84] This was highly unusual. As previously stated, the Muscovite grand princes consistently insisted not only on negotiating and concluding their treaties in Moscow – as had indeed been the case in this instance – but also on issuing and cross-kissing their letters of treaty immediately upon the closing of an agreement, only later to receive the original letter of the foreign monarch.

The reason for the reversal of the standard procedure in 1506 is unknown, but it may well have been dictated by a simple practical concern. Even though the treaty was to remain unaltered, the names and titles of not just the signatories, but also their common enemies, would have to be updated, and David Cochran may simply not have known which exact Swedes the Danish court wished to include in the text as adversaries. Sending another courier to Copenhagen to find out may have been considered too cumbersome or time-consuming; it was easier to let the Danish king issue his letter first and subsequently have the Russian side copy the names and attributes of the adversaries from it. The remaining parts of the text was accessible to Vasilij III in the shape of the original Danish letter of 1493 located in his archives, a fact that would allow him to control the accordance of the king's forthcoming diploma with the text it was supposed to repeat.

In consequence of the change of procedure, neither the grand prince nor the envoy seems to have issued, sealed and cross-kissed any treaty acts at the conclusion of the negotiations in Moscow.

---

83   For a rather detailed description of the issues facing Vasilij III when assuming power, see Zimin, Rossija na poroge, Chapter 3.
84   Missive by Vasilij III, as n. 80 above.

Cochran left the city for Copenhagen sometime between July 17 and August 31, 1506,⁸⁵ accompanied by the Russian diplomat Grigorij Istoma.⁸⁶ Istoma carried a personal missive from Vasilij III to King Hans in which the grand prince declared his willingness to continue the relationship enjoyed by his father and informed the king of the treaty-making procedures he had agreed with Cochran, as described above.

This was the context in which the royal chancery, possibly the chancellor Ove Bille himself, produced *the surviving copy of the Danish text of the treaty of 1493*, i.e. the document labelled *1493 in this book. As stated above, the purpose of the copy was to serve as a draft of the new treaty, for which reason the copyist entered a number of revisions directly into the copied text.⁸⁷

It is unclear when exactly the king transmitted his original letter of treaty to Moscow. The draft of his covering letter to Vasilij III, still in the Danish National Archives, is undated, but lists the Danish town of Nykøbing as the place of issue.⁸⁸ There is no evidence in extant sources that the king was present in this particular town in 1506, but he is known for certain to have attended

---

85   Opisi, p. 116. The source places the departure from Moscow in 7014, which ended on August 31, 1506. The *terminus post quem* is the date of Vasilij's missive to King Hans, July 17, 1506 (see 80 above).

86   The two knew each other well, as they had travelled together to Copenhagen in 1496 by circumnavigating the Kola Peninsula and northern Norway. The story of the mission is related by Herberstein in his *Rerum Moscovitarum Commentarii* (see the chapter "Navigatio per mare Glaciale" alias "Die Schiffung nach dem Moer das man das Eisig oder gefrorn Moer nennt" in Herberstein, Synoptische, pp. 374-85, esp. 374-80 [1556 and 1557 editions]); Herberstein had the information from Cochran and Istoma personally, as he met them on his first mission to Moscow in 1517. For a detailed study of Herberstein's account, see Šaskol'skij, Ob odnom plavanii, and, for Danish readers, Pape, Fælles Front. Istoma appears several times in the extant sources as translator of Latin. According to Herberstein, he had learned the language at the Danish court ("apud Ioannem Daniae regem" / "bei Khünig Hannsen in Dennemarckht") (Synoptische, p. 374). In 1517, he wrote the Latin version of Vasilij III's letter of treaty to the Grand Master of the Teutonic Order (SIRIO 53, 2, p. 19).

87   The authorship of Bille was suggested by the publisher of the oldest extant Danish archival inventories (ÆDA V/1, p. 20). As the revisions were high politics, they would hardly have been made by a lowly clerk or secretary.

88   Grönblad, Nya källor, 162; Kopengagenskie akty, 6; FMU VI, 5202; Aarsberetninger I, p. 54, 5; Forsten, Bor'ba, p. 156, n. 1, and SGGD V, 112 (with a translation into 19th-century Russian). It is incorrectly listed under the year 1505 in the latter.

negotiations with the Hanse there in June-July 1507.[89] A circumstantial source strongly suggests that this was indeed the occasion on which he produced the letter. Sometime in the summer of 1507, the king's nephew, King James IV of Scotland,[90] wrote letters to the pope in Rome and the kings of France and England informing them that the King of Denmark had been approached by high-ranking legates of the "Emperor of Russia" requesting league and friendship (*foedus et amicitiam*), i.e. an amicable treaty-based relationship, with him. The king king had consented to the request, seeing in the proposed relationship a vehicle for converting the Russians to Catholicism.[91] In all likelihood, this less-than-accurate account was written on the instigation of King Hans himself. On September 18, the Scottish king sent his Danish uncle a missive in which he first acknowledged receipt of a Danish envoy bringing his messages, then wrote that "as far as the Russian emperor is concerned," he, James, had written "abundantly" to the abovementioned rulers asking them individually to work towards a successful outcome of the matter ("ut felicem negocij successum pro se quisque curaret").[92] The exchange leaves little doubt that King Hans informed James IV in mid-1507 that he had just entered into a treaty with the Russians and simultaneously asked the Scottish king to help him put a spin on the controversial matter vis-à-vis the bigger powers in Europe.

Further to the question of the date, no sources mention a Danish diplomatic mission to Russia in the fall of 1506,[93] whereas David Cochran was demonstrably on his way to Moscow by way of Visby, Reval, Narva and Novgorod "with two Russians" (one of whom would have been Istoma) in the fall of 1507,

---

89   Regesta diplomatica I/1, 5351.
90   James' mother was King Hans' sister Margaret who had married his father, James III, in 1469.
91   A draft of the letter to Pope Julius II is printed in Epistolæ Jacobi Quarti I, XLV, pp. 85-86. The draft is undated, but letter No. XLII is dated April 10, 1507, and No. XLVII September 1507, while a letter to King Hans referring to the letter to the pope is dated September 18, 1507 (Aarsberetninger I, p. 57, No. 8).
92   Aarsberetninger I, p. 57, No. 8, referred to by Allen I, pp. 369-70.
93   David Cochran was apparently in Poland that fall (Regesta diplomatica II/I.2, 9125; Aarsberetninger I, p. 4, 4).

arriving in Narva in late September and Novgorod a little later.⁹⁴ The reason it took the Danish side so long to issue the king's letter of treaty to Vasilij could well be that Cochran brought with him to Russia a large shipload of military equipment plus four Scottish cannon founders – probably requested by Vasilij III and certainly delivered by King Hans in an attempt to ingratiate himself with the grand prince – which would have taken considerable time to put together.⁹⁵ There is no proof that Cochran and Istoma brought King Hans' diploma to Moscow on this particular journey, but it is a safe assumption. Landing in Narva, Cochran let it be known that Finland would be "torched and overrun" by the Russians before Christmas.⁹⁶ The Danish envoy would not have had the slightest chance of inducing Vasilij III to launch an attack on Finland unless he showed up in Moscow with King Hans' sealed and cross-kissed letter of treaty.

Vasilij III probably issued *his* treaty diploma to King Hans in the course of 1508 or early 1509. We are informed by one source that the act was brought to Denmark by the Russian envoy Dmitrij Laskirev, but not when, and his journey seems not to be mentioned in other sources.⁹⁷ The reference to Laskirev implies that the letter was *not* brought to Copenhagen by Cochran when he returned

---

94   The crossing from Visby via Reval to Narva is related in FMU VI, 5283, written October 3, 1507. King Hans had issued a request for a safe-conduct for Cochran to Reval on July 29, 1507, at which point the envoy had apparently just (*jegenwardigen*) left Copenhagen (LUB II/3, 230). He left Reval for Narva and arrived in the border town before October 3 (FMU VI, 5283). His presence in Novgorod before January 11, 1508, is implied in FMU VI, 5306.
95   FMU VI, 5283, 5291 and 5306. The cargo ship of 30 lasts perished without a trace during the crossing from Visby to Reval.
96   FMU VI, 5306 ("brendth och offuergaat").
97   Opisi, p. 25; Zimin, Gosudarstvennyj archiv, p. 54. The document is referred to as a *gramota dokončal'naja* (letter of treaty) with a golden seal appended, clearly indicating that this really is a reference to Vasilij III's corresponding letter of treaty to King Hans. Laskirev is a Russianization of the Greek surname Lascaris. The envoy was a Byzantine-Greek expatriate in the service of Vasilij III. Incidentally, he is portrayed exchanging letters of treaty with Emperor Maximilian in 1514 (p. 55) in the latter's memoirs, *Weisskunig* (vol. 2, ill. 237). See Kämpfer, Ratifizierung, pp. 237-239 and p. 55. Kämpfer fails to mention that Elizar Sukov, Laskirev's second-in-command on the mission to the emperor and the person who accompanied David Cochran to Copenhagen in 1509, appears in the image as well.

to Copenhagen from Moscow with the Russian envoy Elizar Sukov sometime between February 23 and August 31, 1509.[98]

C. The Treaty of 1516

First Step: The Treaty of 1514

King Hans died on February 20, 1513, and was succeeded by his son and heir Christian II (1513-23). Once again, the existing treaty would have to be renewed to remain in force, and this time both rulers were vitally interested in making it happen, though for very different reasons.

Christian II had been elected heir to the Swedish throne in 1497 following the Stockholm coronation of his father and began styling himself *electus* of Sweden immediately after assuming power at home in 1513. However, the disinclination of the Swedes to honor the claim in tandem with the election in 1512 of a young, ambitious regent, Sten Svantesson, or Sten Sture the Younger,[99] boded ill for his prospects. A war for the Swedish crown was looming, for which reason a swift renewal of the treaty with Muscovy constituted an urgent necessity.[100] In the spring of 1513, only a few months into his reign, the new

---

98 The former date is the *datum* of a letter from Turesson (FMU VII, 5369), while the latter appears in Opisi, p. 116, which places the departure in 7017 that ended on August 31, 1509. Sukov is mentioned in the Moscow archival inventory of the 1570s as bringing "the answer" of King Hans to Moscow when returning there (Opisi, p. 25, and Zimin, Gosudarstvennyj archiv, p. 54). It is unclear what is meant by "the answer", and the journey is not dated.

99 The new regent was the son of his predecessor, Svante Nilsson, who had governed the country in 1504-12. He deliberately substituted his patronymic with his grandmother's family name Sture to brand himself as the natural heir of the strong and widely popular regent Sten Sture, who had governed the country in 1471-97 and 1501-3. "The Younger" is a later historiographical epithet introduced to distinguish between the two.

100 Two new Scandinavian biographies of Christian II offer good background analyses of his confrontation with Sweden. Neither has much to say about his relations with Vasilij III, however. See Bisgaard, Christian 2., and Petersson, Furste av Norden. For a brief but concise overview of the conflict, consult Enemark, Fra Kalmarbrev, pp. 124 ff.

king dispatched David Cochran to Moscow to propose, negotiate and conclude a new accord with Vasilij III.[101]

The objectives of the mission are documented in a hitherto unpublished draft of Cochran's instructions held in the Danish National Archives.[102] The envoy was to express his sovereign's desire to renew the previous treaty and ask Vasilij III, in case he consented, to transmit his letter of treaty (implicitly: with the returning Cochran) to the king, who would then forward his corresponding letter to the grand prince. If, on the other hand, the grand prince should reject the request, Cochran was to ask him for a ten-year "truce, peace and friendship".[103] In addition, he was to implore the Muscovite ruler not to enter any alliances (*federationes*) with the Swedes until King Christian had taken possession of the Swedish throne. The letter expresses a certain doubt on the part of the new king concerning the intentions of the Muscovite ruler.

Vasilij III, on his part, had an ongoing conflict with the Jagiellonian ruler Sigismund I of Poland and Lithuania (1506-48) which had erupted into war in 1512.[104] The campaigns of 1512-3 and 1513-4 did not go particularly well

---

101 En route, Cochran wrote a report to the King still preserved in the original in the Danish National Archives. The letter, sent from Narva, offers a highly interesting look at a Danish diplomat hard at work gathering critical information about the current political scene in Russia (TKUA, Rusland: Akter og dokumenter vedrørende det politiske forhold til Rusland, l.nr. 73-13, 1493-1578. Printed in Grönblad, Nya källor, 320). See the image on page p. 70.

102 TKUA, Rusland: Akter og dokumenter vedrørende det politiske forhold til Rusland, l.nr. 73-13, 1493-1578. I am grateful to Markus Hedemann, Editor-in-Chief of *Diplomatarium Danicum*, for deciphering the document which is written in an unusually illegible hand.

103 Importantly, all three were technical terms. Truce (*treuga* in Latin, *Beifrieden* in German), aptly translated by Tiberg into "peace at set terms" (Moscow, Livonia and Hanseatic League, p. 8) was a peace limited in duration, normally because the parties negotiating it could not arrive at a solution to certain issues and therefore stipulated that new negotiations would take place during or at the end of the term. Peace (*pax, Frieden*) and friendship (*amicitia, Freundschaft*) were expressions rooted in classical antiquity of close, amicable, treaty-based political relations. See p. 57 n. 59 for references and pp. 96–7 and 118–9 for a further discussion of the terms.

104 Filjuškin, Vasilij III, pp. 181 ff.; Uebersberger, Österreich, pp. 70 ff. Sigismund had succeeded his brother Alexander as Grand Prince of Lithuania and King of Poland at the death of the latter in 1506.

for the Russians,[105] so the grand prince was looking for allies to participate in the war effort. In this, Christian II was an obvious candidate as the previous treaties had already stipulated a political alliance against the ruler of Lithuania.

Unfortunately for the king, Vasilij III had, as already mentioned, a pronounced interest in avoiding a military confrontation with Sweden, a concern that had guided his Swedish policy since his accession to the grand princely throne in 1505. In 1510 he had prolonged his father's truce of 1504 to no fewer than sixty years, once again sending a Russian embassy to Stockholm for validation of the act.[106] Three years later, only a few weeks before the arrival of David Cochran in Moscow to renew the alliance against Sweden, he confirmed the extension.[107]

Matters were further complicated when in early 1513 Emperor Maximilian launched yet another grandiose political scheme so characteristic of him.[108] The Habsburger had a conflict of his own with Sigismund I over the Hungarian succession (again). To put pressure on the Polish-Lithuanian ruler in this particular matter, he concocted an anti-Polish coalition comprising Denmark, Muscovy, the Teutonic Order in Prussia and Livonia and the electors and houses of Saxony and Brandenburg with the ostensible aim of bringing the feudal subordination of the Prussian Order to Poland to an end and place it under the overlordship of the German-Roman Empire.[109] Denmark was assigned a

---

105 Filjuškin, Vasilij III, pp. 183-8. Vasilij's objective was to conquer Smolensk, which had been annexed by Lithuania more than a hundred years earlier.
106 Treaty of 1510: ST III, 577, and FMU VII, 5446. The embassy to Stockholm: FMU VII, 5452, 5453, 5472, 5485; Opis' I, p. 244.
107 Treaty of 1513: ST III, 581, FMU VII, 5652, and SGGD V, 53. The underlying reason for the unprecedented 60-year timeframe reveals itself in a clause obliging Sweden to abstain from aiding Lithuania and Livonia in a future war with Muscovy. The reason for the confirmation in 1513 was the death of the Swedish regent Svante Nilsson the previous year.
108 The following after Fiedler, Allianz, passim (the text includes reprints of several original documents); Uebersberger, Österreich, Ch. 2; Wiesflecker, Kaiser Maximilian, Vol. IV, Chapter 3; Metzig, Kommunikation, Ch. 3; Wimmer, Livland, pp. 68 ff.; Allen II, pp. 95-123; Pisarevskij, K istorii, passim.
109 Uebersberger, Österreich, p. 78; Fiedler, Allianz, pp. 184-5. The emperor excused himself from participation in the coalition due to ongoing conflicts with France and Venice. The final list of participants appeared in a declaration (*Abscheid*) of the emperor to a departing embassy of the Teutonic Order in August 1514 (Russisch-Livländische Urkunden, CCCXXXIII). It included Wallachia, of all places.

David Cochran's signature
The only extant signature of the Danish envoy to Moscow is in a letter mailed to Christian II from Narva in May, 1513 (printed in Grönblad, Nya Källor, 320). The text, written in Low German, reads: "Danmarck Rex Armorum alias mysyr Dauid van Koran, jwer gnadens trwe dener etc." (Denmark King of Arms, alias master David van Koran, your Grace's faithful servant, etc.). Danish National Archives. Photo: Carsten Pape.

prominent role in the scheme, as the coalition was to be formally founded at a convention in Copenhagen attended by representatives of the various princes, including Vasilij III.[110]

Maximilian dispatched an ambassador to Moscow in early 1514 to initiate the grand prince in the plan and persuade him to send envoys to the founding assembly. Vasilij, however, was wary of grand coalitions and treaties negotiated away from Moscow and instead cajoled the imperial envoy into signing a bilateral Imperial-Muscovite treaty of alliance against Sigismund, on paper turning Maximilian into an ally in Muscovy's conflict with the Polish king. Not only did

---

110 See the diplomatic instructions for the Imperial ambassador to Moscow in Fiedler, Allianz, p. 239, and Pisarevskij, K istorii, pp. 9-21 (Russian translation). The scheme said something about the growing importance of Muscovy as a potential partner and ally in Western political thinking. As late as 1497, the Teutonic Order had vetted a plan for a grand coalition bringing together the Order, Poland, Livonia, Sweden, and the Hanse *against* "the infidel Russians, Tatars and Turks" who threatened Christendom with invasion and destruction (LUB II/1, 629, p. 459).

the unfortunate ambassador exceed his mandate on this occasion, he also made the additional *faux pas* of addressing Vasilij III as *kayser* (emperor) throughout the preliminary letter of treaty he issued in Moscow,[111] thereby recognizing, on behalf of his sovereign, the grand prince as the titular equal of the supposedly universal Christian emperor. Maximilian felt obligated to reciprocate the letter more or less word for word, though in German, but later in the year issued an altered version of the diploma with only a single reference to the imperial title, a letter which Vasilij in turn refused to accept.[112]

Maximilian's initiative placed King Christian II under considerable pressure. He had no political or strategic interest in joining an anti-Polish coalition and even less in fighting a costly war with the Polish king. Quite the contrary. King Hans had concluded a treaty of alliance with Sigismund in 1510, and Christian II would conclude a successor treaty in 1516.[113] Relations between the two kingdoms were amicable, and the Poles were as important to Denmark as the Russians in a coming war with the Swedes, if only because they could prevent merchants from Danzig from supplying Sweden during a conflict.[114] There was a dilemma, though. Concurrently with the launching of Maximilian's grand scheme in 1513, Christian II had begun exploring the possibility of a prestigious and lucrative marriage to the emperor's granddaughter Isabella of Burgundy,

---

111 That he issued a preliminary letter of the kind discussed in Chapter 1 is corroborated in Opisi, p. 18, Box 8, and Opis' I, p. 153.

112 Uebersberger, Österreich, pp. 77 ff.; Fiedler, Allianz, pp. 186 ff.; Kudrjavcev, Kayser vnnd herscher, pp. 47-50; Pisarevskij, K istorii, pp. 10 ff. Maximilian de facto revoked the treaty in 1517 (Agoštun, Titul Moskovskogo, p. 134). Both imperial texts are printed in Fiedler, Allianz, pp. 244-7 and 253-6, Vasilij's diploma on pp. 247-50 and in SGGD V, 67, and Maximilian's first diploma in SGGD V, 66 (with a translation into Russian).

113 The relevant documents are printed in Codex Diplomaticus I, pp. 355-6 (Sigismund) and 356-7 (Hans). There is a certain enigma about the treaty, as the published texts of the two diplomas differ significantly from one another and the original Polish diploma was never transmitted to Denmark. It is filed in the Polish national historical archive, *Archiwum Głównym Akt Dawnych*, which has kindly sent me a high-resolution image of it free of charge, for which I extend my thanks to archivist Hubert Wajs. On the other hand, the inventory of the documents brought into exile by King Christian II lists a copy of King Sigismund's ratification of the treaty (München-Samlingen, p. 74). Despite the enigma, the treaty was acknowledged by both parties, for it is explicitly referred to in the treaty concluded by Christian and Sigismund in 1516 (see below) (Codex Diplomaticus I, pp. 357-58, Sigismund's diploma).

114 Uebersberger, Österreich, p. 104.

a sister of the future Emperor Charles V. Once the liaison had been proposed and negotiations begun, the matter would surely be used as a bargaining tool for convincing the King of Denmark to join the anti-Polish league of his future de facto father-in-law.[115] Indeed, during the nuptial negotiations in Linz in early 1514, Maximilian demanded not only that Christian II join the projected coalition, but also that he commit to spending one third of the dowry, set at an exorbitant 250,000 Rhenish guilders, on actual warfare against Sigismund.

David Cochran arrived in Moscow on June 24, 1513,[116] but it took until the beginning of March the following year before the new Danish-Muscovite treaty was completed.[117] The delay was caused in part by Vasilij III's absence at the Polish front in the fall of 1513,[118] in part by the arrival of Maximilian's ambassador on February 2, 1514.[119] Negotiations with Cochran could well have begun by that date, but the grand prince undoubtedly wished to clench his imperial alliance ahead of entering into a treaty with the Danes. A compact in which Maximilian bound himself to participate in Vasilij's war with Sigismund

---

115 Isabella (known in Denmark as Elisabeth) was the daughter of Maximilian's son Philip of Burgundy (Philip the Fair or Handsome), who had died in 1506. The Danish-Imperial negotiations are still treated in the greatest detail by 19th-century Danish historian C. F. Allen (Allen II, pp. 101-15. See also Bisgaard, Christian 2., pp. 148-66).

116 PSRL VI/2, col. 396, PSRL XX, p. 386. The latter refers to the arrival under the year 7022, but this is an obvious error (the correct year is 7021). Among other things, the next entry in the chronicle is "February 7022" which should have preceded June 7022 by a wide margin if the latter were correct. Also, the letter written by Cochran to Christian II on his way to Russia is dated Narva, May 22, 1513 (Grönblad, Nya källor, 320, and Kopengagenskie akty, 10).

117 Swedish archbishop Jakob Ulvsson's statement of June 24, 1513, that David Cochran had returned from Russia is clearly incorrect (Grönblad, Nya källor, 327).

118 The grand prince left Moscow for the second time on June 14, 1513, ten days before the arrival of Cochran, and returned on November 21, only to plan for a new military campaign which was launched at the end of February 1514 (Filjuškin, Vasilij III, p. 188). Cochran, writing from Narva on May 22, 1513, told Christian II that he had been informed of the absence of Vasilij, then on his first campaign against the Poles, and that "yk furchte my dat er my eyn langhe Resenn wyll maken" (and I fear that he will make me a long journey) – a fear which certainly came true (Grönblad, Nya källor, 320).

119 PSRL VI/2, cols. 396-397, PSRL VIII, pp. 253-254, PSRL XIII, pp. 16-17, PSRL XX, p. 386. The imperial ambassador was dismissed on March 7 and subsequently left the city carrying Vasilij III's sealed letter of treaty to Maximilian (ibid.). The diploma is printed in SGGD V, 67; Fiedler, Allianz, pp. 247-250; and Vertrag Vasilijs III, 34.

would put maximum pressure on the Danish envoy to accede to the inclusion of a similar provision in the new treaty, not least in view of the ongoing negotiations for the marriage contract. The Muscovite grand prince will most likely have learned about the marriage plans from Maximilian's ambassador.[120]

A third reason for the delay may have been the absence of a proper mandate on the part of Cochran. The instruction of 1513 did not empower the Danish envoy to commit his sovereign to active participation in Vasilij's Polish war – the issue had not been raised when the instruction was written – forcing him in all likelihood to send a courier back to Copenhagen to obtain a mandate, as Vasilij would refuse to negotiate a treaty without his foreign interlocutor being in possession of *plena potestas*. In the end, an agreement was struck, whereupon Cochran issued, sealed and cross-kissed the required preliminary letter of treaty while Vasilij issued, sealed and cross-kissed his original diploma to the king.[121]

In general terms, the parties agreed that the new treaty would once again be a word-for-word copy of the preceding one, but with the addition of a new anti-Polish clause (see below for documentation). Both acts have been lost, but the clause is easily identifiable in Vasilij III's surviving letter of treaty of 1516 (i.e. *1516), in which it forms a very wordy departure from the purely political anti-Lithuanian articles in the Danish texts of 1493 and 1506 (Appendix, items 16-16ª). The corresponding clause of the 1514 acts will doubtless have been near-identical, for it appears almost verbatim in Vasilij's letter of treaty to Maximilian issued just a month before his letter to Christian II.[122] The only difference between the two appearances was a rather unconventional

---

120 The treaty of marriage was concluded on April 29, 1514. For a transcript of the original, see Lindbæk, Christiern, or Historiske aktstykker, pp. 3-10. According to Wiesflecker, the willingness of Maximilian to consider the marriage was caused by the role he intended Denmark to play in his anti-Polish coalition plans (Kaiser Maximilian, IV, pp. 173-74). In fact, the contract does oblige Christian II to join the proposed coalition if the north German electors were willing to do so as well (Historiske aktstykker, p. 9).

121 The negotiation process, the reaching of an agreement, the inclusion of the anti-Polish clause, and the issuing and cross-kissing of the pertinent acts are referred to in the subsequent Russian ambassadorial orations before Christian II in 1514 and 1515 (Russkie akty, 2, col. 5 and 4, col. 9). As the orations have been preserved in the original in the Danish National Archives – they were normally handed over to the receiving princes – the evidence is incontrovertible, as further documented by two additional sources cited below.

122 Fiedler, Allianz, pp. 248-9.

inclusion in *1516 of a reference to the treaty against Sigismund just concluded by Vasilij and Maximilian – a thinly veiled piece of political blackmail meant to put pressure on Christian II to fulfill his new obligation.[123] The Muscovite ruler would continue to nudge the Danish king into compliance by referring to his treaty with the emperor and the latter's promise to join the fight against Sigismund in the ambassadorial orations of his envoys to Copenhagen in both 1514 and 1515.[124] The overall political priorities of the grand prince were amply revealed by the fact that it took until the end of both orations before any mention was made of his willingness to take action against the Swedes – once Christian had moved against Sigismund, that is.[125]

Cochran left Moscow in mid-April 1514 and arrived in Copenhagen with the treaty acts sometime in June accompanied by the Russian diplomats Ivan Nikolaevič [*Mikulin syn*] Zabolockij and Vasilij Aleksandrov.[126] On July 3,

---

[123] The text states that when or if Christian II engages in war with Sigismund and informs Vasilij thereof, the latter "will also, for our brotherly love and for the friendship and pact (*zaveščanie*) we have entered into with our brother Maximilian, Roman emperor-elect and most august king, your father, move against [Sigismund] united with you" (Appendix, item 16ª). For the term "your father" in this context, see the explanation of *otcem* on p. 120.

[124] 1514: Russkie akty, 2, cols. 6-7. 1515: Ibid, 4, cols. 11-12. The information about Maximilian's intentions was false, as demonstrated below, but Vasilij would not have known this when he dispatched his envoys to Copenhagen. As late as 1521, the grand prince once again exhorted Christian II to aid him in his fight with Sigismund according to the treaty of 1516 (Russkie akty, 10).

[125] Russkie akty, 2, cols. 6-7, and 4, cols. 11-12.

[126] Cochran was formally dismissed (*otpustilsja*) on April 9 (PSRL VI/2, col. 397, PRSL VIII, p. 254, PSRL XIII, p. 17, PSRL XX, p. 386), and Vasilij's letter of credence for his envoys is dated April 10 (Russkie akty, 1). On May 4, Narva informed Reval that one of its citizens was escorting Cochran there (Hanserecesse III/6, 551). On June 1, the customs officer in Elsinore, based on information received from Reval, informed King Christian that the envoy had left that city accompanied by "some 30 Russians" (Grönblad, Nya källor, 342). In a draft letter to Vasilij III drafted on July 5, the king writes, *inter alia*, that the grand princely envoys had arrived in Copenhagen "a few days ago" (*his diebus peractis*) (Grönblad, Nya källor, 344). The Russian envoys are identified as Ivan Mikulin [syn] Zabolockij and Vasilij Aleksandrov in the 1514 and 1515 letters of credence, the 1516 inventory of the tsars' archive, and the Russian ambassadorial orations of 1514 and 1515 (Russkie akty, 1 and 3; Opisi, p. 117; Russkie akty, 2 and 4) and as Ivan Jaryj son of Mikula and Vasilij Belyj in several Russian chronicles (PSRL VI/2, col. 397, PSRL VIII, pp. 254, 259, PSRL XIII, стр. 17, PSRL XX, p. 386). In the hitherto unpublished Latin translations of the two orations, produced in Moscow,

the royal chancery drew up and subsequently revised *the surviving copy of the treaty of 1506 (i.e. *1506)* as a preliminary draft of Christian II's corresponding letter of treaty,[127] and two days later it drafted a royal missive to Vasilij III acknowledging receipt of his consent to conclude the new treaty as well as an instruction for David Cochran concerning his upcoming return mission.[128] As early as August 14, 1514, the Danish and Russian envoys were back in Moscow with the king's sealed and cross-kissed corresponding letter of treaty.[129] Speed was clearly of the essence.

The Treaty Annulled

What happened next was exceptional, though not entirely without precedent: Vasilij III refused to accept Christian II's act and simultaneously annulled his own.[130] In April 1515 he dispatched a new embassy to Copenhagen to explain his reasons and present Christian II with the text he expected him to

---

the envoys are named Johannes Nicolaij filius Zabolotzco and Vasilius Alexandri (1514) and Johannes Nicolai and Vasilius filius Alexandri (1515) (National Archives, TKUA, Rusland: Akter og dokumenter vedrørende det politiske forhold til Rusland, l.nr. 73-13, 1493-1578).

127 Grönblad, Nya källor, 343.
128 The draft missive: Grönblad, Nya källor, 344, and Kopengagenskie akty, 12. The draft instruction: Grönblad, Nya källor, 345, and Kopengagenskie akty, 13. On the same date, Christian II issued a letter to Reval requesting the city council to facilitate Cochran's upcoming passage through the town (Russisch-Livländische Urkunden, CCCXXXII).
129 PSRL VI/2, col. 397, PSRL VIII, p. 254, PSRL XIII, p. 17, PSRL XX, p. 386. Opisi, p. 117, places the arrival in 7023 AM, i.e. between September 1, 1514 and August 31, 1515.
130 Russkie akty, 4, col. 10. The precedent: In 1506, soon after his accession to the throne, Vasilij III sent an envoy to the Crimean Tatars to suggest a renewal of the treaty between Ivan III and Khan Mengli-girej. When presented with the khan's new letter of treaty the following year, the grand prince rejected it. Unfortunately, no explanation is offered in the chronicles recording the event (e.g. PSRL XIII, p. 4).

employ in a new letter of treaty if he, Vasilij, were to accept it and issue his own corresponding diploma.[131] What had gone wrong?

Unfortunately, the Russian envoys did not explain the cause of the matter in their 1515 oration before the king. Austrian historian Hans Uebersberger suggested that it was Christian II who rejected Vasilij's letter of treaty because of the inclusion of the new anti-Polish clause in its text. Instead, he claims, the king produced a diploma that was an exact copy of the Danish letter of 1493, which in turn was the reason for the grand prince's rejection of it.[132] The thesis is feasible in view of the opposition of the king to the alliance against Sigismund, but it is not supported by compelling evidence, nor by situational logic. Christian II must have acceded to the Polish clause and somehow, most likely by a courier, empowered David Cochran to close the deal. *Not* including the clause would potentially have damaged his relations with both Vasilij III and Maximilian and put any hope of Russian intervention against Sweden or a swift disbursement of the Habsburg dowry in jeopardy. Conversely, he risked little by accepting the clause. His negotiators in Linz had managed to insert a paragraph in the marriage contract with Maximilian making his participation in the anti-Polish league conditional on the simultaneous accession of the north German electors, and they had rejected the emperor's grand scheme out of hand by the time Christian produced his letter of treaty to Vasilij III.[133] Additionally, rulers were seldom punished for not living up to their treaty obligations as long as their mutual diplomatic relationships remained desirable at a general level, as evidenced by Vasilij III's truces with the very Swedes he was supposed to fight according to his treaties with the Danish kings.

---

131   Russkie akty, 4 (the ambassadorial oration). The Russian envoys were the same as the previous year. The date of departure is given in e.g. PSRL VI/2, col. 405, PSRL VIII, p. 259, PSRL XIII, p. 24, PSRL XX, p. 390. Likewise, Vasilij III's letter of credence for his envoys is dated "April 7023", i.e. April 1515 (Russkie akty, 3).

132   Uebersberger, Österreich, pp. 89-90. Tiberg concurs in placing the blame on Christian II, but offers no reason for his reaction (Moscow, Livonia and the Hanseatic League, pp. 156-7). Uebersberger evidently does not know the text of Vasilij III's 1516 letter of treaty to Christian II, neither is he aware of the existence of the treaty of 1506.

133   Allen II, pp. 115, 152-3; Bisgaard, Christian 2., p. 153. The paragraph is on p. 9 of the treaty as published by Reedtz in Historiske aktstykker. David Cochran would not have known this result of the Linz negotiations when he negotiated the treaty terms with his Russian counterparts.

In terms of hard evidence supporting Uebersberger's thesis, it is true that the draft of the new treaty produced by the royal chancery on July 3 (i.e. *1506) does not include the anti-Polish clause. The document, however, is clearly an *early* draft, not the final version from which the king's original letter of treaty was eventually drawn up.[134] Among other things, the titles of the signatories are by and large substituted by an "etc.". Furthermore, the draft missive to Vasilij III and the draft instruction to David Cochran, produced two days later after further political deliberations, both promise the grand prince that the king will issue a letter of treaty repeating the 1506 accord verbatim while adding the article against Sigismund ("addendo articulum contra regem Polonie", in Danish "oc luder oc samme confederacion mod konungen aff Paalen"),[135] which is said to have been demanded by Vasilij III.[136] Christian II clearly accepted the inclusion of the anti-Polish clause in the treaty, meaning that an omission to do so was *not* the reason for the rejection of his treaty diploma by Vasilij. More evidence in favor of this view will follow below.

Uebersberger is unaware of the drafts discussed above, even though Grönblad's volume in which they are printed is on his list of literature. He therefore misses the one feature of the king's communication with the grand prince which might, on the face of it, have roused the ire of Vasilij III. This is a statement in both the draft missive and the draft instruction requesting that the grand prince issue, *upon receipt of the king's letter of treaty*, an identical (i.e. corresponding) diploma written in Latin.[137]

---

134 In his introduction to the document, Grönblad calls it the "draft of the original" (*original-konceptet*), but this is obviously not the case (Grönblad, Nya källor, 343).
135 Grönblad, Nya källor, 344 and 345.
136 Grönblad, Nya källor, 345.
137 "[…] instanter fratrem nostrum charissimum rogantes, quatenus velit nobis quam primum similes literas suas, sigillo suo sigillatas et in latino conscriptas, cum haraldo nostro Dauid remittere" (asking without delay our most beloved brother whether he will forthwith send back his identical letter, sealed with his seal and written in Latin, with our herald David) (Grönblad, Nya källor, 344). The draft instruction for David Cochran states the same: "Oc begerer at then stoore forste will oc sende met mester Dauid myn herre [Christian II] hanss breff, liige swaa ludendis paa sijne vegne oc screiffuet paa latine" (Grönblad, Nya källor, 345).

The request is odd, and not only for the suggestion that Vasilij formulate his act in Latin.[138] It is glaringly out of step with the ongoing treaty-making process. The orations of the Russian envoys to Copenhagen in 1514 and 1515 make it abundantly clear that Vasilij III had issued, sealed and cross-kissed his original letter of treaty, and David Cochran his preliminary royal letter, in Moscow in April 1514, and that the diplomats had brought the acts to Copenhagen in June of that year.[139] All Christian II had to do according to the standard Russian treaty-making procedure *and* the Russian oration of 1514 was to transfer the text of Cochran's preliminary act word for word to his own letter of treaty. In other words, the king's diploma was clearly and correctly considered the *corresponding* letter of treaty. Yet Christian II apparently reversed the chronological order of issuing the two letters, in effect canceling the letter of Vasilij III that he had just received. Obviously, this would be cause enough for the Muscovite grand prince to annul the letter of Christian II once it arrived in Moscow.

We need not take the argument this far, however. In their 1514 ambassadorial oration, made just days before Christian II issued his ill-fated act, the Russian envoys first went over the details of the ongoing treaty-making process, then continued:

"And when you, God willing, King-elect Christian of Denmark and Sweden and Norway, are crowned, you should send your envoys to us [asking for] friendship and brotherhood. And when, God willing, your envoys are then with us, we will then enter friendship and brotherhood in the same manner in which we were in friendship and brotherhood with your father Hans, King of Denmark and Sweden and Norway."[140]

---

138 This *could* be explained by the fact that the Russian orations of both 1514 and 1515 and the credential of 1515 were accompanied by translations into Latin produced by the *Russian* side. These are unpublished, but preserved in the Danish National Archives (TKUA, Rusland: Akter og dokumenter vedrørende det politiske forhold til Rusland, l.nr. 73-13, 1493-1578).

139 Russkie akty, 2, col. 5, and 4, col. 9.

140 "A kak ty ožo dast" bog izbrannyj korol' Kristern" datckii i sveiskii i norveiskii koronueššja i ty by k nam prislal svoich poslov o družbe i o bratstve. I kak ožo dast" bog budut u nas togdy tvoi posly i my togdy s toboju učinimsja v družbe i v bratstve po tomu ž kak esmja byli s" otcem s tvoim s Yvanom korolem datckim i sveiskim i norveiskim v družbe i v bratstve". Quoted from the original (TKUA, Rusland: Akter og

The statement is key to a correct understanding of the king's action and the full treaty-making process of 1514-6. As previously explained, "friendship and brotherhood" (*družba i bratstvo*) was a standard Muscovite metaphor for an amicable, treaty-based political relationship, in effect a synonym for a treaty of alliance. In this light the statement must be interpreted to mean that Vasilij III considers the treaty concluded with Cochran in 1514 an incomplete accord due to the fact that Christian II is still *electus*, i.e. not yet properly crowned and therefore inferior to the Muscovite grand prince in terms of regal status.[141] Once the coronation has taken place, however, a new full-fledged treaty between equals ("in *the same manner* in which we were in friendship and brotherhood with your father Hans") will have to be made. In other words, the envoys' invocation of the 1506 treaty is not just a casual allusion to the most recent accord but a deliberate reference to a fully constituted treaty between two rulers of equal standing in the hierarchy of princes. Accordingly, if in 1514 Vasilij agreed to enter "friendship and union (edinačestvo)" with Christian II, a year later he would substitute "union" with "brotherhood".

By coincidence, Christian II was crowned King of Denmark on June 11, 1514, a couple of weeks before David Cochran and the Russian envoys arrived in Copenhagen with Vasilij III's first letter of treaty. At that point, his Norwegian coronation on July 29 had also been arranged. He was therefore in the required position to initiate the second step in his diplomatic relationship with the Muscovite grand prince, the full-fledged treaty, and *this* will explain his restarting the treaty-making process, as well as his suggestion that Vasilij issue a new letter of treaty upon receipt of his own.

This conclusion is supported by the fact that the draft of the treaty drawn up on July 3 (*1506) addresses Christian II *Rex* of Denmark, the Slavs and the

---

dokumenter vedrørende det politiske forhold til Rusland, l.nr. 73-13, 1493-1578) and printed with minor errors in Russkie akty, 2, col. 5.

141   According to two Russian chronicles that relate the arrival of David Cochran in 1513, he arrived from "the *elected* King Christian of Denmark and Sweden" (PSRL VI/2, col. 396, PSRL XX, p. 386. Emphasis added). Significantly, in his ambassadorial oration of 1514, Vasilij named King Hans, but not the as yet uncrowned Christian II, his brother. A year later, however, when the coronation had taken place, Christian was addressed *brat* (Russkie akty, 1-4).

Goths and *Electus* of Sweden and Norway (pp. 103, 105, items 2 and 33).[142] Furthermore, now that the meaning of the reference to the 1506 treaty in the oration of 1514 has been correctly understood, it is easy to see that the king himself announced the proper status of his letter of treaty in the (draft) missive to Vasilj III, writing "Dearest brother, we have ordered the drawing up of a letter of our side on *the kind of confederation* that existed between our dearest father and your serenity [Vasilij]."[143] It also becomes apparent that David Cochran actually explained the new situation to the grand prince and urged him to enter into a new, fully equal relationship with the Danish king. In the Russian ambassadorial oration of 1515 Vasilij III relates how Cochran, having arrived in Moscow, suggested concluding a treaty *like the one* Vasilij had had with King Hans, and how the envoy had brought King Christian's new pertinent letter of treaty with him.[144]

Vasilij explicitly accepted the change in the king's status as well as the new treaty-making procedure in his 1515 ambassadorial oration – in which he announced his non-acceptance of the letter of treaty – and demonstrated it by

---

142 The "Electus of Norway" part of the title may appear odd, as the crown of Norway was considered an inheritance of the Danish Oldenborg dynasty, not an elective office. In theory, however, it did assume both an election and a coronation to take place (Riis, Kongen, p. 311; Bisgaard, p. 165). Vasilij III correctly entitled Christian II *istinnyj naslednik norvejskij*, a direct translation of the Danish "ret arving til Norge" (rightful heir to Norway) in the letter of credence for his envoys as well as the ambassadorial oration of 1514 (Russkie akty, 1 and 2).

143 "Carissime frater, super tali confederacione de verbo ad verbum, que inter genitorem nostrum charissimum [King Hans] et serenitatem vestram [Vasilij III] fuerat, literas nostra jussimus conficere pro parte nostra" (Most beloved brother, we have ordered that our letter on the kind of alliance that existed between our most beloved father [King Hans] and your serenity [Vasilij III] be produced word for word on our part) (Grönblad, Nya källor, 344). In the draft instruction to Cochran, the king likewise emphasized that the letter of treaty brought to Moscow by the envoy was *identical* to the 1506 treaty: "item ath myn herris nade [Christian II] sender hannum [Vasilij III] hanss nadis breff om venskab oc confederacion, at ville halde med then staare forste ligerwiiss som hanss nades herre fader [King Hans] halth met hanum, ludendis ord fran ord som thet gamle confederacionis [letter of treaty] lude" (item that my lord grace [Christian II] sends him [Vasilij III] his grace's letter of friendship and alliance which he will hold with the grand prince in the same manner his father [King Hans] held with him, sounding word for word like the previous letter of alliance) (Grönblad, Nya källor, 345).

144 Russkie akty, 4, col. 9. See the previous footnote for Cochran's instruction.

addressing Christian II King of Denmark, Norway and, rather oddly, Sweden.[145] In other words, the change of procedure initiated by Christian II was not the reason for Vasilij III's rejection of his letter of treaty.

(Incidentally, the explanation offered above solves another puzzle. If Christian II's 1514 letter of treaty had been corresponding in relation to Vasilij III's initial diploma, as commonly assumed, there would have been no reason at all to make a draft of it. All that the chancery would have had to do was to transcribe David Cochran's preliminary royal letter issued in Moscow word for word, as indeed the Russian envoys urged the king to do in their 1514 oration.)

◎ ◎ ◎

If the rejection of the king's 1514 letter of treaty was unrelated to the Polish issue and to the change of procedure by Christian II, what *did* cause it? Norwegian historian Kåre Selnes suggested that in his diploma the king had placed the *intitulatio* before the *inscriptio*, i.e. his own name and title before those of the grand prince, thus offending Vasilij III with a protocollary blunder.[146] This is unlikely, however. The Danish texts of 1493 and 1506 both place the intitulation before the inscription, as was indeed standard protocol in European treaties at the time, and there is no evidence in other contemporaneous Muscovite treaties that Vasilij III had changed his preferences in this respect. For instance, Maximilian's letter of treaty of 1514, which was received in Moscow almost simultaneously with Christian II's diploma, places the intitulation first,[147] as

---

145 Russkie akty, 4, cols. 9-10 (the oration). The credential is printed by Ščerbačev as well (Russkie akty, 3), but in a highly flawed manner, as he omits Norway, the Slavs, and the Goths as well as the term "elected" before "to the kingship of Sweden" (*na kralevstvo sveiskoe*) from the king's title. The original as well as an accompanying Latin-language version are held in the Danish National Archives (TKUA, Rusland: Akter og dokumenter vedrørende det politiske forhold til Rusland, l.nr. 73-13, 1493-1578). The king's Norwegian coronation had taken place on July 29, 1514 (Bisgaard, Christian 2., p. 165), but Cochran will not have known this when he arrived in Moscow in August. The reason for the inclusion of Sweden in the title in the oration could well be that Christian II, in his draft instructions to Cochran, ordered the envoy to explain that the Swedes were about to accept him as king in the near future – an illusion, as it turned out (Grönblad, Nya källor, 345).
146 Selnes, König Christiern, p. 307.
147 Fiedler, Allianz, pp. 244-7.

did other communications by Maximilian to Vasilij.[148] So did the Polish letter of the Polish-Muscovite treaty of 1509 as well as Sigismund I's ratifications of his truces with Moscow in 1523 and 1527,[149] and the King of Poland ranked on a par with the King of Denmark vis-à-vis the grand prince, as both were sovereign rulers not subordinate to the German-Roman Empire. If anything, Vasilij could well have forced Sigismund, his arch enemy, to place the *inscriptio* first in his diplomas, but he did not.

Selnes does have a point, though, in suggesting that the reason for the rejection was protocollary or in some other way minor, not one of substance, for the rupture did not harm the relations between Christian II and Vasilij III in the least.[150] Quite the opposite. In 1517, a year after the eventual conclusion of the treaty (see below), Vasilij III granted Christian II a unique concession: a privilege permitting Danish merchants to establish a fenced-in trade yard with a Catholic church and priest in both Novgorod and Ivangorod and confirming the right granted them in the previous treaties to trade all through the grand prince's lands.[151] This was more than the Hanse had ever possessed in terms of commercial rights in Russia.[152] Even before this, probably in 1515, Vasilij had acceded to a request by Christian II to receive a number of young Danes for Russian language training.[153] As a further sign of goodwill, the Russian

---

148 SGGD V, 56, 83, 84.
149 SGGD V, 59, 97 and 102.
150 On June 1, 1516, Vasilij wrote to Christian that "we wish to maintain our friendship with and love for you, our brother, henceforth, as much as God helps us" (Russkie akty, 5, col. 14).
151 Tiberg, Moscow, Livonia and the Hanseatic League, pp. 154-60; Šaskoľskij, Èkonomičeskie svjazi, p. 20, and, in particular, Kazakova, Russko-datskie torgovye otnošenija, pp. 94-102, which provides a meticulous analysis of the privilege. The act is held in the Danish National Archives (Udenrigsministeriet, Forholdet til udlandet (traktater): E 1 Forholdet til udlandet. Pergamentsbreve (1454-1751) b-425: Rusland 1517 7 2a) and printed in Russkie akty, 9. Further, the privilege is mentioned briefly by Allen II, p. 155; Rasmussen, Historie og diplomati, p. 14, and Selnes, König Christian, p. 308.
152 Kazakova, Danija, Rossija i Livonija, pp. 116-7.
153 Russkie akty, 6. The students were brought to Russia by Cochran and, against the will of Christian II, placed in the Russian interior instead of Ivangorod for faster learning and better supervision; they were taught Russian by a certain "doctor Michail". On a personal note, I was a Russian language student at Moscow State University in 1971-2 and consider the young Danes my earliest predecessors!

and sometimes Imperial diplomats journeying between Moscow and Emperor Maximilian after 1514 typically went by way of Copenhagen, not Lübeck as had been the custom under Ivan III.[154]

In other words, the relationship between the two monarchs was intensified after the debacle of 1514-5 by the realization for the first time of some of the commercial potential inherent in the previous treaties. King Hans had never taken the relationship this far, nor had Ivan III.[155] The eventual foundering of the commercial projects can be attributed to the war with Sweden which Christian II began in 1517, and which was to embroil him for the remaining years of his rule.

In the end, there is no evidence in the extant sources explaining the reason for Vasilij III's rejection of Christian II's first letter of treaty. The issue could well be one of intitulation, however. Vasilij III had expanded his title significantly in the treaty with Maximilian in early 1514 and, by implication, in the treaty he issued to Christian II shortly thereafter, and the Danish chancery may have missed the point when producing the first letter of treaty of Christian II. Or Vasilij wanted the king to retroactively add the term *Smolenskij* to his title, even though he had not seized Smolensk until after issuing his initial letter of treaty of 1514. But again, this is conjecture, although it is based on numerous examples of "title wars" between Muscovy and its allies and enemies.[156]

---

154 Russkie akty, 4, 5; Neizdannye akty, 7; Russkie akty Revel'skogo archiva, 8; Bantyš-Kamenskij, Obzor, p. 208.

155 In 1508, however, Lübeck apparently suspected that entrepôts were about to be established in both Copenhagen and Ivangorod. The news led to some fear of the negative effects of the measure on many Hanseatic towns. See Tiberg, Moscow, Livonia and the Hanseatic League, p. 154, with a reference to LUB II/3, 337.

156 The best known of these is the introduction of the title "Sovereign of all Russia" in early 1493 in a correspondence with Grand Prince Alexander of Lithuania (SIRIO 35, 19), which the latter correctly interpreted as a Muscovite claim to lands that had once been part of Kiev Rus' but were currently under the sovereignty of Lithuania. Closer to home, the conflict over Ivan's title cost David Cochran a six-month prolongation of a stay in Moscow in the winter of 1503-4 (SIRIO 35, pp. 397, 440-1, 450-4, 459, 467-8).

The Treaty of 1516

Vasilij III's original letter of treaty of 1516 to King Christian II, written on parchment and with the grand princely seal, a golden bull, appended. Note that the scribe first constructed a grid with lines and margins before engrossing the document. The design of the act, including bull, initial and grid, is nearly identical to Vasilij's letter of treaty to Emperor Maximilian in 1514, which is reproduced in Ideja Rima v Moskve, p. 432.

The Treaty Completed

The final steps in the process of completing the treaty of 1516 are unknown, but it is a fair assumption that Christian II simply produced a new letter of treaty in accordance with the grand prince's requirements and sent it to Moscow. When and by whom is uncertain, but it may well have been by David Cochran in the fall of 1515.[157] Vasilij III issued, sealed and cross-kissed his still extant letter of treaty (*1516) on August 9, 1516,[158] and there is little doubt that he would not have done so had he not received the king's corresponding act in advance. The letter was brought to Copenhagen by David Cochran and the Russian envoy Nekras Charlamov sometime after August 9.[159]

◎ ◎ ◎

---

157   Cochran and the two Russian diplomats who had visited Copenhagen in 1515 arrived in Moscow in 7024 AM, i.e. between September 1, 1515, and August 31, 1516 (Opisi, p. 117). Within this time span, a date in the fall of 1515 or early 1516 seems likely. On September 2, 1515, Christian II informed Reval that he had recently dispatched his envoy, master David king-of-arms, to Russia (Russisch-Livländische Urkunden, CCCLIII). Cochran arrived in the town before September 29 (FMU VII, 5835). Once the party reached Ivangorod, however, it was held up by what looks like a pestilence which killed several participants, including some Russians. The party was still in the town on November 20 (FMU VII, 5849).

158   The date appears in the document itself; see p. 112, item 40. Allen has August 2, 1517, as the date of issue (Allen II, p. 155), possibly because some of the translations into German give this date (see pp. 120–1).

159   In the letter of June 1, 1516 (p. 82, n. 150), Vasilij III informed Christian II that he would soon dispatch David Cochran to Copenhagen with his secretary Nekras Charlamov (Russkie akty, 5). Several Russian chronicles state that Cochran and Charlamov were dismissed (*otpustilis'*) by the grand prince in June, and that the latter brought Vasilij's letter of treaty to Copenhagen (PSRL VI/2, col. 406, PSRL VIII, pp. 259-60, PSRL XIII, pp. 24-25, PSRL XX, pp. 390-1). For unknown reasons, considerable time apparently went by between the farewell audience (*otpusk*) and the issuing of the treaty in August. In all likelihood, Cochran and Charlamov did not leave the city until after August 9, the date of Vasilij's letter of treaty, Charlamov's letter of credence (Russkie akty, 7) and a grand princely letter to Reval asking the city not to put obstacles in the way of the envoy. Reval wrote back on September 20 informing Vasilij of Charlamov's arrival and subsequent departure for Copenhagen (Hanserecesse III/6, p. 774, n. 1, full text in Russkie akty Revel'skogo archiva, 10). On the same date the Reval council informed Lübeck that Cochran and a Russian company had left the city for Copenhagen *on that day* (Hanserecesse III/6, 727, p. 819, n. 2).

To wind up the 1514-6 episode: Maximilian abandoned his grand anti-Polish plan and thus his anti-Polish alliance with Vasilij III at the so-called First Congress of Vienna in the summer of 1515, at which the epochal Habsburg-Jagiellonian double marriage was agreed and performed.[160] The new dynastic constellation would subject Bohemia and Hungary to Habsburg rule for the next four centuries.[161] Since it was a prerequisite for the conclusion of the pertinent treaties that Sigismund I accede to the agreement, Maximilian gave up his protection of the Teutonic Order and left its fate to its feudal overlord since 1466, the King of Poland – i.e. to Sigismund. The emperor subsequently launched a serious diplomatic campaign to persuade Vasilij III to make peace with the latter which was to last until the emperor's death in 1519, the political reason being a desire to align Russia and Poland-Lithuania against the ever more threatening Turks.[162] In 1515, for instance, he exhorted the warring rulers to use Christian II as arbiter in their conflict.[163] The Muscovite grand prince continued the warfare, however, until eventually signing a five-year truce in 1523. Rather than giving in to their nominal Polish overlord, the Teutonic Order concluded a short-lived anti-Polish defensive treaty with Vasilij III in 1517.[164] In 1526, diplomatic missions to Moscow from the German-Roman Empire and the papacy came to an end with Sigismund von Herberstein's second journey to Russia.

Christian II confirmed his father's 1510 treaty with Sigismund I in the summer of 1516,[165] exactly two months before Vasilij III issued his letter of treaty to the Danish king obliging the latter to wage war on the Polish-Lithuanian ruler and promising to aid him in his fight with the Swedes with whom Vasilij had

---

160 In brief, Vladislav, the Jagiellonian King of Bohemia and Hungary and brother of Sigismund I, married off his two surviving children, Anna and the future King Louis II, to two of Maximilian's grandchildren, among them the later emperor Ferdinand I. At the death of Louis in the battle of Mohacs in 1526 his kingdoms fell to the Habsburgs.
161 Fiedler, Allianz, pp. 198 ff.; Metzig, Diplomatie Maximilians, pp. 265 ff.
162 E.g. SGGD V, 83, 85 (1518). Sigismund von Herberstein's famous mission to Moscow in 1517 was but one instance in this diplomatic effort.
163 Fiedler, Allianz, p. 228-34; Uebersberger, Österreich, p. 101. Both princes were against the idea, however.
164 For a short outline of the treaty and its aftermath, see Filjuškin, Vasilij III, pp. 210-14. Full documentation in SIRIO 53.
165 Uebersberger, Österreich, p. 104.

confirmed a truce of sixty years just three years earlier.[166] In 1523, Christian was deposed by a noble rebellion against his rule and Danish-Muscovite diplomatic relations came to a forty-year standstill.

---

166 Sigismund's diploma, dated June 8, 1516, is in the Danish National Archives (Udenrigsministeriet, Forholdet til udlandet (traktater): E 1 Forholdet til udlandet. Pergamentsbreve. Polen. Nr. 10. It is printed in Codex Diplomaticus I, pp. 357-8. The Danish diploma is presumably lost.

познаньскои секратарь королевскои
и князь станиславъ городетскои

А литовскіе послы панъ станиславъ
глѣбовичь намѣстникъ полотцкіи
да пан тѣ и поповичь намѣстникъ соде
нескіи. да писарь ивашко сопѣжичь
поехаша со княземъ дмитромъ иваномъ
васильевичемъ во всея русіи. перемиріе
на шесть лѣтъ ѿ благовѣщеніева дни

3. The Texts

The texts of the three surviving documents published and translated below are my transcriptions of the original records in the Danish National Archives conferred with prior publications.

Publication Principles

I have "straightened" the texts by expanding all abbreviations and entering all text elements originally appearing in the margin or above the line – superscripted letters, tildes, etc. – into the text flow. All three originals are devoid of systematically used punctuation marks, indentations, capital letters and other visually organizing features, so to enhance their legibility I have broken them down into "items" – titles, formulae and articles, in some cases further divided into sub-units – indicated by a line return and numbered in the margin. For uniform referencing across the three documents, the numbering is applied consistently to all appearances of identical items in all published texts in this and the following chapter as well as in the Appendix. Consequently, references to individual text units are to *items*, not to page and line numbers or "articles". The quickest way for readers to identify an item across texts is to consult the Appendix.

← Producing a treaty with Muscovy
The image shows the negotiations of a truce between Ivan III and envoys of the Polish-Lithuanian ruler Alexander in Moscow in 1503. Once agreement on the wording of the treaty was reached, secretaries of both sides set about drawing up their diplomas (bottom). These were sealed and cross-kissed and subsequently exchanged (top). Ivan is seated on his throne on the left, while a boyar of his is effecting the actual hand-over.
Miniature from the Russian "Illustrated Chronicle Compilation". Copyright: AKTEON Publishing House, Moscow.

To further enhance legibility, I divide each of the published texts into four sections by a blank line: the formal opening section, or protocol, the alliance section of the *dispositio* (clauses establishing the alliances against Sweden and Lithuania), the cooperation section of the *dispositio* (clauses establishing future cooperation between the treaty partners), and the formal closing section, or eschatocol.[1]

In the Danish documents, words that have been crossed out by the copyist are crossed out in the published text as well, while words that have been added in the margin or above the line are rendered in italics, with Text Notes explaining their exact position in the manuscript.

The text of the 1516 Russian letter of treaty is rendered in the modern Russian alphabet, but in the syntax and orthography of the original. Words are separated according to modern convention.

All proper and geographic names are capitalized except when appearing in adjectival form.

Each of the publications-cum-translations is immediately followed by a set of Text Notes, Translation Notes, Realia Notes and a Publication History.

Note on Translations

I have chosen to translate the texts relatively literally; first, because a free translation would blur the subtle semantic differences existing between identical clauses in the Latin and Russian texts – important for reasons explained in Chapter 4 – and second, to provide readers with a sense of the syntax and semantics of the originals. This may give the impression that the texts are somewhat awkward, but in fact this is what they often are, what with their many literal or faulty translations from Latin to Russian and vice versa and their frequently odd formulations of complex matters in each of the two languages. I have consulted several contemporaneous English-Scottish documents to find English translations sounding "authentic" while still making sense to modern readers. Also, I apply normal interpunctuation in the translations.

---

1   For the form of medieval treaties, see pp. 29–31.

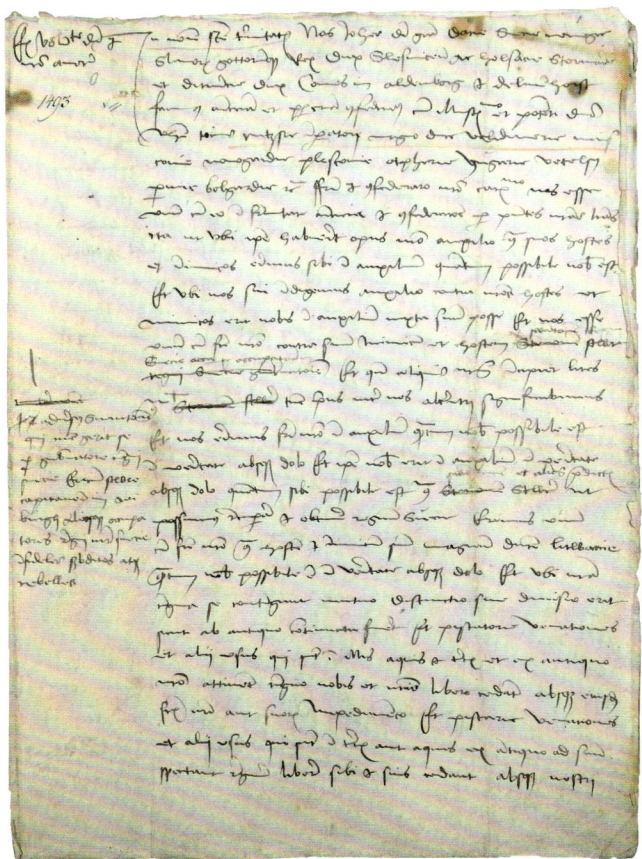

The Treaty of 1493
First page of the transcript of King Hans' letter of treaty of 1493 to Grand Prince Ivan III (*1493). The copy was produced as a draft of the Danish version of the Treaty of 1506, for which reason revisions were added directly in the original text. Danish National Archives. Photo: Carsten Pape.

A. The Preserved Danish Text of the Treaty of 1493

The text published and translated below is the surviving transcript of the chancery copy of King Hans' original letter of treaty to Grand Prince Ivan III issued on November 8, 1493, i.e. the document labelled *1493 in this book. The copy was produced in 1506 as a first draft of the letter of treaty that was to be issued by King Hans to Grand Prince Vasilij III according to the agreement to renew the treaty of 1493 reached in Moscow earlier in the year (pp. 62–63). The copied text was revised by the copyist to adapt it to the realia of 1506 by crossing out obsolete names, titles and epithets and replacing them with currently relevant alternatives in the margins or above the lines, or by changing the text directly in the process of transcription. As the revisions as well as the greater part of the text which was *not* revised were meant to constitute the text of the new treaty, the document is a source for the perished original Danish texts of both 1493 and 1506.

Superscripted Arabic numbers denote Text Notes, while superscripted Latin numbers (i, ii, iii, iv, etc.) indicate Translation Notes. The numerals appearing in the left margin of the text are item numbers as explained on p. 89.

	Text	**Translation**
00	Jn nomine sancte trinitatis	In the name of the Holy Trinity.
01	*ex voluntate dei et nostro amore*[1]	By the will of God and our love,
02	nos Johannes dei gracia Dacie Suecie Noruegie slauorum gottorumque rex dux slesuicensis ac Holsacie Stormarie et Ditmercie dux comes in Oldenborg et Delmenhorst	We Hans, by the grace of God King of Denmark, Sweden, Norway, the Slavs and the Goths, Duke of Schleswig and Duke of Holstein, Stormarn and Ditmerschen, Count in Oldenburg and Delmenhorst,[i]
03	facimus amiciciam et perpetuam confederacionem	make friendship and perpetual union[ii]
05 ▲ ⋮ ▼	cum illustrissimo et potenti domino Johanne tocius Rutzsie imperatore magno duce Volodimerie Muscouie Nouogardie Plescouie Otpherie Vngarie Vetolsy Permie Bolgardie etc	with the most excellent and mighty[iii] lord[iv] Ivan, Emperor of all Russia, Grand Prince of Vladimir, Moscow, Novgorod, Pskov, Tver', Jugra, Vjatka, Perm', Bulgar etc.,[v]
04	ffratre[2] et confederato nostro carissimo	our most beloved brother and confederate.
	– – –	– – –
06	nos esse vnum cum eo in fraternitate amicicia et confederacione	We shall be one with him in brotherhood, friendship and union[ii]
07	per presentes nostras literas	by our present letter,[vi]
08	ita ut vbi ipse habuerit opus nostro auxilio contra suos hostes et inimicos erimus sibi in auxilium quantum possibile nobis est	so that when[vii] he needs our aid against his enemies and adversaries, we will come to his aid as much as we can.
09	et vbi nos sui indigemus auxilio contra nostros hostes et inimicos erit nobis in auxilium iuxta suum posse	And when[vii] we need his aid against our enemies and adversaries, he will come to our aid in accordance with his ability.
10 X	et nos esse vnum cum fratre nostro contra suum inimicum et hostem ~~Stenonem Stwre regnj Suecie gubernatorem~~ Swantonem regni Suecie ~~occu~~ occupatorem[3]	And we shall be one with our brother against his adversary and enemy, ~~Sten Sture, regent of the kingdom of Sweden~~ [viii] Svante, ~~occu~~ occupier of the kingdom of Sweden.[ix]
11	et qum aliquis nostrum incipiet lites contra + ~~Stenonem Stwre~~ *inimicum*	And when one of us joins battle against ~~Sten Sture, our adversary,~~ *and versus*

92   The Early Danish-Muscovite Treaties, 1493-1523

	~~nostrum~~ et aduersus Swantonem qui nunc gerit se pro gubernatore regnj Suecie Ericum Stwre capitaneum in Wiburgh aliosque occupatores regnj nostri Suecie infideles subditos atque rebelles[4]	Svante who now purports to be regent of the kingdom of Sweden, Eric Sture, governor at Viborg, and the other occupiers of our kingdom of Sweden, disloyal subjects and rebels,
12	tunc prius inter nos alterutrj significabimus	then we will first notify the other,
13	et nos erimus fratri nostro in auxilium quantum nobis possibile est in veritate absque dolo	and we will come to the aid of our brother as much as we can, in truth and without guile.
14	et ipse nobis erit in auxilium in veritate absque dolo quantum sibi possibile est contra ~~Stenonem Stwre~~ Swantonem et alios predictos[5]	And he will come to our aid in truth and without guile as much as he can against ~~Sten Sture~~ Svante and the aforementioned [persons]
15	ut possimus recuperare et obtinere regnum Suecie	so that we can regain and obtain[x] the kingdom of Sweden.
16	erimus vnum cum fratre nostro contra hostem et inimicum suum magnum ducem Litwanie quantum nobis possibile est in veritate absque dolo	We will be one with our brother against his enemy and adversary, the grand prince of Lithuania, as much as we can, in truth and without guile.
	– – –	– – –
17	et vbi nostra regna se contingunt mutuo distinctio siue diuisio erit sicut ab antiquo continuata fuerit	And where our realms border upon each other, the boundary or division will be as it will have been delimited as of old.[xi]
18	et piscatorie venaciones et alij vsus quj sunt in illis aquis et terris et ex antiquo nostro attinent regno nobis et nostris libere cedant absque eiusdem fratris nostri aut suorum impedimento	And fishing, hunting and other rights which exist in these waters and lands and belong to our realm as of old shall freely pass to us and ours without impediment by our brother or his [people].
19	et piscarie venaciones et alij vsus, qui sunt in terris aut aquis ex antiquo ad suum spectant regnum libere sibi et suis cedant absque nostrj aut nostrorum impedimento	And fishing, hunting and other rights which exist in [these] lands or waters and belong to his realm as of old shall freely pass to him and his [people] without impediment by us or ours.
20	et que hactenus hucusque ad istud nostrum pactum inter ambo regna nostra et nostrorum subditos facta sunt per spolia rapinas et lites de cetero non accusentur nec menti tradentur	And what has hitherto, up to [the conclusion of] this our pact, been done between our two realms and our subjects in terms of plunder, theft, and strife shall henceforth not be prosecuted, nor brought to mind.
21	et que postmodum ex vtraque parte inter nostros subditos contingunt iudicium et expedicionem absque temporis longa prolongatione habebunt	And what comes to pass from this day forth,[xii] on both sides, between our subjects, shall be given justice and due process[xiii] without long delay.[xiv]

22	et isdem *isdem*[6] frater noster suj officiales et procuratores secundum suam consuetudinem nostros homines foueant et expediant sicut suos proprios in veritate absque dolo
23	et nos nostrique officiales et procuratores suos homines quemadmodum nostros nostra consuetudine foueamus et expediamus in veritate et absque dolo
24	et nostri nuncij et ambasiatores in suo regno viam mundam in terris et aquis absque impedimento habebunt
25	et sui ambasiatores et nuncij in nostro regno viam mundam in terris et aquis absque impedimento habebunt
26	mercatores et institores et alij negotiatores regnorum vtrorumque in vtrisque nostris regnis ex alterutro in terris et aquis ambulare equitare et libere negocianda tractare possint absque timore et perturbacione
27	consuetis solutis theoloneis iuxta morem terre
28	eosque ex vtraque parte fouere et expedire debemus in veritate absque dolo
29	et si casu aliqui de nostris vento agitati in et ad regna sua deuenerint vel aliqui de suis in nostro tunc nos aut ipse nostri uel sui officiales et procuratores ex vtraque parte eorum bona uel mercancias nullatenus impediamus sed eos iuuare absque precio et impedimento debemus
30	et quod soluere tenentur nostre terre soluant consuetum
31	sclaui et sclaue debitores et fideiussores fures fugitiuj raptores et ceteri malefactores qui veniunt de vno regno in alterum cum expedicione restituantur ex vtraque parte
	− − −
32	jn et per omnia ista
33	nos Johannes dei gracia Dacie *Suecie*[7] Noruegie slauorum gottorumque rex

	And our brother, his officials and procurators shall watch over and give justice[xv] to our people like to their own according to their custom, in truth without guile.
	And we and our officials and procuratores shall likewise watch over and give justice to his people like to our own according to our custom, in truth and without guile.
	And our envoys and ambassadors will have safe passage[xvi] in his realm, in lands and waters, without impediment.
	And his ambassadors and envoys will have safe passage in our realm, in lands and waters, without impediment.
	Merchants and vendors and other traders of both realms shall, in both our realms, [coming] from the other, have the right to walk and ride about and freely do business in lands and waters, without fear and perturbation,
	having paid customary dues according to the habit of the land,
	and we must watch over and give them justice, on both sides, in truth without guile.
	And if by accident some of ours, driven by the wind, come into or up to his realms, or some of his into ours, then we or he, our or his officials and procurators, on both sides, shall nowise seize their goods or merchandise,[xvii] but assist them without cost and impediment.
	And what they must pay to our land, they pay according to custom.
	Male and female slaves, debtors and guarantors, thieves, fugitives, robbers and other malefactors who come from one realm into the other shall be returned with due process,[xiii] on both sides.
	− − −
	On and by all this
	we Hans, by the grace of God King of Denmark, *Sweden*, Norway, the Slavs

	~~electus in regem Suecie~~ dux slesuicensis ac Holsacie Stormarie et Ditmercie dux comes in Oldenborg et Delmenhorst	and the Goths, ~~elected King of Sweden~~, Duke of Schleswig and Duke of Holstein, Stormarn and Ditmerschen, Count in Oldenburg and Delmenhorst,
34	osculati sumus crucem	have kissed the cross
35	fratri nostro carissimo	to our most beloved brother,
36	domino ~~Johanne~~ Basilio[8] imperatori tocius Russie magno duci Voledimorie Muscouie Nouegardie Plescouie Otpherie Vngarie Vethelsie Permie Bulgarie etc	lord ~~Ivan~~ Vasilij, Emperor of all Russia, Grand Prince of Vladimir, Moscow, Novgorod, Pskov, Tver', Jugra, Vjatka, Perm', Bulgar etc.,
37	ad tenendum amiciciam et veritatem	to observe friendship and truth
38	cum nostris presentibus literis patentibus	by this our letter patent,
39	appendens hiis nostris fortibus literis sigillum nostrum	appending our seal to this our confirmed letter.[xviii]
40	datum in castro nostro haffnensi anno diuine incarnacionis millesimo quadringentesimo nonagesimo tercio octaua die menssis nouembris	Given in our Copenhagen castle in the year of the Holy Incarnation one thousand four hundred ninety-three, on the eight day of the month of November.

Text Notes

1. The sentence is added in the margin and referred to its place in the text by a slightly curving line ending in a loop.
2. The double ff is one way in which scribes could render the letter f in their manuscripts. The same is true of *haffnensi* in item 40. The reversed order of items 4 and 5 is explained on p. 128.
3. The revision is placed above the words it substitutes and marked with an "X" placed immediately before *Stenonem*.
4. The italicized words, including the deleted *inimicum nostrum*, are added in the margin and referred to their place in the text by the "+" immediately preceding *Stenonem*.
5. The italicized words are added above the words they substitute.
6. The copyist first wrote *isdem*, then crossed out the "s" with a vertical stroke and added a word above the line which looks like isdem once again. The reason for this is unclear, but grammatically speaking the correct form is idem. *1506 has idem.
7. *Suecie* has been entered above the line, with an oblique line between *Dacie* and *Noruegie* marking its place in the text.
8. *Basilio* is placed immediately above the blurred-out *Johanne*.

Translation Notes

i. The title is translated using modern geographical names (German in the case of the duchies and counties). The ethnonym *slavorum* (often rendered *sclavorum* in Danish and European texts), i.e. "of the Slavs," is the contemporaneous Latin version of the original Danish *de venders*, i.e. "of the Vends." The Vends were a group of Slavic tribes settled in what is today the northern parts of eastern Germany and Poland. The Latin version was introduced in Danish usage sometime between 1187 and 1193, not long after the so-called

"Vendish crusades" by the Danes.² The word Schleswig is an adjective ("Schleswigian") in the Latin original.

ii. I use the term "union" rather than "alliance" as my translation of *confoederatio* in items 03 and 06. The semantic connotations of *confoederatio* when appearing in this position in medieval treaties are broader than "alliance" understood as a defensive or offensive league directed against one or more common enemies. To illustrate the point by a modern reference, we speak about the European Union and the Nato Alliance, but not vice versa.

Confoederatio derives from the classical term *foedus* which may mean both treaty, alliance, league and union, in German *Bündnis* and *Bundesvertrag*,³ as well as covenant in the biblical sense, bond, or "agreement between private persons with reference to kinship or friendship, and marriage".⁴ Accordingly, the verb *confoederare* may mean to unify or connect by treaty, in German "durch ein Bündnis vereinigen, verbinden".⁵

To convey the innate meaning of *confoederatio* in a translation, it should be taken into consideration that the Danish envoy uses the term twice, in items 03 and 06, where the Russian text of 1516 (and, as I shall argue in Chapter 4, of 1493 and 1506 as well) uses two different terms, viz. *dokončanie* and *edinačestvo*. The Danish envoy will have discussed the terms he used with his Russian counterparts, so it may be concluded that *confoederatio* as used by Hans Claussen was broad enough in terms of semantic content to cover the meaning of both Russian words and that, *vice versa*, these had themselves had their original individual definitions blurred by conventional diplomatic use in late medieval Russian texts (further, see Translation Note v on pp. 118–9).

Lesaffer writes of the word *amicitia* (friendship), another standard medieval treaty term, that it "was used in the enumerations of terms which indicated the *general condition* and relationship that was brought about by the peace or alliance treaty" in which it "appeared among other terms and concepts such as alliance, concordia, confoederatio, foedus, fraternitas, intelligence, liga, pax and unio. […] Alliance, confoederatio, liga and unio refer to the *condition of alliance*. The use of the words referring to alliance is not restricted to treaties that actually constitute an alliance" as these "radiate a willingness for lasting understanding and peaceful relations." Consequently, "the use of these terms is from a strictly juridical point of view incorrect and indicates that the terms were loosely chosen and easily confused."⁶

---

2   Riis, Kongen, p. 391.
3   Ausführliches lateinisch-deutsches Handwörterbuch, Vol. 1.
4   Dictionary of Medieval Latin, Vol. 1.1.
5   Ordbog over dansk middelalderlatin; Ausführliches lateinisch-deutsches Handwörterbuch, Vol. 1.
6   Lesaffer, Amicitia, pp. 85-87. Emphasis added. For a similar point of view, see Roshchin, Friendship, pp. 62-65. A typical example of the blurring of individual definitions appears in Henry VII's proposed text of the Danish-English treaty of 1490, according to which the parties conclude "perfectam pacem, amicitiam, guerrarum abstinentiam, ligam, unionem, & confoederationem" (perfect peace, friendship, abstention from war, league, union and confederation) (Rymer XII, p. 375s). Henry's mandate to his envoys further included the terms *concordia*, *affinitas* and *intelligentia* (concord, affinity and

The italicized words are key to the point I am making. In the context in which it appears in *1493, *confoederatio* does not so much mean alliance *per se* as the *condition of alliance* brought about by the treaty at hand. It is the personal bond inherent in or expressed by the treaty-based alliance that matters, as exemplified by the numerous occurrences in European treaties of parallel terms such as *vinculum pacis*,[7] *amicitiæ vinculum*,[8] and *confoederationis vinculo*,[9] in which *vinculum* means bond: the bond of peace, the bond of friendship, and the "bond of being allied". The point is underscored by the fact that the adjective and verbal noun *confoederatus* may and often does mean "allied" and "ally" in the narrow sense, but that it can only refer to an overarching state of unity and connectedness when used in the superlative, as does King Hans in letters to James IV of Scotland and the grand prince of Moscow, calling each of his correspondents his "confederatissimus," i.e. "most confederate" brother.[10] In sum, "union" seems an apt translation of *confoederatio* in the given context, as the term is semantically broader than "alliance" or "treaty" and at the same time connotes some form of prior agreement to have come into existence.

iii. The superlatives used in most regal titles in contemporaneous English and Scottish documents are rendered either "the right …" or "the most …," e.g. "the Right Excellent and Myghty Prince Henry, by the Grace of God, King of England [etc.],"[11] or "the maist Excellent and maist Mithti Prince Edwarde, be the Grace of God, King of Ingland,"[12] both of which clearly correspond to the terms *illustrissimus et fortissimus* in the title of Ivan III (English-Scottish treaties written in English use "excellent" for "illustrious" as revealed by an electronic search in Rymer XII). Though the latter formula appears to be used slightly more infrequently than the former, I have chosen to use it as the more idiomatic to modern readers.

iv. For my use in this place of the term "lord" for Latin *dominus* and Russian *gospodar'*, see the discussion on pp. 114–8, notes i–iii.

v. The title is translated using modern geographical names.

vi. Cf. "by their *present letters*" (Rymer XII, p. 160s).

vii. The Latin *ubi*, which appears in this place in both Danish texts, normally means "where" but may also mean "when." (The same is true of the corresponding Russian *gde* in

---

consensus) (Rymer XII, p. 373d). „S" and „d" refer to left and right columns, respectively.

7 Rymer XII, p. 250s («pacis, foedus, & caritatis vinculum»).
8 Corps Universel III/1. p. 521d.
9 Codex Diplomaticus I, p. 357s (Denmark-Poland, 1510).
10 Aarsberetninger I, p. 9, no. 13 and Grönblad, Nya källor, 150. Many medieval treaties include the word *connexus* in the series of positive terms connoting a bond between two rulers, e.g. "Potentissimus Scotorum Princeps Confrater & Consanguineus noster carissimus, cum quo & Affinitate & Amicitiae Foedere connexi fuerimus" (the most mighty prince of the Scots, our most beloved brother and relative, with whom we have been connected by a pact of both affinity and friendship) (Rymer XII, p. 53d).
11 Rymer XII, p. 440s.
12 Rymer XII, p. 161s

*1516).¹³ The latter meaning seems to me to be the most appropriate here as the article is probably one of timing, not of place. In a similar clause in the 1517 treaty of alliance between Muscovy and the Teutonic Order, the word used by the Grand Master in his letter of treaty is *quando* which can only mean when, not where.¹⁴ Likewise, a Latin translation of Vasilij III's 1514 letter of treaty to Emperor Maximilian (p. 70–1), most likely produced by the Moscow chancery, uses *quando* and *ubi* in parallel.¹⁵

viii. I use "regent" to render the Swedish *riksföreståndare* ("praeses of the realm," i.e. interim ruler in the absence of a duly crowned king) which was Latinized to *gubernator* in contemporaneous texts.

ix. Cf. "against the *occupiers* of the crown of France" (Rymer XII, p. 174d).

x. The Latin verb *obtinere* may mean both "to obtain" (acquire) and "to retain." The choice of translation will depend on a contextual analysis of the text.

xi. The reason why the perfect form *fuerit* in item 17 is in the subjunctive is unclear. It is hardly an error. The handwriting of the copyist is unmistakable here, as is the hand of the copyist of *1506 who also wrote *fuerit*. For a speculative explanation, the use of subjunctive may reflect a piece of realia. As I have pointed out in a prior publication, items 17-19 probably refer to an old Norwegian-Novgorodian border in northern Norway established in 1326 and were most likely brought to the negotiation table in Moscow by the Danish envoy in order to stop Russian hunting and fishing on the Norwegian side of this border.¹⁶ Having annexed Novgorod as late as 1478 and not yet transferred the archives of the republic to Moscow, the Russian side may have been surprised to learn about the ancient border from the envoy. This thesis is strongly supported by the circumnavigation of Northern Norway and the Kola Peninsula by the Russian and Danish envoys returning from Copenhagen to Moscow in the spring of 1494 (pp. 56–7). The purpose of this enormous detour would almost certainly have been to inspect the "new" Muscovite border. In this context, the subjunctive may have been deliberately used to express some doubt on the part of the grand prince and his negotiators as to the validity of the claim presented by the envoy at the negotiation table. I have reflected this explanation by conditionally translating the verb "will have been."

xii. Cf. "*from this day forth*" (Rymer XII, p. 173d).

xiii. The Latin syntagm *iudicium et expeditionem* does not exist as a stock phrase in European diplomatic parlance. It is the Danish envoy's attempt at translating the Russian standard term *sud i isprava* which appears in this place in *1516 (item 21) and translates into something approximating "justice and due process" which I consequently use here. In item 31, *cum expedicione* likewise means "with due process", being a translation of the likewise standard Russian term *po isprave* appearing in *1516. For comparison, the Latin

---

13 Slovar' russkogo jazyka XI–XVII vv., Vol. 4, p. 16.
14 SGGD V, 82, p. 77s.
15 Fiedler, Allianz, p. 251.
16 Pape, Rethinking, passim.

text of the 60-year border peace concluded in 1510 between Sweden and Novgorod (read: Muscovy) translates *po isprave* into "secundum iusticiam" in an identical clause.[17]

xiv. Cf. "to be put to a *longer delay*" (Rymer XII, p. 157s).

xv. Again, *fovere et expedire* does not exist as a stock phrase in Western treaties. It is the Danish envoy's translation of the Russian standard term *bljusti i uprava dati*, the meaning of which approximates "watch over and give justice" which I consequently use here.[18]

xvi. *Via munda* ("clean way," i.e. safe passage) is the envoy's translation of the Russian standard term *čistyj put'*. It, too, is non-existent as a fixed term in Western diplomatic language, except that it was calqued by the Hanseatic League and Sweden in their treaties with Novgorod, e.g. "[…] mogen de Russzen eynen *reynen wech* hebben" (Hanserecesse III/4, p. 48) and "the skulle hafve *reen wegh*" (ST III, 525).

xvii. Cf. "all our *goods, merchandise* and things" (Rymer XII, p. 161s).

xviii. Cf. "in witness whereof we have done *these our letters* to be made patents" (Rymer XII, p. 166d).

Realia Notes

Item 02: *Johannes*

Hans (Johann in German, Johannes after the biblical John), born 1456, King of Denmark and Norway 1481-1513, King of Sweden 1497. Deposed from the Swedish throne in 1501 by an insurgency of Swedish nobles subsequently deemed illegitimate by the German-Roman emperor, for which reason he considered and styled himself King of Sweden to the end of his days. Before 1497, his "Swedish" title had been *electus in regem Suecie* (elected King of Sweden, King-elect of Sweden).

Item 05: *Johanne*

Ivan III (ablative of Johannes, in Russian Ivan), born 1440, Grand Prince of Moscow 1462-1505.

Item 10: *Stenonem Stwre regnj Suecie gubernatorem*

Sten Gustavsson Sture (Sten Sture the Elder), *c.* 1442-1503. Regent of Sweden 1470-97 and 1501-3. (King Hans was King of Sweden in the intervening years.) The epithet "the Elder" was introduced by later historians to distinguish him from Sten Sture the Younger (see the comments to item 10 of *1506 on p. 106).

Item 10: *Swantonem regni Suecie occupatorem*

See the comments to item 10 of *1506 on p. 106.

Item 11: *Ericum Stwre capitaneum in Wiburgh*

Copyist error for *Ericum Turesson capitaneum in Wiburgh*. See p. 106, item 11, for further details on Turesson.

---

17 "Et si fugam dabit aliquis profugus ex terra Nouagardie in terram Suecie, slauus vel slaua, debitor vel fideiussor, restituere ipsum secundum iusticiam et secundum crucis osculacionem" (FMU VII, 5446).

18 Hanseatic sources use "vorwaren" and "recht geven" to translate the two terms, e.g. GVNP, 62. In Latin, *uprava dati* reads "iusticiam dare" (FMU VII, 5446), in Swedish "gifua rätt" (ST III, 525).

Item 16: *[cum] magnum ducem Litwanie*

Grand Duke Alexander of Lithuania (1492-1506, additionally King of Poland 1501-1506), commonly referred to as Alexander Jagiellon in English, Aleksander Jagiellończyk in Polish and Aleksandras Jogailaitis in Lithuanian due to his being a scion of the central European Jagiellonian dynasty. Married the daughter of Ivan III in 1495 as part of the peace settlement of 1494 mentioned on pp. 25–8.

Publication History

The document has been published quite widely, possibly because it is the founding act of the late-medieval Danish-Muscovite diplomatic relationship, and because historians have typically focused on the founding of the relationship to the neglect of its subsequent history.

The first person to prepare the document for publication was the Icelander Grimur Thorkelin who served as Chief Archivist (*gehejmearkivar*) of the Royal Archives (*Gehejmearkivet*) in Copenhagen in 1791-1829. His transcript was eventually printed in the fifth volume of the Russian "Collection of State Papers and Treaties" (*Sobranie gosudarstvennych gramot i dogovorov,* henceforth SGGD) published in 1894.[19] A postscript to the publication, evidently written by Thorkelin himself, reads: "Ex charta coæva accurate exscripsi Sacræ Regiæ Majestatis Archivorum secretariorum præfectus Grimus Iohannes Thorkelin" (accurately transcribed from a contemporaneous charter by the Head of Secretaries of his Sacred Royal Majesty's Archives). Thorkelin was presumably approached by the early editors of the collection, of which Volumes I–IV were published in 1813-26,[20] and asked to provide transcripts of Russian treaties held in the Royal Archives for Volume V which was to publish Russian treaties with foreign powers. The Foreword to the volume states that Count N. P. Rumjancev, the driving force of the project until his death in 1826, "solicited copies of such acts from foreign archives and handed them over to the Moscow archive with the purpose of subsequently having them printed."[21] In tune with its editorial policy, the publication of the document in SGGD V is accompanied by a translation into what was then contemporary Russian. The publication contains a limited number of inexact readings of the original.

In 1835, Danish historian F. H. Jahn published the document in the Appendix to his posthumous political-military history of Denmark.[22] His reading of the record was so flawed, however, that the publishers of the manuscript felt compelled to check and revise it.[23] Even so, the transcript is unreliable as printed, and researchers are advised not to use it.

---

19   SGGD V, 110. Thorkelin also provided copies of the initial correspondence between King Hans and Grand Prince Vasilij III in 1506-7 (ibid., 111 and 112).

20   The history of the publishing project is outlined in the Foreword (*Predislovie*) to SGGD V.

21   SGGD V, p. XXXI.

22   Jahn, Danmarks politisk-militære historie, pp. 569-70.

23   Jahn, Danmarks politisk-militaire historie, Foreword, p. v. In the list of published documents, p. 592, the treaty is labelled "King Hans' Alliance with Grand Prince Johan Basilius of Russia"!

In 1859, Finnish historian Edvard Grönblad published what is easily the most reliable reading of the document in his collection of sources illuminating the history of Finland.[24] He does, however, overlook a few of the revisions made to the text by the copyist and omits a couple of words of the original in his transcript.

All subsequent publications are more or less accurate replicas of Grönblad's version, whether acknowledged or not by the individual publishers. These include, by date of appearance, Forsten (1884),[25] Rydberg (1895),[26] Ščerbačev (1915)[27] and Hausen (1928).[28] The listing of the document in Vol. I of the 19th-century Danish repertory of medieval sources refers to Jahn's publication, naming the document *Confoederatio* without qualifying it as a *copy* of the treaty.[29] Vol. I.2 in Series 2 of the publication mistakenly presents it as a *draft* of the treaty of 1493, but correctly states that it was later re-used as a draft of the treaty of 1506.[30] The 20th-century repertory correctly presents it as a near-contemporaneous copy of the 1493 treaty and as a draft of the treaty of 1506.[31] The notion that *1493 should have been a draft of the treaty can be rejected on purely technical grounds. The copied text is entered on pages 1, 2 and 3 of two folios folded and inserted one into the other and is immediately followed by a copy of Vasilij III's 1506 missive to King Hans on pages 3, 4 and 5, written in the same hand.[32] Had *1493 been a draft of the treaty of 1493, it would have been written on a single sheet of paper, not over three pages of two different sheets, sharing page 3 with a copy of an incoming letter dated 1506. See the illustration on p. 61.

---

24 Grönblad, Nya källor, 43. In his introductory remarks, Grönblad erroneously calls the document "the draft of the original" of the Danish 1493 letter of treaty and does not relate it to the treaty of 1506.
25 Forsten, Bor'ba, pp. 597-9.
26 ST III, pp. 701-2.
27 Kopengagenskie akty, 2. Ščerbačev's introductory remarks present it as a contemporaneous copy or "perhaps" a draft of the 1493 letter, but he is aware that the document was used as a draft for the 1506 treaty. The document is listed and correctly identified in his Datskij archiv, pp. 1-2.
28 FMU V, 4521.
29 Regesta Diplomatica I, 5017.
30 Regesta Diplomatica II/I.2, 5017.
31 Repertorium Diplomaticum II/4, 7494.
32 I number the pages of the outer folio 1-2-7-8 and of the inner one 3-4-5-6. Pages 6-7-8 are empty except for a note on p. 8 written in a different hand: "Contra et aduersus Swantonem, quj nunc se gerit pro gubernatore regnj Suecie, Ericum Stwre, capitaneum in Viborgh, aliosque occupatores regnj nostri Suecie, infideles subditos atque rebelles", a quote of item 11 of the treaty text.

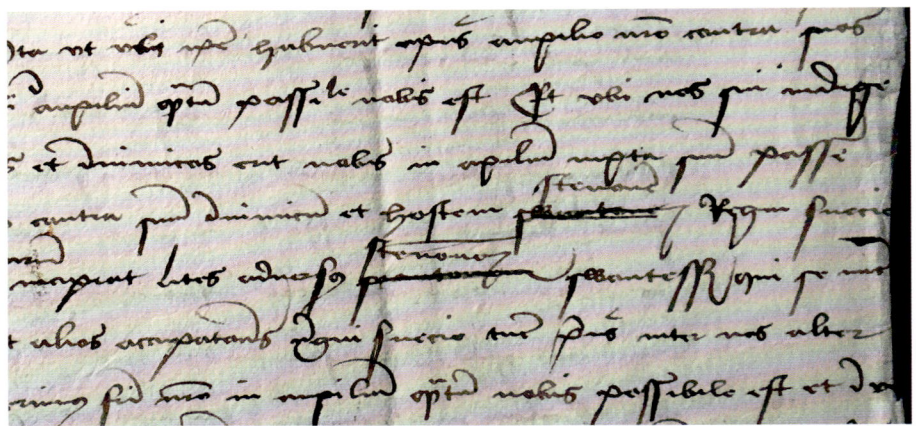

The Treaty of 1506
Detail of the copy of the Danish letter of the Treaty of 1506 (*1506). The image shows, *inter alia*, the replacement of *Swantonem* with *Stenonem* in items 10 and 11 of the text (see p. 103). Danish National Archives. Photo: Carsten Pape.

B. The Preserved Danish Text of the Treaty of 1506

The text published and translated below is the surviving transcript of the chancery copy of King Hans' original letter of treaty to Grand Prince Vasilij III, i.e. the document labelled *1506 in this book. The copy was produced in 1514 as a first draft of the letter of treaty to be issued by King Christian II to Vasilij III according to the agreement to renew the treaty concluded in Moscow earlier that year (pp. 72–74). The copied text was revised by the copyist to adapt it to the realia of 1514 by crossing out obsolete names, titles and epithets and replacing them with currently relevant alternatives in the margins or above the lines; by replacing parts of the titles of the signatories with an "etc." (awaiting later fill-in); and by changing the text directly in the process of transcription. There is an example of the latter in item 02 which referred to King Hans in the 1506 original but lists Christian II as King of Denmark etc. without visible revisions. As the revisions, as well as the greater part of the text which was *not* revised, were meant to constitute the text of the new treaty, the document is in fact a source for the Danish texts of both 1506, 1514 and 1516.

The Translation Notes of *1493 above are relevant for the translation here as well.

	Text	Translation
01	ex voluntate dei et nostro amore	By the will of God and our love,
02	nos Cristiernus dei gracia Dacie slauorum et gotorum rex et electus in regem Suecie et Noruegie etc dux slesuicensis etc	We, Christian, by the grace of God King of Denmark, the Slavs and the Goths and elected King of Sweden and Norway etc., Duke of Schleswig, etc.,
03	facimus amiciciam et perpetuam confederacionem	make friendship and perpetual union
05	cum jllustrissimo et potentissimo principe [et][1] domino Basilio totius Rutzie imperatore magno duce Wolodimerie Muscouie Nouogardie Plescouie Muscouie Nouogardie Plescouie[2] Otpherie Jugorie Wetkie Permie Bulgardie etc	with the most excellent and mighty prince and lord Vasilij, Emperor of all Russia, Grand Prince of Vladimir, Moscow, Novgorod, Pskov, Moscow, Novgorod, Pskov, Tver', Jugra, Vjatka, Perm', Bulgar, etc.,
04	fratre et confederato nostro charissimo	our most beloved brother and confederate.
	– – –	– – –
06	nos esse vnum cum eo in fraternitate et amicicia et confederacione	We shall be one with him in brotherhood, and friendship and union
07	per presentes literas nostras	by our present letter,
08	jta ut vbj ipse habuerit opus auxilio nostro contra suos hostes et inimicos erimus sibi in auxilium quantum possibile nobis est	so that when he needs our aid against his enemies and adversaries, we will come to his aid as much as we can.
09	et vbi nos sui indigemus auxilio contra nostros hostes et inimicos erit nobis in auxilium iuxta suum posse	And when we need his aid against our enemies and adversaries, he will come to our aid in accordance with his ability.
10	et nos esse vnum cum fratro nostro contra suum inimicum et hostem Swantonem *Stenonem*[3] regni Suecie occupatorem	And we shall be one with our brother against his adversary and enemy Svante Sten, occupier of the kingdom of Sweden.
11	et qum aliquis *nostrum*[4] incipiet lites aduersus Swantonem *Stenonem*[5] Swantesson qui se nunc gerit gubernatorem regni et alios occupatores regni Suecie	And when one of us joins battle against Svante Sten Svantesson, who now purports to be regent of the kingdom of Sweden, and the other occupiers of the kingdom of Sweden,
12	tunc prius inter nos alter alteri significabit	then he will first notify the other,
13	et nos erimus fratri nostro in auxilium quantum nobis possibile est et in ver*itate* **absque*[6] dolo	and we will come to the aid of our brother as much as we can and in truth without guile.
14	et ipse nobis erit in auxilium in veritate absque dolo quantum sibi possibile est absque dolo contra Stenonem et alios	And he will come to our aid in truth and without guile as much as he can without guile against Sten and the aforemention-

15	predictos vt possumus recuperare et optinere[7] regnum Suecie	ed [persons] so that we can regain and obtain the kingdom of Sweden.
16	erimus vnum cum fratre nostro contra contra[8] hostem et inimicum suum regem Polonie et ducem Letuonie quantum nobis possibile est in veritate absque dolo	We will be one with our brother against his enemy and adversary, the King of Poland and [Grand] Prince of Lithuania, as much as we can, in truth without guile.
	– – –	– – –
17	et vbi nostra regna se contingunt mutuo distinctio et diuisio erit sicut ab antiquo continuata fuerit	And where our realms border upon each other, the boundary or division shall be as it will have been delimited as of old.
18	et piscatorie venaciones et alii vsus qui sunt in illis aquis et terris et ex antiquo nostro attinent regno nobis et nostris libere cedant absque eiusdem fratris nostri aut suorum impedimento	And fishing, hunting and other rights that exist in these waters and lands and belong to our realm as of old shall freely pass to us and ours without impediment by our brother or his [people].
19	et piscatorie venaciones et alij vsus qui sunt in terris aut aquis ex antiquo ad suum spectant regnum libere sibi et suis cedant absque nostri et nostrorum impedimento	And fishing, hunting and other rights that exist in [these] lands or waters and belong to his realm as of old shall freely pass to him and his [people] without impediment by us or ours.
20	et que hactenus hucusque ad istud nostrum pactum inter ambo regna nostra et nostros subditos facte sunt per spolia rapinas et lites de cetero non accusentur nec menti tradentur	And what has hitherto, up to [the conclusion of] this our pact, been done between our two realms and our subjects in terms of plunder, theft, and strife shall henceforth not be prosecuted, nor brought to mind.
21	et que postmodum ex vtraque parte inter nostros subditos contingunt iudicium et expedicionem absque temporis longa prolongacione habebunt	And what comes to pass from this day forth, on both sides, between our subjects, shall be given justice and due process without long delay.
22	et idem frater noster sui officiales et procuratores secundum suam consuetudinem nostros homines foueant et expediant sicut suos proprios in veritate absque dolo	And our brother, his officials and procurators shall watch over and give justice to our people like to their own according to their custom, in truth without guile.
23	et nos et nostri officiales et procuratores suos homines quemadmodum nostros nostra consuetudine foueamus et expediamus in veritate absque dolo	And we and our officials and procurators shall likewise watch over and give justice to his people like to our own according to our custom, in truth and without guile.
24	et nostri nuncii et ambasiatores in suo regno viam mundam in terris et aquis absque impedimento habebunt	And our envoys and ambassadors will have safe passage in his realm, in lands and waters, without impediment.
25	X V *et sui ambasiatores et nuncii in nostro regno viam mundam in terris et*	And his ambassadors and envoys will have safe passage in our realm, in lands

	aquis absque impedimento habebunt[9]	and waters, without impediment. Mer-
26	mercatores ceterique negociatores	chants and other traders of both realms
	regnorum vtrorumque in vtrisque regnis	shall, in both realms, [coming] from the
	in terris et aquis ambulare equitare	other, have the right to walk and ride
	et libere negocianda tractare possint	about and freely do business in lands and
	absque timore et perturbacione	waters without fear and perturbation,
27	solutis consuetis theloniis iuxta morem	having paid customary dues according
	terre	to the habit of the land,
28	eosque ex vtraque parte fouere et	and we must watch over and give them
	expedire debemus in veritate et absque	justice, on both sides, in truth and
	dolo	without guile.
29	et si casu aliqui de nostris vento agitati in	And if by accident some of ours, driven
	et ad regna sua deuenerint vel aliqui	by the wind, come into or up to his
	de suis in regno nostro peruenerint	realms, or some of his into our realm,
	tunc nos aut ipse nostri vel sui officiales	then we or he, our or his officials and
	et procuratores ex vtraque parte	procurators, on both sides, shall
	eorum bona et mercancias nullatenus	nowise seize their goods or merchandise,
	impediamus sed eos iuuare absque pretio	but assist them without cost or impedi-
	et impedimento debemus	ment.
30	et quod soluere tenentur more terre	And what they must pay according to
	soluant consuetum	the habit of the land, they pay according
		to custom.
31	sclaui et sclaue debitores fures	Male and female slaves, debtors, thieves,
	fugitiui[10] raptores fideiussores et ceteri	fugitives, robbers, guarantors, and other
	malefactores qui veniunt de vno regno in	malefactors who come from one realm
	alterum cum expedicione restituantur ex	into the other shall be returned with due
	vtraque parte.	process, on both sides.
	– – –	– – –
32	Jn et per omnia	On and by all [this]
33	nos Cristiernus dei gracia Dacie	We, Christian, by the grace of God King
	slauorum et gotorum rex electus in	of Denmark, the Vends and the Goths,
	regem Suecie et Noruegie etc	elected King of Sweden and Norway etc.,
34	osculatj sumus crucem	have kissed the cross
35	fratri nostro charissimo	to our most beloved brother,
36	[principi et] domino Basilio imperatori	[prince and] lord Vasilij, Emperor of all
	totius Rutzie etc	Russia etc.,
37	ad tenendum amiciciam et veritatem	on observing friendship and truth
38	cum hiis nostris litte patentibus litteris	by this our letter patent.
39	et ad fortificationem harum nostrarum	And for the confirmation of this our
	litterarum sigillum nostrum apposuimus	letter we affix our seal to it.
40	datum in castro nostro hafnense etc 3ª	Given in our Copenhagen castle etc. on
	die mensis julii anno xiiij	the 3rd day of the month of July in the
		year xiiij.

3. The Texts

Text Notes

1. Between *principe* and *domino* there is a sign which may be meant by the copyist to read "et" although it is not a standard abbreviation or rendering of the word.
2. *Muscouie Nouogardie Plescouie* are repeated in the copied text.
3. *Stenonem* is added directly above *Swantonem*. See the image on p. 102.
4. *Nostrum* is added above the line between *aliquis* and *incipiet*.
5. As note 3. The fact that "Svantesson" is uncorrected shows that the copyist crossed out Swantonem immediately after having written it, added Stenonem above the deleted word, and entered the correct patronymic of the latter when continuing the process of copying.
6. An asterisk is added above the "a" in *absque*, while *tate* is added in the margin.
7. Sic.
8. *Contra* is repeated in the copied text.
9. The "X" is placed in the line between *habebunt* and *mercatores* while the "V" introduces the forgotten (here italicized) text above the line.
10. *Fugitivi* is added above the line. Its place in the text is marked by an oblique line between *fures* and *raptores*.

Realia Notes

Item 02: *Cristiernus*
   Christian II, born 1481, son of King Hans, King of Denmark and Norway 1513-23, King of Sweden 1520-1, in exile and later Danish captivity between his deposal in 1523 and death in 1559.

Item 05: *Basilio*
   Vasilij III (ablative of Basilius, in Russian Vasilij), born 1479, son of Ivan III, Grand Prince of Moscow 1505-33.

Item 10: *Swantonem*
   Svante Nilsson Natt och Dag, 1460-1512, regent of Sweden (*riksföreståndare* in Swedish, *gubernator* in Latin, i.e. interim ruler in the absence of a king) 1504-12.

Item 10: *Stenonem*
   Sten Svantesson Sture, 1493-1520, son of Svante Nilsson, regent of Sweden 1512-20. He deliberately adopted his great grandmother's family name Sture to brand himself as a relative of the widely popular regent Sten Sture, who had governed the country in 1470-97 and 1501-3. "The Younger" is a later epithet introduced to distinguish between the two.

Item 16: *[contra] regem Polonie et ducem Letuonie*
   Alexander Jagiellon (see p. 43 n. 14) died in August 1506 and was succeeded in that year by his younger brother Sigismund I (1506-48) on the thrones of Lithuania and Poland.

Publication History

   The document has been published only once, by Grönblad.[33] Unlike his publication of *1493, the transcription of *1506 is imprecise in the sense that it does not include the revisions made to the copied text by the copyist.

---

33 Grönblad, Nya källor, 343. Hausen prints Grönblad's introductory summary verbatim in FMU VII, 5733.

In the 19th-century Danish repertory of medieval sources, the document is erroneously listed as a "Treaty of friendship and alliance made between Christian II, King of Denmark etc. and Basilius, Emperor of all Russia, and confirmed by Christian II" (*Tractatus amicitiæ et confoederationis inter Christiernum II^{dum}, regem Daniæ etc., et Basilium, totius Rutziæ imperatorum, factus, et a Christierno II^{do} [secundo] rege confirmatus*).[34] There is no statement to the effect that the document is an incomplete, revised copy of the treaty of 1506, nor does the editor explain its relation to "an alliance between Grand Prince Basilius [and] King Christian" entered in the volume under August 2, 1517.[35]

The document is listed and correctly identified in Ščerbačev's 1893 publication Datskij archiv, p. 7, Nr. 14, except that it is not "of the same content" as the Russian text of the treaty of 1516 (it does not include the anti-Polish clause discussed on pp. 71 ff.).

---

34 Regesta Diplomatica II/I.2, 9990.
35 Regesta Diplomatica II/I.2, 10,223, with a reference to Regesta Diplomatica I, 6071, which dates it August 2, 1516.

C. The Original Russian Text of the Treaty of 1516

The text published and translated below is the original letter of treaty issued by Grand Prince Vasilij III to King Christian II in 1516.

Text

01	По божией воле и по нашей любви	
02	мы великий господарь[1] Василей божиею милостию царь и господарь всея Русии и великий князь владимерский московский новгородцкий псковский смоленский тферский югорский пермьский вятцкий болгарский и иныхъ господарь и великий князь новагороданизовские земли и черниговский и рязанский и волотцкий и ржевский и белский и ростовский и ярославский и белозерский и удорский и обдорский и кондинский и иных	
03	взяли есмя любовь и вечное докончанье	
04	съ своим братом	
05	с Кристерном королем датцким и свейским и норвеиским и словунским и готцким и князем слезвитским и олшатскимъ и сторманским и дитмерским и комит алдемболским[2] и дельменгорским и иныхъ	
	– – –	
06	быти нам с нимъ в братстве и в любви и во единачстве	
07	по сей грамоте	
08	где будет тебе брату нашему Кристерну королю надобе наша помочь на твоих неприятелей и нам тебе помогати где будеть нам мочно	
09	а где будет нам надобе твоя помоч на наших неприятелей и тебе нам помогати где будет тебе мочно	

Translation

By the will of God and by our love,

We, the great lord[i] Vasilij, by the grace of God Emperor and Sovereign[ii] of all Russia and Grand Prince of Vladimir, Moscow, Novgorod, Pskov, Smolensk, Tver', Jugra, Perm', Vjatka, Bulgar and others, Sovereign[iii] and Grand Prince of Nižnij Novgorod and Černigov and Rjazan' and Volokolamsk and Ržev and Bel'sk and Rostov and Jaroslav and Beloozero and Udora and Obdora and Konda and others,[iv]

have taken friendship and eternal union[v]

with our brother,

with Christian, King of Denmark and Sweden and Norway and the Slavs and the Goths and Duke of Schleswig and Holstein and Stormarn and Ditmerschen and Count in Oldenburg and Delmenhorst and others.[iv]

We shall be in brotherhood and in friendship and in union[v] with him

by this letter.

When[vi] you, our brother King Christian, need our aid against your enemies, we shall aid you as much as we can.

And when[vi] we need your aid against our enemies, you shall aid us as much as you can.

10	а на твоих неприятелей на свеиского обдержателя на свантова сына на Стенстура³ и на выборского наместника и на всю землю свеискую быти нам с тобою съ своим братом заодинъ	And we shall be one with you, our brother, against your enemies, the occupier of Sweden Sten Sture, son of Svante, and the governor of Viborg and all of Sweden,
15	и свеиские земли доставати нам с одного⁴	and together we shall obtain Sweden.
11	а как нам будеть валка почати с свеиским обдержателем с свантовым сыномъ Стенстуром и со всею землею свеискою	And when we join battle with the occupier of Sweden, with the son of Svante, Sten Sture, and with all of Sweden,
12	и нам межъ себя сослатися	we shall send [messages] to each other.
13	и мне тебе на свантова сына на Стенстура и на всю землю свеискую помогати в правду без хитрости	And I shall aid you against Sten Sture, son of Svante, and all of Sweden, in truth without guile.
14	а тебе нам на свантова сына на Стенстура и на всю землю свеискую помогати в правду без хитрости	And you shall aid us against Sten Sture, son of Svante, and all of Sweden, in truth without guile.
16	Также и на нашего неприятеля на Жигимонта короля полского и великого князя литовского тебе нашему брату быти со мною заодинъ и помогати тебе на Жигимонта короля полского и великого князя литовского в правду без хитрости	Likewise, you, our brother, shall be one with me against our enemy Sigismund, King of Poland and Grand Prince of Lithuania, and you shall aid me against Sigismund, King of Poland and Grand Prince of Lithuania, in truth without guile.
16ᵃ	а поидем мы великий господарь Василей божиею милостию царь и господарь всеа русии и великий князь на того на нашего недруга короля полского и великого князя литовского или воевод нашихъ на его землю пошлем и мы тогды тебе весть учиним и вы Кристернъ король сами ли на него поидете или князей и воевод ваших с вашею силою на его землю пошлете и делати тебе то дело с нами заодинъ и также пойдете вы Кристернъ корол на того на того⁵ нашего недруга на Жигимонта короля полского и великого князя литовского или князей и воевод ваших на его землю пошлете а нам весть пришлете и мы тогды также для братские наши любви и для дружбы и завещанья	And if we, the great lord Vasilij, by the grace of God Emperor and Sovereign of all Russia and Grand Prince, move against this our enemy, the King of Poland and Grand Prince of Lithuania, or send our commanders against his land, we will then give you notice, and you, King Christian, will either move against him yourself or send your vassals and commanders with your forces against his land, and you shall do this together with us. And if you, King Christian, move against this our enemy Sigismund, King of Poland and Grand Prince of Lithuania, or you send your vassals and commanders against his land, and you send us news of this, we will then for our brotherly love and for the friendship and agreement made with our brother

	учиненаго з братом нашим с Максимилияном избранным цесарем римским и навышшим королем отцем вашим будем с вами заодинъ на того на нашего недруга сами ли на него поидемъ или воевод наших с нашею силою на него пошлем сколко намъ мощно	Maximilian, Roman Emperor-Elect and August King,[vii] your father, be one with you against this our enemy, whether we move against him ourselves or send our commanders with our forces against him, as much as we can.
	– – –	– – –
17	а которые наши земли сошлись с твоими землями ино рубежь ведати на обе стороны по старине	And where our lands border with your lands, the boundary shall be observed on both sides as of old.
18	которые земли и воды и ухожаи и ловища и всякие угодья издавна потягли к нашим землям и в те земли и в воды и в ухожаи и в ловища и во всякие угодья тебе и твоим людем у нас и у наших людей не вступатись	You and your people shall not intrude in our and our people's lands and waters and hunting grounds and fishing waters and other rights which have belonged to our lands as of old.
19	а которые земли и воды и ухожаи и ловища и всякие угодья издавна потягли к вашимъ землям и в те земли и в воды и в ухожаи и в ловища и во всякие угодья нам и нашим людемъ у тебя и у твоих людей не вступатись	And we and our people shall not intrude in your and your people's lands and waters and hunting grounds and fishing waters and other rights which have belonged to your lands as of old.
20	а что будет учинилось межи нашими людми наперед сего до сего нашего докончанья наезды и воинами и татбами и розбои того всего не искати ни поминати на обе стороны по се наше докончанье	And what has previously been perpetrated between our people, before [the conclusion of] this our treaty, in terms of incursions and wars and theft and robberies, all of this shall neither be prosecuted nor remembered, on both sides, by this our treaty.
21	а впред что учинится межи нашими людми каково дело в сей нашей любви тому всему судъ и изправа без перевода	And what is henceforth committed between our people, no matter the case, during this our friendship, shall all be given justice and due process without delay.
22	а блюсти тебе наших людей и управа им давати с своими людми во всяких делех в своих землях и твоим наместником и всем твоим приказчиком какъ и своим людем по вашему обычею в правду без хитрости	And you shall watch over our people and give them justice in all matters by your people, in your lands, by your governors and all your bailiffs, like your own [people], according to your custom, in truth without guile.
23	а нам блюсти твоих людей и	And we shall watch over your people

	управа им давати с своими людми во всяких делех в своих землях и нашим наместником и всем нашим приказчиком какъ и своим людем по нашему обычею в правду без хитрости	and give them justice in all matters by our people, in our lands, by our governors and all our bailiffs, like our own [people], according to our custom, in truth without guile.
24	а посломъ нашимъ по твоим землям землею и водою путь чистъ без всяких зацепок	And our ambassadors shall have safe passage around your lands, by land and water, without any impediments.
25	также и твоим послом по нашим землям землею и водою путь чистъ без всяких зацепок	Likewise, your ambassadors shall have safe passage around our lands, by land and water, without any impediments.
26	а гостем нашим и купцом и иным всяким делным людем ездити по нашимъ землям землею и водою торговати и всякое дело делати доброволно на обе стороны без всякие боязни	And our merchants and traders and other tradespeople may freely travel around our lands, by land and water, and trade and do all sorts of business, on both sides, without any fear.
27	а пошлины и мыта им пълатити как есть обычай в которой земле	And they shall pay dues and taxes according to custom in each land.
28	а управляти их и обороняти на обе стороны в правду без хитрости	And they shall be given justice and protection, on both sides, in truth without guile.
29	также которых наших людей занесет ветром неволею по морю в твои земли или твоих людей занесет в наши земли и нашим наместником и всем нашим приказчиком товару у тех людей ничем не двинути а пособляти им безпосулно на обе стороны без всякие задержки	Further, if some people of ours are involuntarily driven by the wind across the sea to your lands, or your people driven to our lands, then our governors and all our bailiffs shall nowise cause harm to[viii] the goods of these people, but assist them without remuneration, on both sides, without any obstruction,
30	а где прилучится им которая пошлина дати и им та пошлина платити	and where they may have to pay a due, they shall pay the due.
31	а холопа робу должника поручника татя беглеца розбоиника рубежника по исправе выдавати на обе стороны	And male and female slaves, debtors, guarantors, thieves, fugitives, robbers, borderers should be handed over with due process, on both sides.
	– – –	– – –
32	а на том на всемъ	And on all this
33	мы великий господарь Василей божьею милостию царь и господарь всеа русии и великий князь володимерский московский новгородцький псковский смоленский тферский югорский	We, the great lord Vasilij, by the grace of God Emperor and Sovereign of all Russia and Grand Prince of Vladimir, Moscow, Novgorod, Pskov, Smolensk, Tver', Jugra, Perm', Vjatka, Bulgar and others, Sovereign and Grand Prince

3. The Texts 111

	пермьский вятцкий болгарский и иных господарь и великий князь новагороданизовскои земли и черниговский и рязанский и волотцкий и ржевский и бельский и ростовский и ярославский и белозерский и удорский и обдорский и кондинский и иных	of Nižnij Novgorod and Černigov and Rjazan' and Volokolamsk and Ržev and Bel'sk and Rostov and Jaroslav and Beloozero and Udora and Obdora and Konda and others,
34	целовали есмя крестъ	have kissed the cross
35	к брату своему	to our brother
36	х Кристерну королю датцкому и свеискому и норвеискому и словунскому и готцкому и князю слезвитцкому и олшатцкому и сторманскому и дитмерскому и комить алдемборскому и делменгорскому и иных	Christian, King of Denmark and Sweden and Norway and the Slavs and the Goths and Duke of Schleswig and Holstein and Stormarn and Ditmerschen and Count in Oldenburg and Delmenhorst and others,
37	по любви в правду	out of friendship and in truth.
38	а по сей нам грамоте и правити	And we shall observe this letter.
39	а к сей нашей утверженной грамоте и печать нашу привесили есмя	And we have appended our seal to this our confirmed letter.
40	писанъ в нашемъ государстве в нашем граде Москве о созданьи мира лета 7024 августа въ 9 день	Written in our realm in our city Moscow in the year 7024 since the creation of the world, on the 9th day of August.

Text Notes

1. In Russian documents of the late Middle Ages, the title of the ruler is normally abbreviated *gdr'* (гдрь) with a tilde (титло) above it. Russian historians have for generations expanded the abbreviation into *gosudar'*, but, as pointed out by several modern scholars, this is probably incorrect for the 15th and early 16th centuries. At that time it was expanded into *gospodar'*. This, for example, was the case on the wax seals of Ivan III and Vasilij III (though not on their golden bulls) and on coins minted by two different grand princes in 1446-1447.[36] Apparently, *gosudar'* did not acquire widespread usage until the end of the 16th century.[37] For this reason, I use *gospodar'* throughout this book.

---

36   Krom, Roždenie gosudarstva, p. 63.
37   Zoltan, K predystorii, pp. 103-5. Zoltan's conclusion is explicitly accepted by M. M. Krom (Roždenie gosudarstva, p. 64, note *) and implicitly by for instance M. Agošton who consistently uses *gospodar* in her works, except when citing previous source publications (Titul moskovskogo and Titul pravitelja, passim). Ščerbačev pointed out that the wax seal of Vasilij III used *gospodar'* instead of the usual abbreviation *gdr'* (Datskij archiv, p. 6, no. 12). Vasilij's golden bull on the 1516 letter of treaty to King Hans has *cr' i gdr'*, abbreviations for *car' i gospodar'* (ibid., p. 10, and original in the archive).

The Treaty of 1516. Details of the Russian original diploma

Left: The initial, an illuminated P made in red ink and gold leaf. Line 1 begins "Po božiej vole" (By the will of God). Top right: Obverse of Vasilij III's pendant golden bull showing a horseman slaying a winged serpent or dragon with his spear, a symbol of the grand prince fighting evil. (Not until 1722 was the figure officially proclaimed a representation of St George.) Bottom right: Reverse with a crowned double-headed eagle, an ancient and ubiquitous symbol of power adopted by Ivan III for his seal in the closing decade of the 15th century. The inspiration may well have been the Habsburg eagle, the intention purportedly being to equalize Ivan's rank with that of the German-Roman emperor. Danish National Archives. Photos: Carsten Pape.

2. The second "л" is an error. It is rendered correctly as an "р" (i.e. a Russian "r") when reappearing in the eschatocol (item 33). The name of the county is Oldenburg in modern German.
3. "Stenstura" is clearly written in one word in items 10, 11, 13 and 14, but it should be mentioned that the name is written in two words in other documents, e.g. the ambassadorial oration before King Christian II in 1514.[38] Scribes were not too particular about the spelling of proper names in the Middle Ages.

---

38   TKUA, Rusland: Akter og dokumenter vedrørende det politiske forhold til Rusland, l.nr. 73-13, 1493-1578. Printed in Russkie akty, 2.

4. I have numbered the sentence "item 15" because it appears as such in the two Danish texts, though in a different place in the text. See the Matrix, item 15.
5. "na togo" is repeated in the original.

Translation Notes

i–iii. The term *gospodar'* appears three times in the title of Vasilij III (item 2) which had been significantly expanded in his treaty of 1514 with Maximilian and would be used, with slight changes, for years to come.[39] On the face of it, this would call for translating *gospodar'* using the same foreign term in all three instances. Indeed, this is precisely what the grand princely chancery did when it prepared a Latin version of Vasilij's letter of credence for his envoys to Copenhagen in 1515, employing the Latin appellation *dominus* (column 1 in the chart below).[40] Christian II would copy this usage in his known correspondence with the grand prince.[41] In contemporaneous European parlance, the English translation for *dominus* (when referring to rulers and notables at higher levels) would be *lord*, corresponding to *seigneur* in French.

---

[39] The *intitulatio* of Vasilij's letter of treaty to Maximilian is identical to the one appearing in *1516 except for subtle differences of spelling (Fiedler, Allianz p. 247).

[40] The Russian-language original is printed in Russkie akty, 3. The Latin-language version, which is held by the Danish National Archives, is unpublished (TKUA, Rusland: Akter og dokumenter vedrørende det politiske forhold til Rusland, l.nr. 73-13, 1493-1578). In the Latin version of the ambassadorial oration of 1514, likewise unpublished, Vasilij styles himself "[de] magno domino Vasilio Dei gracia imperatori et domino tocius Russie et magno duci", leaving little doubt that he employed his new title vis-à-vis Denmark only little over a month since first using it in his Habsburg treaty (ibid.). The same thing happened in a missive to the Grand Master of the Teutonic Order of January 1515 (Lobin, Poslanija Vasilija III, No. 2, pp. 146-7).

[41] Kopengagenskie akty, 14 and 15. As some of his communications are only preserved as drafts, they do not write out Vasilij's title.

	1.[42]	2.[43]	3.[44]	4.[45]
1.	Ex magno *domino* Vasilii	Nos Magnus *Dominus* Basilius	[per] magni *domini* nobilissimi [...] Basilii	Magnus *dominus* Basilius
2.	dei gracia imperatoris ac *domini* tocius rucie et magni ducis	Dej gratia Caesar et *Dominator* totius Russiæ, et magnus Princeps	Imperatoris ac *dominatoris* totius Russiae	Imperator ac *dominator* totius Rusiae
3.	et *domini* et magni ducis	Et *Dominus* ac magnus Princeps	*dominatoris* et magni ducis	*dominator* et magnus dux

However, the grand princely chancery soon changed tack. In the Habsburg treaty of 1514 it had already replaced dominus with *dominator* in instance 2 (column 2 above),[46] and in all subsequent treaties known in Latin translation the Russians and their treaty partners (most likely copying the new Muscovite usage) would use *dominator* in instances 2 and 3 (examples in cols. 3 and 4 above). What lay behind the change and the differentiated translation of *gospodar'* by the Russians themselves?

In Biblical Latin, *dominus* and *dominator* are synonyms and, as such, both translated Lord in English bibles.[47] In the Middle Ages, however, *dominator* seems to have yielded to *dominus* in general usage, as the latter became the preferred appellation for people of substance, so to speak: prelates, peers, lawyers, dukes, kings and even the pope (*dominus*

---

42 1515 letter of credence by Vasilij III to Christian II, translated into Latin by the Moscow chancery (TKUA, Rusland: Akter og dokumenter vedrørende det politiske forhold til Rusland, l.nr. 73-13, 1493-1578). Vasilij had used the same terminology in his first letter to King Hans in 1506: "Basilius Dei gracia Imperator ac Dominus tocius Rutzsie et Magnus Dux" (Grönblad, Nya källor, 149).

43 The 1514 Habsburg-Muscovite treaty, clearly translated into Latin by the Moscow chancery itself (Fiedler, Allianz, pp. 250-2).

44 1517 Muscovite-Teutonic Order treaty, Grand Master's letter in Latin, probably copied from the Muscovite translation of Vasilij's preceding letter into Latin (SGGD V, 82).

45 1522 missive from Vasilij III to Emperor Charles V, translated into Latin by the Moscow chancery (Lobin, Poslanie gosudarja, No. 2, p. 136).

46 Maximilian's original letter of treaty in German had *Herr* (lord), *Herrscher* and *Herrscher* (ruler), respectively (Fiedler, Allianz, pp. 244-7).

47 Thus, in the Vulgate Isaiah 3:1 reads: "Ecce enim *Dominator, Dominus* exercituum, auferet a Jerusalem et a Juda validum et fortem, omne robur panis, et omne robor aquae" (www.biblegateway.com/passage/?search=Isaias %203&version= VULGATE;RSV&interface=amp. Emphasis added). The translation in the King James Bible reads: "For, behold, the *Lord*, the LORD of hosts, doth take away from Jerusalem and from Judah the stay and the staff, the whole stay of bread, and the whole stay of water" (www.kingjamesbibleonline.org/Jude–Chapter–1/).

summus pontifex).⁴⁸ From the vantage point of Vasilij III there was a problem with the term, though. Unlike *gospodar'* in the Russian context, *dominus* was never used in European titulature as, or as part of, the title proper – the designation of the office and the subject political unit – of a ruler of a *de facto* sovereign land (as for instance "Rex Angliæ", "Duc de Bourgogne", "Comes in Oldenburg", etc.). It was only used as, or as part of, the title of a ruler of inferior, not fully autonomous entities,⁴⁹ or as an honorific preceding the title proper, as in instance 1 in the chart above. Consequently, once the Russians began to adapt the grand princely title to the European model, they had to distinguish semantically between the three appearances of *gospodar'* in their translations into Latin, and this was probably the reason for the introduction of dominator. The distinction must be clear in a modern translation of the title. I therefore suggest the following renditions of *gospodar'*:

i. In all likelihood, the prefixed element of the title of Vasilij III, *velikij gospodar'* / *magnus dominus*, is a Russian approximation of the standard European honorific which typically (and with some variations) consisted of one or two adjectival attributes in the superlative drawn from a limited number of standard terms⁵⁰ plus one or both of the appellations *princeps* and *dominus*. Examples include "Christianissimus Princeps & Dominus Ludovicus Dei gratia Francorum Rex" and "Serenissimus & Potentissimus Princeps Dominus

---

48   *Dominator* was used in the generic sense of "ruler" and as such gets about 250 hits when searched in *Monumenta Germaniae Historica* (see the search facility at https://www.dmgh.de). *Dominus*, on the other hand, gets thousands. As a title proper, *dominator* appears very rarely. After the seizure of Constantinople in 1204, the Doge of Venice became "Venetorum, Dalmatorum atque Croatorum dux, quarti partis & dimidiae totius Imperii Romaniae *dominator*" (e.g. Corps Universel I, CCCLIV), and Emperor Charles V at some point became "*Dominator* in Asia et in Africa" (Corps Universel IV/3, IV), but apart from that there seem to be few other examples, if any. (Emphasis added.)

49   Thus, the full title of English medieval kings was, e.g., "Serenissimus & Potentissimus Princeps Dominus Edwardus Dei gratia Angliæ & Franciæ Rex Dominusque Hiberniæ" (the most serene and mighty prince lord Edward, by the grace of God King of England and France, Lord of Ireland) (Rymer XII, p. 92s. Likewise, the title of Polish rulers was "Serenissimus Perpotensque Dominus Joannes Albertus, Poloniæ Rex Supremus Dux Litvaniæ Russiæ Prussiæque Dominus" (The most serene and mighty lord John Albert [Jan Olbracht], King of Poland, Grand Prince of Lithuania, Lord of Russia and Prussia" (Codex Diplomaticus I, p. 443d. *Perpotens* is a variant of fortissimus). In the latter title, "Russia" was a reference to the former Russian principalities that had later been conquered by the Lithuanians and now formed semi-feudal entities within the grand principality, while "Prussia" was a reference to the Teutonic Order that had been feudally subordinate to Poland since 1466.

50   The most frequently used were *excellentissimus*, *inuictissimus*, *illustrissimus*, *potentissimus* and *altissimus*. The term *cristianissimus* was reserved for the French monarchs.

Edoardus, Dei gratia Rex Franciæ & Angliæ &c."[51] It is noteworthy in this connection that both *1493 and *1506 employ the standard European model of the title when addressing the grand princes in their inscriptions (item 05). The reason why Vasilij III does not embrace the full model with its twin attributes in the superlative may well be that Ivan III had used "velikij gospodar'" on and off as a title proper (e.g. *velikij gospodar' vsea Rusi* or *velikij gospodar' car' vsea Rusi*),[52] and that Vasilij simply converted this pre-existing formula to an honorific without caring to fully adapt it to the European template. For the translation I have not been able to find a contemporaneous English-language equivalent of the standard Latin honorific, but there is a good French example in a 1458 treaty of marriage between the "tres-haulte & Puissante Dame Charlotte Fille du Roy de Chypres […] & Treshault & Puissant Prince Monseigneur Loys de Savoye Comte de Geneve, Fils de Tres-haut & Tres-excellent Prince Monseigneur le Duc de Savoye [etc.]."[53] In this title, *Tres-hault[e] & Puissant[e]* is the French equivalent of "altissimus et potentissimus",[54] *Dame* the female equivalent of "dominus" and *Prince Monseigneur* the French equivalent of "princeps dominus" (though in this exalted case the normal *seigneur* is substituted by *monseigneur*).[55] As (mon)seigneur indisputably translates into lord in English, this term will be an appropriate rendering of *gospodar'* in the case at hand. Hence my translation of "velikij gospodar'" into "great lord."

ii. The composite appellation *car' i gospodar'* followed by the territorial designation *vsea Rusii* is a title proper at the level of *rex* and *duc* (duke) – a supreme ruler of a *de jure* or *de facto* sovereign political entity – in the examples cited above. Unfortunately, there is no obvious English equivalent of *gospodar'* in this particular sense of the term. English-speaking historians of Russia typically translate it "Sovereign",[56] but this is not a particularly apt rendition as it does not convey an essential semantic connotation of *gospodar'* in the Russian political-ideological context. The original meaning of the word is, or includes the notion of, "head of a household seen as an economic unit" or "master of a landed property with workhands ascribed to it", as is also the case with some appearances of

---

51 "The most Christian prince and lord, Louis, by the grace of God King of France" and "The most serene and mighty prince lord, Edward, by the grace of God King of France & England &c." (Corps Universel III/1, pp. 306s and 488s).

52 PDS I, cols. 15-16 (1489) and col. 88 (1492); Neizdannye akty, nos. 5 and 6; Agoŝton, Titul pravitelja, p. 7.

53 "Most exalted and mighty Dame Charlotte, daughter of the King of Cyprus, and the most exalted and mighty prince lord Louis of Savoy, Count of Geneva, son of the most exalted and excellent prince lord, the Duke of Savoy" (Corps Universel III/1, p. 251s. Emphasis added).

54 Cf. "Cum inter Altissimos & Potentissimos Principes Fernandum Regem & Helesabetham Reginam Castellæ […]" (Rymer XII, p. 413s).

55 In other contexts, the French used "prince et seigneur" (e.g. Rymer XII, p. 306s).

56 E.g. Fennell, Ivan III, p. 147. This meaning is borne out by a less frequently used title of Ivan III, *samoderžec*, which is a calque of the Greek "autokrator". The sovereignty implied by the titles was perceived as being both international and domestic (Krom, Roždenie gosudarstva, p. 66).

lord and seigneur.⁵⁷ Muscovy's patrimonial ideology did not operate with "the crown" as a concept distinct from "the ruler" as in the West, but perceived the incumbent grand prince as the proprietor of the Russian lands in the same way a seigneur was the owner of a landed estate with people ascribed. In this respect, "lord" would be a reasonable translation, except that it does not convey the notion of supreme ruler well. For an alternative, contemporaneous English and Scottish documents employed an honorific (but not a title) which actually conveys both meanings, viz. *sovereign lord*, as exemplified in syntagms such as "our *Soverane Lord* James, King of Scotland",⁵⁸ "[le] Treshault & Tresexcellent Prince nostre Tresredoubte & *Souverain Seigneur* Charles, par la Grace de Dieu, Roy de France Tres Christien",⁵⁹ or in the common shorthand refence to the English king as "oure *Soverain Lord*" in contexts where it is not part of the full title.⁶⁰ I will, however, leave the idea of translating *gospodar'* with "sovereign lord" for further discussion and for the time being retain the conventional "sovereign" as the title proper of Vasilij III in English translation. As for *car'* (tsar), Vasilij clearly intended the term to be the equivalent of the Latin *imperator* as demonstrated in the chart above, for which reason I use "Emperor" for the translation.

iii. In its third appearance, *gospodar'* is at the same hierarchical level as *velikij knaz'* (grand prince). Since Vasilij III deliberately had the term translated into *dominator* in this position as well, thereby semantically equalizing it with its second appearance (ii), I again translate it "sovereign", though for lack of a better alternative.

iv. I employ modern geographical names for the translation of the titles. In the Russian original, the designations of the subject lands are adjectives, but I use substantival proper names as this was commonplace in European treaties at the time. *Volockij* refers to Volok Lamskij, or simply Volok, i.e. present-day Volokolamsk. The ducal and comital possessions of Christian II are located in present-day Germany and therefore rendered in modern German. The Muscovite chancery misses the point that Christian II appears as duke twice in his official title, separating Schleswig from his other dukedoms.

v. In continuation of the discussion of *confoederatio* in Translation Note ii on p. 96, the terms *dokončanie* and *edinačestvo* in items 03 and 06 may both reasonably be translated "union". *Dokončanie* can and often does refer to a treaty⁶¹ and *edinačestvo* to an alliance (like the Latin *unio* it derives from the numeral "one"), but the fact that they are used together or even interchangeably in Russian sources blurs their original definitions and turns them, like their Latin counterparts, into formulaic abstracta connoting a state of

---

57 Krom, Roždenie gosudarstva, p. 62.
58 Rymer XII, p. 160s. Emphasis added.
59 Rymer XII, p. 506s. Emphasis added.
60 Rymer XII, p. 479s. Emphasis added.
61 Slovar' drevnerusskogo jazyka, Vol. III; Slovar' russkogo jazyka XI–XVII vv., Vol. 4. An example from the Muscovite-Lithuanian peace negotiations in early 1494 reads: "Panove! Veleli esmja pisati diakom dokončan'ja, i oni načisto napisali" (My lords! We have ordered the secretaries to draw up the treaty, and they have engrossed it) (SIRIO 35, 24, p. 124).

benevolent treaty-based relations.⁶² A particularly apt example of the double meaning of *dokončanie* appears in the accounts of the Muscovite-Lithuanian peace negotiations in early 1494, during which the Lithuanian ambassadors expressed the wish of their sovereign to establish "peaceful living and friendship and union ["dokončjanja"] according to the treaty ["dokončan'ju"] that our father concluded with your father".⁶³ The Habsburg Imperial chancery was conscious of these broader connotations when it translated Ivan III's 1490 letter of treaty to Maximilian into German, using *verstentnuss* ("understanding") for *dokončanie*⁶⁴ and *aynigung* (*Einigung*, in one web translation "amicable arrangement") for *edinačestvo*,⁶⁵ i.e. terms not denoting formally constituted treaties and alliances.

vi. The Russian *gde* normally means "where" but may also mean "when".⁶⁶ For my choice of the latter translation, see the discussion on p. 97, Translation Note vii.

vii. I use *august* for *navyššii* ("the most high"), as Maximilian's full title included the epithet "semper augustus".⁶⁷

viii The verb *dvinuti* may mean "to touch, disturb, offend". In all likelihood, during the negotiations the Russian side did not quite catch the Danish envoy's point which was to prevent locals from appropriating the goods of the shipwrecked.

Realia Notes

Item 02: *Vasilei*

Vasilij III (see p. 106, item 05)

Item 05: *Kristernom*

Instrumental of Kristern, Russian for Christian II (often spelled Christiern or Kristiern in contemporaneous Danish sources). King of Denmark-Norway 1513-23.

Item 10: *[na] svantova syna na Stenstura*

Sten Svantesson Sture (Sten Sture the Younger) (see p. 67 n. 99 and p. 106, item 10).

---

62 Thus, the Grand Prince of Tver' had been in "brotherhood, friendship and *dokončanie*" with Kazimir IV of Lithuania (PDS I, col. 169), but Ivan III in "brotherhood, friendship and *edinačestvo*" with Matthias Corvinus of Hungary (PDS I, col. 166; the two statements appear only three columns apart in the source). At one point Ivan stated that he had entered into "friendship and *dokonczanie* and *edynaczestwo* and eternal amity" with Alexander of Lithuania (Lietuvos metrika, p. 81s; in this example, the Lithuanian chancery renders the Russian terms in Latin letters and Polish orthography). Also, Slovar' russkogo jazyka XI–XVII vv., Vol. 4, defines *dokončanie* not only as "treaty" (*dogovor*), but also as "treaty-based relations" (*dogovornye otnošenija*).

63 SIRIO 35, 24, p. 113. The treaty in question was concluded by Kazimir IV and Vasilij II in 1449.

64 Lichnowsky, Geschichte, Del C, No. IX, p. DCCLII. Note that Lesaffer uses the same word, understanding, in the quote p. 96, Translation Note ii.

65 Lichnowsky, Geschichte, Del C, No. IX, p. DCCLII. For the web translation, see https://www.dict.cc/?s=einigung (accessed February 27, 2020).

66 Slovar' russkogo jazyka XI–XVII vv., Vol. 4, p. 16.

67 E.g. Corps Universel III/2, p. 219s, Corps Universel IV/1, p. 99s.

Item 16: *[na] Žigimonta*
>Accusative of *Žigimont*, Russian for Sigismund I of Poland and Lithuania (1506–48).

Item 16ª: *[s] Maksimilijanom izbrannym cesarem rimskim i navyššim korolem otcem vašim*
>Maximilian I of the house of Habsburg was effectively German-Roman Emperor 1493-1519. As previously stated, he was never crowned but eventually given the title Emperor-elect. Hence the syntagm *izbrannym cesarem rimskim* (Roman Emperor-Elect). Maximilian had been elected successor to his father, Emperor Friedrich III, in 1486 and was given the standard title of the emperor-elect, *Romanorum Rex* (King of the Romans), hence the word *korolem* (king) in the citation. As stated in Translation Note vi above, the adjective *navyššim* (supreme) is probably a reference to the epithet *semper augustus* (always august) in Maximilian's official titles, *Romanorum Rex Semper Augustus* and *Electus Romanorum Imperator Semper Augustus*.
>
>The word *otcem* in the syntagm *otcem vašim* (your father, "your" referring to Christian II) is an example of so-called metaphorical kinship and does not imply that Maximilian was in any way related to the Danish king. However, Christian II would not have missed the point that Maximilian was his *de facto* father-in-law at the time the treaty was drawn up (see p. 72 n. 115).

Publication History

>Surprisingly, the Russian original diploma has only been published once, by Ščerbačev.[68] Ščerbačev, however, omitted the titles of the two signatories in both the protocol and the eschatocol, meaning that these are published for the first time in the present volume. He also made a few other errors of transcription which have been corrected here.
>
>The Danish National Archives holds two translations of the act into German.[69] For convenience I label them A and B in the following. A is printed in Grönblad,[70] while B remains unpublished. There is little doubt that they were produced in connection with the diplomatic overture by King Frederik II to Tsar Ivan IV in 1558-62, and there is little doubt that document A is the primary of the two, even though Ščerbacev reverses the order.[71] First, on the back of B a modern hand has written "Bilag til relation fra Klaus Urne m.fl., Danzig 13/11 1558" (Annex to a relation from Klaus Urne et al., Danzig Nov. 13, 1558). On the given date, a Danish embassy headed by Urne was on its way to Moscow to open negotiations about the status of Livonia,[72] and it may be surmised that the translation it had brought along (and for some reason sent back from Danzig) was not the original, but a copy. Second, the text of A is characterized by a curious, but significant detail: the person who translated it was unable to render the two Russian terms *ugod'ja* (rights of use) and *potjagli k* (belonged to) in Danish and instead entered the words *ugoddi* and *potegli* without further explanation (items 18 and 19) in the text.

---

68   Russkie akty, 8. Grönblad maintained that the original had been lost (Grönblad, Nya källor, Introduction to 365).
69   TKUA, Rusland: Akter og dokumenter vedrørende det politiske forhold til Rusland, l.nr. 73-13, 1493-1578. See Datskij archiv, pp. 10-11.
70   Grönblad, Nya källor, 365.
71   Datskij archiv, p. 10.
72   Venge, Københavnertraktaten, pp. 21 ff. = Venge, Kopengagenskij traktat, pp. 21 ff.

In B, a margin note explains one of the terms, indicating that the document was copied from A.

The 1516 Russian original was published in Danish translation by Arild Huitfeldt in the tome of his Chronicle of the Danish Realm covering the reign of Christian II.[73] To produce the translation, Huitfeldt clearly translated the German text A, for he retained the two untranslated Russian terms, though actually making notes of their meaning in the margin:

> "oc det saaledis at udi huilcke lande oc vand som fiskerij ere oc allehaande *potegli* udi vore lande oc udi de land oc vand huor som helst fiskefang for haanden er oc allehaande **ugoddi* dig oc dit folck […].
> * irrige trætagtige stæder [margin note]
> ** irrige stæder [margin note]"[74]

Like the German translation, Huitfeldt dates the treaty August 2, 7024 = 1516, but places the translation under 1515 in his book.

The act was further printed in German translation (and without any introduction) in *Büschings Magazin*, vol. III, 1769, pp. 179-82, in a section on "Rußland" and subsection on "Verträge zwischen den Norwegern und Nowgorodern von 1326 und zwischen Rußland und Dänemark von 1517. Von Archiv-Urkunden abgeschrieben." It is based on the German document A as well, retaining the two Russian terms untranslated and erroneously dating the treaty August 2, 1517.

An excerpt of *1516 comprising items 18 and 26 is published in Russian translation in SGGD V, 80. The text is a rather loose translation of the version appearing in *Büschings Magazin*, from which it retains the incorrect date August 2, 1517.

The 19th-century Danish repertory of medieval sources lists *1516 as "an alliance between Grand Prince Vasilij […] and King Christian," naming August 2, 1516, as the date of issue (Regesta Diplomatica I, 6071). In the second Series of the publication, the date is changed to August 2, 1517, probably following *Büschings Magazin* (see above) which it refers to (Regesta Diplomatica II/I.2, 10,224).

The diploma is listed, correctly identified and described, but not published in Ščerbačev's Datskij archiv, pp. 9-11.

---

73 Huitfeldt, Christian II, pp. 39-42.

74 "[…] and that in such a way that in which lands and waters there is fishing and all kinds of [* disputed, contested places] *potegli* in our lands and in land and water wherever fishing is at hand and all kinds of [** disputed places] *ugoddi* you and your people […]". The translation of * is incorrect, as it parallels the translation of ** instead of conveying "belong to" in Danish.

о посѣхъ. Того же лѣта и ною. ѿпоу
стилъ князь велїкїи да цесого корола
крестерпопа его посла до старого.
да с нїмъ вмѣсте послалъ князь велїкїи
к королю дацескому дьика своего нек͠р
саха рламопа. да и грамотꙋ
докончалную с нїмъ
к королю
посла
лъ.

4. Reconstructing the Lost Originals

To recapitulate the preceding chapters: of the eight letters of treaty constituting the Danish-Muscovite treaties of 1493, 1506 and 1516 and the abortive treaty of 1514 only one, the Russian letter of 1516, has been preserved in the original. The Danish originals of 1493 and 1506 were copied and amended in 1506 and 1514, whereas any trace of the Russian originals of 1493, 1506 and 1514 has been lost. In no case have both texts of one and the same treaty been preserved.

This state of affairs is deplorable, for it diminishes the heuristic value of the surviving documents in more than one way. Two examples will illustrate why and point up the uses of attempting to reconstruct the missing texts.

The Uses of Reconstructions

As previously stated, the constituent acts of most European medieval treaties were formulated in one and the same language, be it Latin, French, German, English, Danish, Swedish, etc., i.e. languages reflecting more or less identical

◄ **Bringing Vasilij III's letter of treaty to Copenhagen in 1516.**
In the background, Grand Prince Vasilij III hands over his letter of treaty of 1516 to the Danish envoy David Cochran, who subsequently rides off to Copenhagen accompanied by his Muscovite colleague Nekras Charlamov.
In the foreground, Cochran and Charlamov hand over the diploma to King Christian II in Copenhagen.
Miniature from the Russian "Illustrated Chronicle Compilation". Copyright: AKTEON Publishing House, Moscow.

political cultures.[1] As the texts would also typically be identical, though reciprocal, it is normally possible to ascertain the content of a given treaty even if only the acts of one side have been preserved.[2] This, however, is not entirely the case with treaties concluded with Muscovy. The treaty diplomas were written in two different languages – effectively Russian and Latin or German – reflecting significantly different political, confessional, and diplomatic cultures. In consequence, the letters of any given treaty were not necessarily fully congruent in the sense of being correct, unequivocal translations of each other.[3] Technical terms connoting socio-political and even spatial phenomena might differ between the two languages or simply be lacking in one of them, and negotiations mediated by more or less proficient interpreters could lead to subtle inaccuracies or blatant incoherencies between the texts. To arrive at a proper understanding of the formulaic and substantive content of such treaties it will therefore be necessary to analyze *both* versions of an agreement in a comparative manner.

As an example, the Danish (Latin) text of 1493 and the Russian text of 1516 have a paragraph in common that instructs the parties how to handle a situation

---

1 Mattingly, pp. 15-19; Lesaffer, Medieval Canon Law, p. 180. Luciana Duranti writes about diplomas in general: "Any written document in the diplomatic sense contains information transmitted or described by means of rules of representation […]. These rules, which we call form, reflect political, legal, administrative, and economic structures, culture, habit, myths, and constitute an integral part of the written document, because they formulate or condition the ideas or facts which we take to be the content of the documents" (Duranti, Diplomatics, p. 41).

2 Feldbrugge makes the point the following way, speaking of "princes whose legal relationships are determined by documents which they address to each other and in which the mutual rights and duties are spelled out. Such letters then appear as each other's complements". Consequently, "if only one part of the set of letters survived, almost no information is lost and we may regard the surviving letter, in a material sense, also as a treaty" (Feldbrugge, Treaties, p. 159).

3 Marija Grischmanova writes: "Wie eine kontrastive Untersuchung ergeben hat, war [die Inhalts-]Struktur sowohl in den mittelniederdeutschen, als auch in den altrussischen Urkunden in der Regel ähnlich. Trotzdem unterscheiden sich die mittelniederdeutschen und altrussischen Texte darin, dass sie über unterschiedliche Formulierungen für die Ausdrücke der gleichen kommunikativen Einheiten verfügen" (As evidenced by a contrastive study, [the content] structure of the middle low German and the old Russian diplomas was normally similar. Yet, the middle low German and the old Russian texts differ between them in that they employ different formulations to express identical communicative units). See Grischmanova, Sprachkontakt und Textstruktur, p. 2).

in which a vessel from one side is driven onto the shores of the other by inclement weather (item 29). The article concludes with the following stipulation:

1493	1516 [1493]
Et quod soluere tenentur nostre terre soluant consuetum.	A gde prilučitsja im kotoraja pošlina dati, i im ta pošlina platiti.
– – –	– – –
And what they must pay to our land, they pay according to custom.	*And where they may have to pay a due, they shall pay the due.*

Imagine for the sake of argument that the Russian text of 1493 were identical to that of *1516 (as indeed I shall argue in this chapter). A comparative reading of the two letters would then reveal that the Russian version speaks of a certain duty using a standard Russian technical term, *pošlina*, whereas the Danish version does not specify the type of duty to be paid; it simply requires an unspecified, but obligatory payment (*quod soluere tenentur*) to be made according to custom (*soluant consuetum*), a not unimportant requirement which, on the other hand, is absent in the Russian text. In addition, the Danish version is specific about the recipient of the duty (*nostre terre*) whereas the Russian version is non-specific (*gde*). The two versions are not widely different, yet being in possession of only one would not necessarily yield a correct interpretation of the dispositive content of the clause as understood by the negotiators who clinched the agreement. Both letters would be needed for that.

There is more to it, however. The potential and often real inconsistencies between two letters of treaty written in two different languages may, correctly interpreted, offer significant insights into the negotiation process itself. As a case in point, consider the clause determining how to deal with future conflicts between the border populations of the two realms (item 21):

1493	1516 [1493]
Et que postmodum ex vtraque parte inter nostros subditos contingunt, iudicium et expedicionem absque temporis longa prolongatione habebunt.	A vpered čto učinitsja meži našimi ljudmi kakovo delo v sej našej ljubvi, tomu vsemu sud i isprava bez perevoda.
– – –	– – –
And what comes to pass from this day forth, on both sides, between our subjects, shall be given justice and due process without long delay.	*And what is henceforth committed between our people, no matter the case, during this our friendship, shall all be given justice and due process without delay.*

Again, the two versions are close enough to be basically identical in terms of the actions they mandate, although it should be noted, with regard to the previous argument, that the Danish (Latin) text does not include the term limitation inherent in the Russian version's "in this our friendship," i.e. "for the duration of this treaty". But a critical analysis of the two versions reveals that the Russian text, when compared to the full body of preserved and published Russian treaties, consists of a series of either standard technical terms or fixed diplomatic turns, whereas the Danish text does not.[4] It is largely translated directly from the Russian version without recourse to Western standard diplomatic terms. For instance, if *sud i isprava* is a fixed term in Russian inter-princely treaties, Hans Claussen's Latin equivalent *iudicium et expedicionem* is not a standard syntagm in any European diplomatic act and will have been invented for the occasion by the Danish envoy. Likewise, *absque temporis longa prolongatione* is an unusually clumsy translation of the Russian standard phrase *bez perevoda* which would typically be rendered *sine dilatione*,[5] *sine mora*[6] (both "without postponement"), or *cum omni celeritate*[7] ("with all haste") in Western treaties. Other standard terms typical of Russian treaties in general include *a vpered čto učinitsja, meži našimi ljudmi, v sej našej ljubvi*, and *tomu vsemu*. None of these were translated by the Danish envoy using standard Western terminology.

What should we make of this? It seems fair to assume that the party using standard terminology from its own linguistic arsenal was also the party who brought the given clause and its underlying issue to the negotiation table. This, in turn, makes it possible to pinpoint the particular interests that informed the sides during the talks and from there develop the analysis further. Incidentally, this requires meticulous linguistic scrutiny of the texts.

Not all articles are as clear-cut as the one cited above, however. Comparative readings of the treaty texts reveal paragraphs that appear to be formulated from scratch in a joint effort, while still others may contain standard as well as translated linguistic material on both sides, again reflecting a multifaceted negotiation process. The main point is that it is possible to make conclusions

---

4   I have come to this conclusion by performing electronic searches in a number of standard source publications of the past that have been digitalized in recent years.
5   Cf. Codex Diplomaticus I, XV and XXVI.
6   Cf. Corps Universel III/1, p. 156s, Codex Diplomaticus IV, p. 112s.
7   Cf. Corps Universel III, Suppl. I, XVIII and III/2, CXXXV (both are Danish-English treaties).

about that process itself by approaching the texts in a comparative manner and performing linguistic analyses across multiple treaty texts. Incidentally, this method has been greatly facilitated by the recent advent of digitalized and searchable editions of the standard source publications of the past.

In the examples given above I compare clauses appearing in two different treaties, viz. the Danish letter of 1493 and the Russian letter of 1516, but the point I am making should be clear: if it were possible to perform a comparative reading of the Danish and Russian versions of *one and the same* treaty through a reconstruction of the missing acts, we would potentially gain significant insights into the intended content of the treaties – which is far from always clear, as demonstrated by the examples above – *and* into the diplomatic process of putting forward themes for discussion and of jointly formulating identical content in two languages representing widely different cultures.

The Feasibility of Reconstruction

But can it be accomplished? Under normal circumstances historians should for obvious reasons abstain from any attempt to reconstruct lost acts. I will argue, however, that in this particular case the form of the surviving Danish-Muscovite documents in combination with our knowledge of the conditions under which they came into existence does make it possible to restore the lost treaty texts with a high degree of accuracy, and certainly accurately enough to make comparative readings legitimate and meaningful.

First, as will be remembered, the Danish and Russian negotiators in both 1506 and 1514 agreed that the new treaties produced in those two years would repeat the content of the previous compacts word for word, implying that the formulae and substantive provisions of the treaty of 1493 would remain unchanged in the subsequent agreements, save for the addition of the anti-Polish clause in 1514-6 (pp. 73 ff.). What *would* change from treaty to treaty was the names, titles and epithets of the contracting rulers and their common adversaries plus the dates of issue, but these were essentially substitutions of one set of data for another within otherwise identically formulated clauses.

Second, the juxtaposition in the Appendix of the three surviving documents (plus the Russian letter of the treaty of 1490 between Ivan III and Emperor Maximilian, referred to as *1490 below), representing three *different* treaties and *both* languages, reveals that all three texts were structurally identical in the sense that all textual items of one text have matching items in the others; that no text includes items not present in the others (except for the "Polish" clause in *1516, item 16a); and that the sequence of items is identical across the three texts with only two minor exceptions: (1) Item 04 (*s svoim bratom*) is positioned before the inscription in both *1490 and *1516, but after the inscription in both *1493 and *1506 (*cum ffratre et confederato nostro carissimo*). The reason for the repositioning and reformulation of the latter will have been an attempt by the Danish envoy to adapt the Russian version – which was dictated to him, see below – to standard European and especially Danish-Scottish diplomatic language.[8] (2) The clause determining the objective of the anti-Swedish alliance – to "obtain" Sweden – is positioned after item 10 in *1516 but after item 14 in the two Danish texts. In both cases I take it for granted that these differences were also present in the lost originals.

Third, it turns out – and this is a novel insight – that significant parts of the Russian text of *1516 are direct copies of *1490. The sections in question include the full protocol, the full eschatocol, and the "alliance" part of the *dispositio*, together comprising items 01-09, 24-25 and 32-40. Of these, some are structurally identical in the sense that names, titles, and epithets change between the two treaties, but that the textual framework in which they appear remains identical. In addition, items 10-14 were clearly inspired by the identical clauses of *1490, but these were too different in terms of concrete stipulations to warrant direct copying. In the following I label the sum total of these items *Text Corpus A*. The text was formulated from scratch by the Russian side during the negotiations with Maximilian's envoy in 1490. It had only scant and partial precedents in Muscovite (or Tverian, or Novgorodian) diplomatic usage, and no

---

8   Maximilian's chancery did the same when translating Ivan III's 1490 letter of treaty (Lichnowsky, Part C, No. IX, pp. DCCLII–DCCLIII). While Ivan's letter reads "s svoim bratom s Maksimianom, kralem rimskim [etc.]" (with our brother Maximilian, King of the Romans [etc.]), the translation by the Imperial chancery reads "mit Maximilian Romischen Kunig [etc.], vnnsern lieben Bruder" (with Maximilian, King of the Romans [etc.], our beloved brother). Interestingly, Vasilij III, possibly in an effort to emulate Western practice, used the same syntagm about King Hans in his very first missive to him in 1506 ("serenissimo et potentissimo Johanni, Dei gracia Dacie, Suecie, Noruegie [etc.], fratri nostro et confederato carissimo [...]") (Kopengagenskie akty, 5). In all likelihood, the Moscow chancery copied the syntagm directly from the king's 1493 letter of treaty.

precedents in Imperial custom.⁹ In other words, it was *unique*. Yet it reappears verbatim in *1516. The point is illustrated by the diagram below showing all letters of treaty issued between 1490 and 1516, with the latter two rendered in light grey.

Text Corpus A: Verbatim accordance

Ivan III to Maximilian (*1490) — Reuse → Ivan III to King Hans 1493 → Vasilij III to King Hans 1506 → Vasilij III to Christian II 1514 → Vasilij III to Christian II (*1516)

Translation ↓ King Hans to Ivan III (*1493) → King Hans to Vasilij III (*1506) → Christian II to Vasilij III 1514 → Christian II to Vasilij III 1515

The fact that Vasilij III reused Text Corpus A of *1490 in his 1516 letter of treaty to Christian II makes it a likely proposition that this particular text was used in the Russian letters of 1493, 1506 and 1514 as well. It is inconceivable that Vasilij should suddenly, when issuing his second or third letter of treaty to the King of Denmark in 1514 or 1516, reach 24 or 26 years back in time to search his father's letter to Maximilian for inspiration on how to formulate the protocol, the eschatocol and the alliance clauses of the renewed treaty with Denmark. It is far more reasonable to conclude that the text in question was handed down from treaty to treaty, beginning in 1493 when Ivan III must have found that he could re-use the wording of his Habsburg treaty to formulate the text of the new, nearly identical treaty of alliance with King Hans.

Fourth, the text items of the two surviving Danish documents (dark grey boxes) corresponding to Text Corpus A in *1490 are not only identical between them, again excepting names, titles, and epithets, they are verbatim translations of the Russian text, albeit with some issues discussed in the comments to the reconstructions below. By "filling in" the gap between 1490 and 1516, this too

---

9   The Imperial ambassador visiting Moscow in 1490 was presented with Ivan III's letter of treaty without having been invited to negotiate the terms first. He was not even empowered by Maximilian to conclude a treaty, only to explore the possibility of doing so. See PDS I, cols. 28-30, 32, 49, and Uebersberger, Österreich, pp. 18-25.

supports the argument that Text Corpus A was identical across all treaties in both languages.

Fifth, the "cooperation" clauses of the Danish-Muscovite treaties – comprising items 17-31 and labelled *Text Corpus B* in the following – were genuinely new in 1493 and were consequently formulated from scratch by the negotiators of both sides working through interpreters. The fact that the two Danish texts are virtually identical *and* that they are identical with the Russian text of *1516 in terms of number and sequence of individual clauses clearly expressing identical content, though with some linguistic inconsistencies, allows us to conclude that the missing acts contained the very same text, be it in Danish or Russian.[10]

The Sources Assessed

Before turning to the reconstructions, the accuracy of the surviving sources in rendering the original but perished texts should be briefly assessed. In this respect, Vasilij III's letter of treaty of 1516, being the original, poses no problems, but the remaining documents do.

First, they are all copied from chancery copies of the originals which may themselves contain errors of transcription, quite apart from the fact that the originals may have contained minor errors of their own, as is indeed the case with *1516.[11]

Second, apart from perpetuating possible errors of the chancery copies, the copyists may have made their own mistakes in the copying process in the form of oversights and misreadings. This actually did happen. As an example of an oversight, the person who drew up *1493 forgot to copy the introductory statement *Ex voluntate dei et nostro amore* (item 01) and had to subsequently add it in the margin. While this is a detectable error because it was corrected,

---

10   Ščerbačev agreed, writing about his publication of *1493 in Kopengagenskie akty: "The contents are word for word the same as the contents of the letter of treaty of Grand Prince Vasilij Ivanovic [III] to the Danish King Christian II, only no help from our side against the King of Poland is specified" (Soderžanie doslovno tože samoe, čto soderžanie dogovornoj gramoty velikogo knjazja Vasilija Ivanoviča s datskim korolem Christiernom II, tol'ko s našej storony ne vygovarivaetsja pomošč datčan protiv korol-ja pol'skogo) (Kopengagenskie akty, 2, p. 2).

11   It repeats the words *na togo* in item 16ª.

others may be invisible to the modern researcher. For instance, a misreading may have occurred when the copyist transcribed the words *nostre terre* in item 30 from what may have appeared in the original as *more terre* (see the discussion on p. 137, item 30). If this is the case, the error is undetectable or can only be established circumstantially.

Third, the copyists could make errors when revising the texts once they were copied, as most revisions were carried out by crossing out irrelevant words and entering their substitutes in the margins or above the lines. There is an example of this type of mistake in *1493, item 11, in which the copyist named the Swedish governor at Viborg Erik Sture instead of the correct Erik Turesson (*Ericum Stwre, capitaneum in Wiburgh*). In a case like this it takes knowledge of Swedish prosopography to spot the error.

Finally, to adapt the treaties of 1493 and 1506 to the realities of 1506 and 1514, respectively, the copyists may have revised the texts of the chancery copies directly in the process of transcription without first entering the original text, crossing out obsolete words and adding substitutes in the margins or above the line. Examples appear in the inscriptions of both *1493 and *1506 (items 02 and 33) in which the copyists entered the names and titles of the current monarchs, not the ones appearing in the chancery copies they were transcribing. The problem to the analyst is that not all such corrections are readily detectable.

Restoring King Hans' original letter of 1506 presents a specific problem in that there are two sources for it, *1493 being a draft and *1506 a copy.[12] How does one interpret instances in which draft and copy do not coincide? For example, item 11 of the two documents reads, taking the revisions entered into the former into account:

---

12   *1506 was *not* copied from David Cochran's preliminary letter issued in Moscow and brought to Copenhagen by the envoy in 1514 (pp. 74–5). The copyist has crossed out the name of Svante Nilsson, who was Swedish regent in 1506 and would therefore have appeared in the treaty of that year, but not in Cochran's letter, as Svante had been dead for two years when he issued it.

*1493	*1506
et qum aliquis nostrum incipiet lites contra et aduersus Swantonem qui nunc gerit se pro gubernatore regnj Suecie *Ericum Stwre capitaneum in Wiburgh* aliosque occupatores regnj nostri Suecie *infideles subditos atque rebelles*	et qum aliquis nostrum incipiet lites aduersus Stenonem Swantesson qui se nunc gerit gubernatorem regni et alios occupatores regni Suecie
— — —	— — —
And when one of us joins battle against and versus Svante, who now purports to be regent of the kingdom of Sweden, Eric Sture, governor at Viborg, and the other occupiers of our kingdom of Sweden, disloyal subjects and rebels	*And when one of us joins battle against Sten Svantesson, who now purports to be regent of the kingdom of Sweden, and the other occupiers of the kingdom of Sweden*

The question is whether the italicized Latin phrases of *1493, which were added to the copy-cum-draft in 1506, were left out when King Hans' original letter of that year was engrossed and therefore obviously not copied in 1514, or whether they were left out as an invisible revision when *1506 was produced as a draft of the original letter of King Christian II of 1514. Another example appears in the inscriptions (item 02). In *1493, Ivan III was *dominus*, but in *1506 Vasilij III was *princeps et dominus*, raising the question whether *princeps* was forgotten as an oversight in the copying process in 1506, or added to the engrossed treaty text in that year, or entered in 1514. There is no way to obtain a correct answer, but also no way to avoid dealing with the issues thus raised. See the discussion of these and related examples of invisible changes in the notes to the reconstructions of the Danish acts below.

◦ ◦ ◦

Ivan III's original letter of treaty of 1490 to Maximilian has been lost, as has the chancery copy of it. However, its text is known from a contemporaneous transcript entered into a preserved embassy book (*posol'skaja kniga*) covering Muscovy's relations with the German-Roman Empire in the period 1488-1517.[13] As the production of these books would normally take place after the conclusion of a given diplomatic mission or exchange, the copies of the relevant Russian documents were most likely made not from the outgoing originals, but from

---

13   On "embassy books," see p. 26 n. 20.

their chancery copies, whereas the incoming foreign documents were copied from the originals. In this respect, the status of *1490 is equal to that of the two surviving Danish copies. On the other hand, it differs from its Danish counterparts by not being a draft of a future treaty, for which reason it does not contain any revisions.

The embassy book in question was published in the 19th century in accordance with the prevailing publication principles of the time, including the use of the then modern Russian alphabet and orthography.[14] The original, however, has commendably been made accessible on the internet by the Russian State Archive of Ancient Acts (RGADA).[15] The publication of the text in the Appendix is based on my reading of this version.

As with the two Danish sources, it is impossible to assess the accordance of *1490 with the lost original, as scribes and copyists may have made writing errors at every step of the process from engrossing the originals to producing the copies under review. It is possible, however, to evaluate the accuracy of *1490 in reproducing the *chancery* copy from which it was transcribed and thus eliminate one layer of possible errors. When Ivan III issued his letter to Maximilian, he wished to be sure that the corresponding diploma of the latter would be a verbatim replica of his own act, even to the point of preferably being in Russian.[16] He therefore produced and transmitted a draft of *this* letter to Maximilian, suggesting that the emperor-elect simply copy its Russian text when drawing up his own letter of treaty. The two letters are copied in sequence in the embassy book.[17] As they were meant to be identical, and as Ivan III was extremely particular about the minutest details of his diplomatic instruments, they may be taken to be correct renderings of the chancery copy

---

14   PDS I. Ivan III's 1490 letter of treaty is in cols. 37-38, his suggested draft of Maximilian's corresponding letter (see below) in cols. 38-40. The publication principles include the use of the 19th-century Russian alphabet and orthography, capitalization of titles and proper names, line returns, etc. Bojcov writes that "the quality and specifics of this edition need a separate discussion" (Kak uvideli, p. 165, note 8).

15   http://rgada.info/kueh/index.php?T1=&Sk=30&B1 (click the item named Ф. 32. Оп. 1. Ед. хр. 1 = Книга Посольского приказа по дипломатическим сношениям с Австрией и Германской империей 1488-1517 гг.).

16   PDS I, col. 41. Alef, Origins, pp. 269-270.

17   See note 15 above. Ivan's letter to Maximilian is on folios 40ob–42, his suggested draft of Maximilian's corresponding letter on folios 42–43ob. I am grateful to Professor M. M. Krom for the reference.

if they themselves are identical, presuming that a scribe would not make the same error twice. A comparison reveals a few subtle, insignificant differences between the two copies consisting of three cases of spelling (*tobe/tebe, božieju/ božeju* and *p"skovskii/pskov"skim*), three missing but grammatically unnecessary prepositions, and one change between the personal pronouns *s nami* (with us) and *so mnoju* (with me) Otherwise, the accordance is complete and the embassy book copy therefore an essentially correct rendering of the chancery copy, which in turn was most likely a correct or near correct rendering of the original.

A. The Danish Texts

Below I reconstruct the missing originals of the treaties of 1493, 1506, 1514 and 1516 based on the following general considerations:

Text Corpus A:[18] Items being verbatim identical between *1493 and *1506 represent the text of all original acts and need no reconstruction. They are omitted from the reconstructions that follow. Items being *structurally* identical between the two need reconstruction of persons, titles, epithets and dates, but not of the text framing them.

Text Corpus B: The text of *1493 is taken to represent the text of all original acts. The text of *1506 exhibits a few minor discrepancies in items 12, 20, 23, 26, 29 and 31, but these are either errors of transcription or deliberate changes entered during the copying of the 1506 treaty in 1514 when Christian II could have used the reversal of the treaty-making procedure (p. 78) to fine-tune a few words and syntagms for purely stylistic reasons. They may or may not have been entered in the original Danish acts of 1514 and 1516, but they are so minimal that they can be disregarded in the reconstructions, not least because they are not reflected in the Russian text of *1516. A more serious discrepancy in item 30 is discussed on p. 137 and the changed sigillation formula in item 39 on p. 141. Only items in need of revision are included in the reconstructions below.

Each of the reconstructions is followed by comments explaining my arguments for changing individual items into what I consider to have been the wording of the lost original acts.

---

18 For Text Corpus A and B, see pp. 128–30.

1. King Hans to Ivan III, 1493

	Reconstructed Text Items	Translation
00	~~Jn nomine sancte trinitatis~~	In the name of the holy trinity.
02 & 33	Nos Johannes, Dei gracia Dacie, Noruegie, slauorum gottorumque rex, electus in regem Suecie, dux slesuicensis ac Holsacie, Stormarie et Ditmercie dux, comes in Oldenborg et Delmenhorst	We Hans, by the grace of God King of Denmark, Norway, the Slavs and the Goths, Elected King of Sweden, Duke of Schleswig and Duke of Holstein, Stormarn, and Ditmerschen, Count in Oldenburg and Delmenhorst
05	cum illustrissimo et potentissimo [principe et] domino Johanne, tocius Rutzsie imperatore, magno duce Volodimerie, Muscouie, Nouogardie, Plescouie, Otpherie, Vngarie, Vetolsy, Permie, Bolgardie etc	with the most excellent and mighty [prince and] lord Ivan, Emperor of all Russia, Grand Prince of Vladimir, Moscow, Novgorod, Pskov, Tver', Jugra, Vjatka, Perm', Bulgar etc.
10	Et nos esse vnum cum fratre nostro contra suum inimicum et hostem Stenonem Stwre regnj Suecie gubernatorem	And we shall be one with our brother against his adversary and enemy Sten Sture, regent of the kingdom of Sweden
11	Et qum aliquis nostrum incipiet lites contra Stenonem Stwre	And when one of us joins battle against Sten Sture
13	Et nos erimus fratri nostro in auxilium contra Stenonem Sture quantum nobis possibile est in veritate absque dolo	And we shall come to the aid of our brother against Sten Sture as much as we can, in truth and without guile
14	et ipse nobis erit in auxilium in veritate absque dolo quantum sibi possibile est contra Stenonem Stwre	And he will come to our aid in truth and without guile as much as he can against Sten Sture
19	Et piscatorie venaciones et alij vsus […]	And fishing, hunting and other rights […]
20	Et que hactenus hucusque ad istud nostrum pactum inter ambo regna nostra et nostros subditos […]	And what has hitherto, up to [the conclusion of] this our pact, been done between our two realms and our subjects […]

30	Et quod soluere tenentur [nostre/more] terre, soluant consuetum	And what they must pay [to our land/ according to the habit of the land], they pay according to custom.
36	[principi et] domino Johanne, tocius Rutzsie imperatori, magno duci Volodi- merie, Muscouie, Nouogardie, Plescouie, Otpherie, Vngarie, Vetolsy, Permie, Bolgardie etc	[prince and] lord Ivan, Emperor of all Russia, Grand Prince of Vladimir, Moscow, Novgorod, Pskov, Tver', Jugra, Vjatka, Perm', Bulgar etc.

Comments
Item 00

The invocation of the holy trinity does not appear in *1490, *1506 or *1516. In addition, it is absent in Maximilian's corresponding letter to Ivan III of 1491.[19] In general, Russian inter-princely treaties do not use invocations,[20] whereas grand princely *testaments* do.[21] It is therefore unlikely that the original diploma of King Hans included one. The reason why the copyist entered it in the transcript-cum-draft is unknown.

Items 02 and 33

The *intitulatio* in *1493, item 02, is incorrect. Up to his Swedish coronation in 1497, King Hans did not use the title *rex Suecie*, but consistently referred to himself as *electus in regem Suecie* (elected King of Sweden) in his entire known correspondence.[22] It may safely be assumed that the person who produced *1493 in 1506 entered the *then* correct title in the text directly in the process of copying the chancery copy of the 1493 treaty. By contrast, he clearly forgot to do the same once he got to the eschatocol (*1493, item 33). Here he first copied the title as it appeared in the 1493 chancery copy, then crossed out the parts no longer valid and entered the correct 1506 title above the line, as evident from this image of the document:

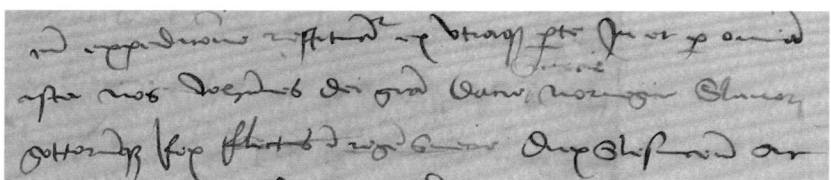

Suecie

Beginning line two word two, the text reads *nos Johannes dei gracia Dacie / Noruegie slauorum gottorumque rex electus in regem Suecie dux Slesuicensis ac [...]*. The revisions support the conclusion that the title used by King Hans in his letter of treaty of 1493 included the *electus* element.

---

19 Lichnowsky, Section C, No. X, pp. DCCLIII–DCCLV.
20 DDG, passim.
21 DDG, passim.
22 Missiver I–II, passim; Aarsberetninger I, passim.

Item 05

The word *potenti* in *1493 must be a copying error. It consistently appears as *potentissimo* in European treaties, including *1506 and Vasilij III's first missive to King Hans in 1506 which was most likely inspired by the latter's letter of treaty of 1493 under review here.[23] On the terms *imperator* and *magnus dux*, see below, pp. 146, 151. On the bracketed *princeps et*, see below p. 140, item 05.

The number and sequence of the lands ruled by Ivan III corresponds to the list in *1490, the two Danish copies, and Vasilij III's 1506 missive to King Hans.[24] I retain the spelling of *1493 in the reconstruction. It could be flawed by the copyist, but is actually maintained, with two exceptions, in Vasilij III's 1506 missive to King Hans, the exceptions being *Ferie* for *Otpherie* (Tver') and *Vetkie* for *Vetolsy* (Vjatka).

Items 10, 11 and 14

The crossed-out sections in *1493 must reflect the original text of 1493 when Sten Sture was the regent of Sweden. They were crossed out to revise them in accordance with the realia of 1506.

Item 13

I add *contra Stenonem Sture* in analogy with item 14 as well as items 13 and 14 in *1516.

Item 19

Piscarie in *1493 must be a copying error, as the word is an adjective. Item 18 has the correct *piscatorie* (fishing waters) as does *1506, items 18 and 19. The error was surely corrected when the 1493 original was engrossed.

Item 20

Nostrorum in *1493 is possibly copied incorrectly and should be *nostros* as in *1506, item 20.

Item 30

Grönblad interpreted the handwriting of the copyists as a dative *nostre terre* (to our land) in *1493 and an ablative-cum-genitive *more terre* (according to the habit of the land) in *1506.[25] The editors who scrutinized Jahn's publication of *1493 (p. 100) opted for *nostre terre* as well, while Thorkelin (ibid.) read *more terre*, which is why the Russian publication of the text uses this version.[26] The difference is far from trivial, as the meaning of the clause changes significantly depending on version. A close look at the source confirms that the copyist of *1493 really did write *nostre,* not *more*, as appears from the images below, but there is no guarantee that this was also the wording of King Hans' original letter of treaty to Ivan III. The fact that *1506, the text of which was meant to be a word-for-word copy of the treaty of 1493, indisputably has *more terre* is an argument against it. On the other hand, any of the several chancery clerks involved in producing the multiple drafts, originals and copies of the treaties of 1493 and 1506 may have made an error at any stage of the transcription processes, and with so many missing documents it is impossible to determine which version of the syntagm was used in the original letters of treaty. In theory, they might even have been deliberately different.

---

23 Grönblad, Nya källor, 149.
24 Grönblad, Nya källor, 149.
25 Grönblad, Nya källor, 43 and 343.
26 SGGD V, 110.

The Russian version of the 1516 treaty, *a gde prilučitsja im kotoraja pošlina dati i im ta pošlina platiti* (and where they may have to pay a duty, they will pay the duty) is of no help in solving the problem. An extrinsic analysis would probably lead to the conclusion that a Western king would not use the word *terra* to describe the political unit governed by him, as in *nostre terre*, but instead employ the politically correct term *regnum*, as is indeed the case whenever Sweden is referred to in the text as well as in item 17 (*nostra regna*); on the other hand, the Danish envoy may in a slip of mind have been influenced by his Russian counterparts when discussing the paragraph as *zemlja*, i.e. *terra*, was the Russian term for a political unit, not just a "land", item 17 again being a case in point.[27] I therefore leave the problem open in the reconstruction of the original letter of 1493.

Details of *1493 showing the copyist's hand when writing morem terre (item 27) and nostre terre (item 30), respectively.

Item 36

In accordance with other Russian treaties, item 36 leaves out the honorific "cum illustrissimo et potentissimo [principe et]" of item 5. The titles proper are in the dative.

2. King Hans to Vasilij III, 1506

	Reconstructed Text Items	**Translation**
02 & 33	Nos Johannes Dei gracia Dacie Suecie Noruegie slauorum gottorumque rex dux slesuicensis ac Holsacie Stormarie et Ditmercie dux comes in Oldenborg et Delmenhorst	We Hans, by the grace of God King of Denmark, Sweden, Norway, the Slavs and the Goths, Duke of Schleswig and Duke of Holstein, Stormarn, and Ditmerschen, Count in Oldenburg and Delmenhorst
05	cum jllustrissimo et potentissimo principe et domino Basilio totius Rutzie imperatore magno duce Volodemirie Muscouie Nouogardie Plescouie Ferie Vngarie Vetkie Permie Bolgardie etc	with the most excellent and mighty prince and lord Vasilij, Emperor of all Russia, Grand Prince of Vladimir, Moscow, Novgorod, Pskov, Tver', Jugra, Vjatka, Perm', Bulgar, etc.
10	Et nos esse vnum cum fratre nostro contra suum inimicum et hostem Swantonem regni Suecie occupatorem	And we shall be one with our brother against his adversary and enemy Svante, occupier of the Kingdom of Sweden
11	Et qum aliquis nostrum incipiet lites	And when one of us joins battle against

---

27   Gorskij, *Russkie zemli*, p. 6.

	contra Swantonem qui nunc gerit se pro gubernatore regnj Suecie Ericum Turesson capitaneum in Wiburgh aliosque occupatores regnj nostri Suecie infideles subditos atque rebelles	Svante who now purports to be regent of the kingdom of Sweden, Erik Turesson, governor at Viborg, and the other occupiers of our kingdom Sweden, disloyal subjects and rebels
14	et ipse nobis erit in auxilium in veritate absque dolo quantum sibi possibile est contra Swantonem et alios predictos	And he will come to our aid in truth and without guile as much as he can against Svante and the aforementioned [persons]
16	Erimus vnum cum fratre nostro contra hostem et inimicum suum regem Polonie et magnum ducem Letuonie quantum nobis possibile est in veritate absque dolo	We will be one with our brother against his enemy and adversary, the King of Poland and Grand Duke of Lithuania, as much as we can, in truth without guile
26	Mercatores et institores et alij negotiatores [..]	Merchants and vendors and other traders […]
29	As in *1493	
30	Et quod soluere tenentur [nostre/more] terre, soluant consuetum.	And what they must pay [to our land/ according to the habit of the land], they pay according to custom
31	Sclaui et sclaue debitores et fideiussores fures fugitiuj raptores et ceteri malefactores […]	Male and female slaves, debtors and guarantors, thieves, fugitives, robbers, and other malefactors […]
32	Jn et per omnia ista	On and by all this
33	Nos Johannes dei gracia Dacie, Suecie, Noruegie slauorum gottorumque […]	We Hans, by the grace of God King of Denmark, Sweden, Norway, the Slavs, and the Goths […]
36	[principi et] domino Basilio totius Rutzie imperatori magno duci Volodemirie Muscouie Nouogardie Plescouie Ferie Vngarie Vetkie Permie Bolgardie etc	[prince and] lord Vasilij, Emperor of all Russia, Grand Prince of Vladimir, Moscow, Novgorod, Pskov, Tver', Jugra, Vjatka, Perm', Bulgar, etc.
39	appendens hiis nostris fortibus literis sigillum nostrum	Appending our seal to this our confirmed letter
40	Datum in castro nostro haffnense, anno diuine incarnacionis [unknown]	Given in our Copenhagen castle in the year of the Holy Incarnation [unknown]

Comments

Items 02 and 33

    As explained above p. 136, the correct title of King Hans in 1506 appears in the direct, "invisible" revision of item 02 of *1493. The revision accords with the title used by the king from his coronation in Stockholm in 1497 to his death in 1513.

Item 05

    For the title of Vasilij III in King Hans' 1506 original, I use the roster of lands ruled by the grand prince, including their spelling, from his first missive to King Hans in 1506,[28] as the Danish chancery would probably have copied the list to use it for writing the king's letter of treaty.

    *1506 adds *principe et* to *domino* in the title of Vasilij III. This is in accordance with European diplomatic custom that routinely used either *princeps* or *dominus* or *princeps et dominus* when addressing the rulers of Christendom.[29] It is impossible to ascertain whether *principe et* appeared in King Hans' original letter of treaty of 1493 and was simply overlooked by the copyist when he produced *1493, for which reason I place it in square brackets in the reconstruction above. It was most likely added to the text no later than in 1506 (as distinct from 1514), for King Hans addressed Vasilij III *exelentissimo* [sic] *et potentissimo principi et domino* in the covering letter which accompanied his 1506 letter of treaty to Moscow.[30]

Items 10, 11 and 14

    The crossed-out *Swantonem* in items 10 and 11 of *1506 must be the original wording of the item. Indeed, Svante Nilsson was Swedish regent in 1506. Item 14 is an example of an "invisible" revision of the text carried out in 1514 by the copyist entering the name of Sten Sture the Younger (*Stenonem*) in the text directly in the process of transcription. In the reconstruction of item 11 I follow the revisions added to the original text in 1506 (i.e. in *1493) and include the person of Erik Turesson in the list of adversaries even though he was deleted again in 1514 (i.e. in *1506). Erik Turesson Bielke was governor at the Swedish stronghold of Viborg in Finnish Karelia from 1499 to his death in 1511, a position with a high degree of independence due to sheer distance from Stockholm. In this capacity he was responsible for managing Sweden's relations with Novgorod, from 1478 effectively Moscow. He is probably singled out among *aliosque occupatores regnj nostri Suecie* because he was highly successful in counterbalancing Danish influence in Moscow. In 1504, two years before the production of *1493, he had concluded the twenty-year truce with Ivan III's lieutenants in Novgorod referred to above p. 60.[31] As medieval treaties were concluded between individuals, not "countries" or "states",[32] it would have been important for King Hans to enter Turesson by name in the new treaty

---

28   Grönblad, Nya källor, 149; Kopengagenskie akty, 5; Forsten, Bor'ba, p. 155, n. 1.

29   King Hans used the extended version in his first missive to Vasilij III (Grönblad, 6) in full accordance with prevailing practice of the royal chancery (Aarsberetninger I, passim).

30   Grönblad, Nya källor, 162. As explained on pp. 64–5, the letter was probably transmitted in 1507.

31   He subsequently negotiated the 60-year truce of 1510 mentioned on p. 69.

32   P. 57 n. 58.

of 1506. There is circumstantial corroboration of this conclusion in item 10 of *1516 in which Vasilij III declares his intent to "be one with" Christian II "against the son of Svante, Sten Sture, and the governor at Viborg and all of Sweden". The mentioning of the governor in this article may be a relic of the 1506 treaty that the Russians forgot to remove in 1516.

The presence of the epithet "disloyal subjects and rebels" in the 1506 original is strongly suggested by the fact that King Hans used identical language in his covering letter to Vasilij III.[33]

Item 16

The addition of "the King of Poland" to the original text will have taken place in 1506, as Grand Prince Alexander of Lithuania had added the Polish crown to his portfolio in 1501 and was succeeded in 1506 by his younger brother Sigismund in both positions. I add a *magnum* before *ducem*, as the omission is probably a copying error. It would surely have been present in King Hans' original letter of treaty of 1506.

Item 26

The wording "mercatores ceterique negociatores" was probably introduced in 1514 to improve the item stylistically. As the change is not reflected in *1516, I conditionally disregard it in the reconstruction.

Item 29

The slight changes to the wording of the item compared to *1493 were probably introduced in 1514 as well and may be disregarded in the reconstruction.

Item 30

See the discussion of item 30 on p. 137, item 30.

Item 31

The word *fugitivi* in *1506 was apparently first overlooked, then added at the wrong place in the sentence by the copyist. It should be restored to the place it holds in *1493.

Item 32

The copyist doubtless forgot the word *ista* when copying the formula which does not work linguistically without it.

Item 33

King Hans, not Christian II, was King of Denmark etc. in 1506. The title should be the one appearing in *1493, item 33.

Item 36

In accordance with other Russian treaties, item 36 leaves out the honorific "cum illustrissimo et potentissimo" of item 5. The title is in the ablative in 05 and in the dative in 36. The surviving text leaves out "principe et" here, which is the reason I place it in square brackets.

Item 39

The sigillation formula appearing in *1506 is significantly different from the formula used in *1493 and from the meaning conveyed by the corresponding item in *1490 and *1516, as the king's seal is said to be applied (*apposuimus*), not appended. The new formula was clearly entered by the copyist in 1514, as King Hans' original letter of treaty will have had a pendant seal. For a possible reason for the deviation in 1514, see the discussion

---

33   P. 59 n. 70.

on p. 141, item 39. There is no doubt that Christian II's final letter of treaty of 1516 was sealed with a *pendant* seal, as he had to reciprocate the expected use by Vasilij III of a pendant golden bull in his forthcoming corresponding letter of 1516. The bull is still attached to the original in the Danish National Archives.[34]

Item 40: Datum

The date of issue of King Hans' original letter of treaty of 1506 (in reality, 1507) is unknown and cannot be reconstructed. It was probably introduced as in *1493: "Datum in castro nostro haffnense, anno diuine incarnacionis […]."

3. Christian II to Vasilij III, 1514 and 1516

As previously stated, it is not possible to identify the "mistake" made by the Danish chancery in 1514 that so offended Vasilij III, but it will have been a minor transgression possibly associated with one of the *intitulationes* (p. 83).

	Reconstructed Text Items	Translation
02 & 33	**1514**: Nos Cristiernus, Dei gracia Dacie slauorum gottorumque rex, electus in regem Suecie et Noruegie, dux slesuicensis ac Holsacie, Stormarie et Ditmercie dux, comes in Oldenborg et Delmenhorst	We, Christian, by the grace of God King of Denmark, the Slavs and the Goths, elected King of Sweden and Norway, Duke of Schleswig and Duke of Holstein, Stormarn, and Ditmerschen, Count in Oldenburg and Delmenhorst
	1516: Nos Cristiernus, Dei gracia Dacie Noruegie slauorum gottorumque rex, electus in regem Suecie, dux slesuicensis ac Holsacie Stormarie et Ditmercie dux, comes in Oldenborg et Delmenhorst.	We, Christian, by the grace of God King of Denmark, Norway, the Slavs and the Goths, elected King of Sweden, Duke of Schleswig and Duke of Holstein, Stormarn, and Ditmerschen, Count in Oldenburg and Delmenhorst
5	cum magno domino Vasilio dei gracia imperatore ac domino tocius Rucie et magno duce vladimerie moscowie nouogradie plescowie [smolencie] tferie jogorie permie wetkie bolgarie et aliis et domino et magno duce novogradie	with the great lord Vasilij, by the grace of God Emperor and Sovereign of all Russia and Grand Prince of Vladimir, Moscow, Novgorod, Pskov, [Smolensk], Tver', Jugra, Perm', Vjatka, Bulgar and others, Sovereign and Grand Prince

---

34 Udenrigsministeriet, Forholdet til udlandet (traktater): E 1 Forholdet til udlandet. Pergamentsbreve (1454-1751) a-83: Rusland 1516 8 2.

	inferioris terre et tzernigowie & rezanie et volock et rsewie et belskie et rostowie et iaroslawie et beloserie et vdorie et obdorie et condinsience et aliis	of Nižnij Novgorod and Černigov and Rjazan' and Volokolamsk and Ržev and Bel'sk and Rostov and Jaroslav and Beloozero and Udora and Obdora and Konda and others
10	Et nos esse vnum cum fratre nostro contra suum inimicum et hostem Stenonem regni Suecie occupatorem	And we shall be one with our brother against his adversary and enemy Sten, occupier of the kingdom of Sweden
11	Et qum aliquis nostrum incipiet lites aduersus Stenonem Swantesson qui se nunc gerit gubernatorem regni et alios occupatores regni Suecie	And when one of us joins battle against Sten Svanteson, who now purports to be regent of the kingdom, and the other occupiers of our kingdom Sweden
14	et ipse nobis erit in auxilium in veritate absque dolo quantum sibi possibile est contra Stenonem et alios predictos	And he will come to our aid in truth without guile as much as he can against Sten and the aforementioned [persons]
16	erimus vnum cum fratre nostro contra hostem et inimicum suum [Sigismundum] regem Polonie et magnum ducem Letuonie quantum nobis possibile est in veritate absque dolo	We shall be one with our brother against his enemy and adversary, [Sigismund,] King of Poland and Grand Prince of Lithuania, as much as we can, in truth without guile
16a	Unknown	
36	magno domino Vasilio dei gracia imperatori ac domino tocius Rucie et magno duci vladimerie [etc. as in item 05]	great lord Vasilij, by the grace of God Emperor and Sovereign of all Russia and Grand Prince of Vladimir [etc. as in item 05]
40	Datum in castro nostro haffnense, anno diuine incarnacionis [??]	Given in our Copenhagen castle in the year of the Holy Incarnation [??]

Comments

Items 02 and 33

> 1514: Christian II was crowned King of Denmark, but not of Sweden and Norway at the time he issued and transmitted his letter of treaty to Vasilij III.
>
> 1516: When he transmitted his second, revised letter, possibly in 1515, he had additionally been crowned King of Norway.

Items 05 and 36

> The Latin title of Vasilij III, as formulated by the *Moscow* chancery, was probably known to the Danish court from a translation into Latin accompanying the Russian letter of

credence to Christian II in 1514.[35] This particular translation has been lost, but the one accompanying the credential of 1515 is preserved in the Danish National Archives.[36] It may be assumed that the credentials were copied rather accurately by the Danish chancery which had no other source for the title when issuing the letters of treaty in 1514 and 1516 (as previously stated, Vasilij had expanded his title significantly in the Habsburg treaty of early 1514, see pp. 83, 114). The title is in the ablative in 05 and in the dative in 36. The abortive letter of 1514 would have left out *smolencie* ("of Smolensk"), as Smolensk had not yet been conquered by the Russians when the Danish envoy David Cochran left Moscow with Vasilij III's original letter of treaty in 1514. Hence I place it in square brackets.

Items 10, 11 and 14

Sten Svantesson, alias Sten Sture the Younger, was elected regent of Sweden in 1512 and died in battle in 1520. Consequently, he is identical to the Swedish adversary in both 1514 and 1516.

Items 16 and 16a

I reuse item 16 from *1506. As *1516 contains the name of the Polish-Lithuanian ruler, Sigismund, it may have been included in the Danish text as well at the behest of Vasilij III, for which reason I place it in square brackets.

As stated on pp. 75–7, item 16 was expanded in 1514 with a long-winded text (marked 16a on p. 109 and in the Appendix) concerning Christian II's participation in Vasilij's projected war against Sigismund, which will have had its Latin counterpart in the Danish letters of 1514 and 1516. As no traces are left of this text, it is not possible to reconstruct its original wording.

Item 36

The item repeats the title of item 05, but in the dative.

Item 40

The date of issue of Christian II's original letters of treaty of 1514 and 1516 is unknown and cannot be reconstructed. The draft of the 1514 treaty, i.e. *1506, has June 3rd, but that may have been changed when the original was engrossed. The item will have been introduced by the phrase *datum in castro nostro haffnense* which appears both in the draft and in *1493.

---

35   Vasilij used his new title in the extant *Russian* version of the 1514 credential. It is omitted from Ščerbačev's publication in Russkie akty, 1, but appears in the original in TKUA, Rusland: Akter og dokumenter vedrørende det politiske forhold til Rusland, l.nr. 73-13, 1493-1578.

36   TKUA, Rusland: Akter og dokumenter vedrørende det politiske forhold til Rusland, l.nr. 73-13, 1493-1578.

B. The Russian Texts

The missing Russian originals of the treaties of 1493, 1506 and 1514 are reconstructed based on the following assumptions:

Text Corpus A: Items being verbatim identical between *1490 and *1516 represent the text of all original acts and need no reconstruction. They are omitted from the reconstructions below. Items being structurally identical between the two documents need reconstruction of persons, titles, epithets and dates, but not of the text framing them. Items 10-14 do not have exactly matching items in *1490 (see above) and need reconstruction of persons, titles and epithets while the framing text of *1516 is taken to represent the text of all missing original acts, with no revisions needed.

Text Corpus B: The text needs no reconstruction, as there is reason to conclude that it did not change between treaties (p. 130). It, too, is omitted below.

Each of the reconstructions is followed by comments explaining my arguments for changing individual items into what I consider to have been the wording of the lost original acts.

1. Ivan III to King Hans, 1493

	Reconstructed Text Items	**Translation**
02 & 33	Мы великий господарь Иоанн божиею милостию царь всеа Русии и великий князь володимерский и московский и новогородский и псковский и тферский и югорский и вятский и пермский и болгарский и иных	We the great lord Ivan, by the grace of God Emperor of all Russia and Grand Prince of Vladimir, Moscow, Novgorod, Pskov, Tver', Jugra, Vjatka, Perm', Bulgar and others
05	с Иоанном кралем датцким и норвеиским и словунским и готцским избранным королем свеиским и князем слезвитским и олшатским исторманским и дитмерским и комит алдемборским и делменгорским и иных	with Hans, King of Denmark and Norway and the Slavs and the Goths, elected King of Sweden and Duke of Schleswig and Holstein and Stormarn and Ditmerschen and Count in Oldenburg and Delmenhorst and others

08	где будет тобе нашему брату Иоанну кралю надобе […]	When you, our brother King Hans, need […]
10	А быти нам с тобою с своим братом заодин на твоего недруга на свейского правителя на Стенстура заодин	And we shall be one with you, our brother, against your enemy, the Swedish regent Sten Sture
11	А как нам будет валка почати с свеиским правителем с Стенстуром	And when we join battle with the Swedish regent Sten Sture
13	И мне тебе помогати на Стенстура в правду без хитрости	And I shall aid you against Sten Sture in truth without guile
14	А тебе нам на Стенстура помогати в правду без хитрости	And you shall aid us against Sten Sture in truth without guile
16	Также и на нашего неприятеля на Александра на великого князя литовского тебе нашему брату быти со мною заодинъ и нам помогати в правду без хитрости	And you, our brother, shall be one with me against our enemy, Alexander, the Grand Prince of Lithuania, and aid us in truth without guile
36	Иоанне кралю дацкому и норвеискому и словунскому и готцскому избранному королю свеискому и князю слезвитскому и олшатскому и сторманскому и дитмерскому и комит алдемборскому и делменгорскому и иных.	Hans, King of Denmark and Norway and the Slavs and the Goths, elected King of Sweden, and Duke of Schleswig and Holstein and Stormarn and Ditmerschen and Count in Oldenburg and Delmenhorst and others
40	А писан на Москве от создания миру в лето [??]	Written in Moscow in the year after the creation of the world [??]

Comments

Items 02 and 33

    I have previously argued in detail that the appellations *velikij gospodar'* (great lord) and *car' vsea Rusi* (Tsar of all Russia), which appear with a slight modification in the title of Vasilij III in *1516,[37] but not in that of Ivan III in *1490, were used for the first time in a Muscovite agreement with a European sovereign in the treaty of 1493 with King Hans.[38] Their use in this particular accord is strongly suggested by the presence in *1493 of the

---

[37] The modification *car' i gosudar'* was introduced by Ivan III towards the end of his life (Pape, Titul Ivana III, p. 71, n. 17).

[38] See Pape, Titul Ivana III, passim, for arguments and documentation.

appellations *illustrissimo et potentissimo domino* and *imperator tocius Rutzsie* which would have been pointless without the use of corresponding Russian terms in Ivan III's letter of treaty, and which must have been entered into the Danish text by the Danish envoy on the suggestion, if not demand, of his Russian interlocutors. (As will be remembered, the Danish text was written at the close of the negotiations in Moscow, not after the return of the envoy to Copenhagen.) The fact that *illustrissimo et potentissimo domino* is not a direct translation of the Russian *velikij gospodar'* is immaterial, as the Danish envoy clearly adapted his translation to prevailing norms in Western treaties (p. 116 n. i).

The syntagm *i velikij knjaz'* (and grand prince) positioned in front of the list of subject lands in the reconstruction is generally absent in Ivan's European correspondence up to the early 1490s, including his letter of treaty to Maximilian (*1490), his draft of the latter's corresponding letter (p. 133),[39] letters of 1492 to the dukes of Mecklenburg and Saxony,[40] letters of 1493 to Maximilian and Archduke Sigismund,[41] and letters of 1491-2 to Lübeck, Narva and Reval.[42] In 1493, however, the title re-appears in a letter to Grand Prince Alexander of Lithuania in January[43] and a credential to Duke Konrad of Mazovia in May,[44] i.e. a few months before the arrival in Moscow of the first Danish envoy.[45] As it is likewise present in *1493 and in general becomes the standard *intitulatio* of the grand prince after 1493,[46] it may safely be assumed that it was used in the 1493 Russian letter of treaty reconstructed here.

The number and order of the subject lands ruled by Ivan III corresponds to their appearance in *1490, *1493 and Vasilij III's first missive to King Hans in 1506.[47] The spelling of the lands is conditionally taken from *1490.

Item 05

The reconstruction of King Hans' title in Russian is based on the fact that Hans was not King of Sweden, but *electus in regem Suecie* ("elected king" or "king-elect" of Sweden) in 1493 (see the discussion on p. 136, items 02 and 33). The equivalent Russian term in sources concerning Christian II is either *izbrannyj korol' sveiskij*,[48] *izbrannyj na kralevstvo*

---

39 PDS I, cols. 38-40.
40 SGGD V, 19, 20.
41 SGGD V, 26; PDS I, col. 111. The reason for the omission in this period was probably a feeling at the Moscow court that "grand prince" as used in Ivan III's title was inferior to the imperial title in the West with which Ivan wished to align himself. In essence, it was the title of a ruler of lesser lands on a par with archduke, duke, *landgraf*, etc. See Agošton, Titul moskovskogo, p. 129. Interestingly, Ivan retained the grand princely title in his Baltic correspondence in the same period in which he shunned it vis-à-vis European rulers (Pape, Titul Ivana III, passim).
42 PDS I, cols. 87, 96-97.
43 SIRIO 35, 19, p. 81.
44 SGGD V, 28 (Konrad Mazowiecki).
45 For these developments, see Agošton, Titul moskovskogo, pp. 128-129.
46 For examples, see SGGD V, 31, 40, 43, 44, 45 et al.
47 Grönblad, Nya källor, 149.
48 Oration of the Russian envoys to Copenhagen in 1514 (Russkie akty, 2, cols. 1, 3, 5, 7).

sveiskoe,[49] or *narečennyj korol' sveiskij*,[50] of which I have tentatively selected the former. The choice of *kral* instead of *korol'* for "king" is motivated by the shorter chronological distance between the texts of 1490 and 1493 relative to those of 1493 and 1516 and the likelihood that Ivan III and his chancery would have used identical terms for Maximilian (who at that point was *Rex Romanorum*) and Hans.

The sequence of the lands governed by King Hans and the corresponding titles follow Danish custom and will have been dictated to the Russians by Hans Claussen, the Danish envoy in 1493. (The Russians missed the point, though, that the Danish royal title used the appellation Dux twice.) The Russian spelling is taken from *1516.[51] It will probably have differed somewhat in Ivan's original letter, as the spelling of foreign proper and geographical names was curiously haphazard in medieval treaties and other diplomatic acts. Note that the Moscow chancery uses the Russian term *knjaz'* (prince) for duke, but the adapted Latin term *komit* (comes, comitem) for count.

Item 10

The structure of the reconstructed item is taken from the two Danish documents with a nod to *1490. It is somewhat different in *1516, probably following the expansion of the paragraph effected by King Hans in 1506 (*1493, item 10), in which year, or the year after, King Hans issued his letter of treaty first pp. 64–5).

I tentatively include the syntagm *na sveiskogo pravitelja* in analogy with *na sveiskogo obderžatelja* in *1516. It is absent in the two Danish texts. The Russian term *pravitel'* (ruler) is used to render the Latin term *gubernator* in *1493. I have found it, albeit used about Sten Sture the Younger (pp. 67 n. 99, 106, item 10), in the oration of the Russian envoys to Copenhagen in 1514.[52]

The syntagm *s svoim bratom* (with my brother) is absent in *1490, but present in *1516 and the two Danish documents, for which reason I include it in the reconstruction, tentatively placing it in the same position as in the Danish documents.

I conditionally use *nedruga* ("adversary") from *1490 instead of the synonymous *neprijatelja* from *1516 because it is chronologically closer to 1493, but either word would be appropriate. However, I put it in the singular, not the plural as in *1516, because there was only one adversary in 1493, as evidenced by the wording of the two Danish documents (*contra suum inimicum*).

For my use of *Stenstura* rather than *Sten Stura*, see the discussion on p. 113.

---

49   Letter of credence from Vasilij III to Christian II in 1515 (Russkie akty, 3). By an apparent mistake, the word *izbrannyj* is missing in Ščerbacev's publication, but it appears in the original document in the Danish National Archives (TKUA, Rusland: Akter og dokumenter vedrørende det politiske forhold til Rusland, l.nr. 73-13, 1493-1578).

50   Letter of credence from Vasilij III to Christian II in 1514 (Russkie akty, 1).

51   The list can also be inferred from the letter of credence to Christian II in 1514 (previous footnote) which has the following alternative spellings: slezvitckomu, olsatckomu, ditmer"skomu, aldenborskomu, and delmengor"skomu. No prior evidence in Russian exists today.

52   Russkie akty, 2, col. 8. Other Russian sources name him either *knjaz'* (duke, prince) or *voevoda* (commander) (SIRIO 35, pp. 85, 255 et al.), but *pravitel'* is more appropriate as it is semantically closer to his position as regent.

Item 11

> I tentatively include the syntagm *s sveiskim pravitelem* in analogy with *s sveiskim obderžatelem* in *1516, item 11.
>
> The adverb *kak* (when) is absent in *1490 but can be inferred from the accordance of *kak* in *1516 with *cuum* in *1493 and *1506.
>
> I include *počati* in the syntagm *valka počati* (join battle, open hostilities) as in *1516 because the Danish version's *incipiet lites* is a calque of it not found in other contemporaneous Western treaties.

Items 13 and 14

> I omit the phrase *i na vsju zemlju sveiskuju* (and against all of Sweden) present in *1516, as it was added to the text by the Danish side in 1506.
>
> The Danish texts include the formula *quantum nobis possibile est* in the item, but since it is absent in both Russian documents, I leave the corresponding Russian formula *gde budet nam močno* out of the reconstruction. The difference between the Danish and Russian items in this respect is not wholly atypical of medieval treaties and probably reflects some of the confusion that will have attended the bilingual negotiations in Moscow. The formula is present in items 08 and 09 in both languages.

Item 16

> The structure of the reconstructed text is based on *1516, item 16 conferred with items 13 and 14 and with a nod to the two Danish texts. It leaves out Poland, as the thrones of Lithuania and Poland were occupied by two different persons in 1493. I include the name of the Lithuanian ruler in analogy not only with *1516, but also *1490, items 10, 11, 13 and 14, despite it being absent in item 16 of the Danish text.

Item 36

> The item repeats the title of item 05, but in the dative.

Item 40

> The date used in *1490, 6998 AM, should be changed to 7001 or 7002 AM in the 1493 reconstruction, the last digit depending on whether the treaty was concluded before or after September 1 which marked the beginning of the new year in the late-medieval Russian calendar (p. 17). Both month and date are unknown. The datum was probably introduced by the words "a pisan na Moskve ot sozdanija miru v leto" as in *1490 (see Appendix).

2. Vasilij III to King Hans, 1506

	Reconstructed Text Items	**Translation**
02 & 33	Мы великий господарь Василей божиею милостию царь [и господарь] всея Русии и великий князь владимерский московский новгородцкий псковский тферский югорский вятцкий пермьский болгарский и иныхъ	We the great lord Vasilij, by the grace of God Emperor [and Sovereign] of all Russia and Grand Prince of Vladimir, Moscow, Novgorod, Pskov, Tver', Jugra, Vjatka, Perm', Bulgar and others
05	с Иоанном королем датцким и свейским и норвеиским и словунским и готцким и князем слезвитским и олшатским и сторманским и дитмерским и комит алдемборским и делменгорским и иных	with Hans, King of Denmark and Sweden and Norway and the Slavs and the Goths and Duke of Schleswig and Holstein and Stormarn and Ditmerschen and Count in Oldenburg and Delmenhorst and others
08	где будет тобе нашему брату Иоанну кралю надобе […]	When you, our brother King Hans, need […]
10	А на твоих неприятелей на свейского обдержателя на Сванта и на выборского наместника и на всю землю свейскую быти нам с тобою съ своим братом заодинъ	And we shall be one with you, our brother, against your enemies, the occupier of Sweden Svante and the governor of Viborg and all of Sweden
11	А как нам будеть валка почати с свейским обдержателем с Свантом и со всею землею свейскою	And when we join battle against the occupier of Sweden, against Svante and against all of Sweden
13	И мне тебе на Сванта и на всю землю свейскую помогати в правду без хитрости	And I shall aid you against Svante and all of Sweden in truth without guile
14	А тебе нам на Сванта и на всю землю свейскую помогати в правду без хитрости	And you shall aid us against Svante and all of Sweden in truth without guile
16	Также и на нашего неприятеля на Жигимонта короля полского и великого князя литовского тебе нашему брату быти со мною заодинъ	Likewise, you, our brother, shall be one with me against our enemy Sigismund, the king of Poland and Grand Prince of Lithuania, and you shall aid me

	и помогати тебе на Жигимонта короля полского и великого князя литовского в правду без хитрости	against Sigismund, the king of Poland and Grand Prince of Lithuania, in truth without guile
36	Иоанне кралю датцкому и свеискому и норвеискому и словунскому и готцскому и князю слезвитскому и олшатскому и сторманскому и дитмерскому и комит алдемборскому и делменгорскому и иных	Hans, King of Denmark and Sweden and Norway and the Slavs and the Goths and Duke of Schleswig and Holstein and Stormarn and Ditmerschen and Count in Oldenburg and Delmenhorst and others
40	[The text of the datum cannot be ascertained]	

Comments

Items 02 and 33

Whether or not the title employed by Vasilij III in his 1506 letter of treaty to King Hans had already then expanded Ivan III's *car' vseja Rusi* with the *1516 term *i gospodar'*, i.e. "Tsar and Sovereign of all Russia", is a moot point. It is highly suggested by the fact that Vasilij in his 1506 missive to the king (p. 64) addressed himself in Latin as "Dei gracia imperator ac dominus tocius Rutzsie et magnus dux Volodemirie [etc.]" (by the grace of God Emperor and Sovereign of all Russia and Grand Prince of Vladimir [etc.]),[53] in which *imperator ac dominus* is a Latin rendition of *car' i gospodar'*. A Hanseatic letter of 1509 testifies to the use of the title in question by that year: *na des Groten Herrn Gebeite* [exhortion] *Wassilie van Gotzs Gnade Keisers unde Herrn aller Russen unde Grotfursten* [of the same lands as above].[54] On the other hand, the Danish text of 1506, if correctly copied in 1514, leaves out *et domino* from the title, but this may well be due to the fact that the person who prepared the Danish letter of 1506 copied the treaty of 1493 directly without noticing the change of title that had taken place in Vasilij's missive. In all likelihood, Vasilij's title had changed in the *Russian* letter of treaty.

The order of Vasilij's subject lands is taken from his missive of 1506 to King Hans (in Latin) in which it differs slightly from both *1490 and *1516 but will probably have been used in the treaty of 1506. I tentatively use the spelling of *1516 for want of a better alternative.

Item 05

King Hans, not King Christian II (as in *1506), was king in 1506. His reconstructed title is confirmed by the inscription in Vasilij's first missive to the king in 1506 in which he appears as *Dei gracia Dacie, Suecie, Noruegie, Slauorum, Gottorumque regi, et duci Slesuicensi, Holsacie, Stormarie, Dytmercieque, comiti in Oldenburg et Delmenhorst etc.* The Moscow chancery overlooked the fact that the term *dux* appears twice in the correct title of King Hans (see p. 118 n. iv).

---

53 P. 115 n. 42.
54 SGGD V, 57.

Item 08

    King Hans (Ioann), not Christian II, was King of Denmark in 1506. Most likely, the phrase used in Ivan's letter of 1493 was reused here.

Item 10

    The reconstructed text is based on the wording of *1516 conferred with the revisions to the text in *1506. It is different from the reconstruction of the item in the letter of 1493 above precisely because of the revisions which will have expanded and probably restructured the Russian text of 1506. Svante Nilsson was regent of Sweden in that year. He will have appeared as *obderžatel'* (*occupator* in the Danish text), not *pravitel'* (ruler) due to the Swedish insurrection against King Hans in 1501.

    I include the section *i na vyborskogo namestnika i na vsju zemlju sveiskuju* in the reconstruction despite its absence in *1506, item 10. It is most likely the Russian version of the revisions to item 11 carried out in 1506, which added the Viborg governor Erik Turesson and *aliosque occupatores regnj nostri Suecie* to the original text of the 1493 treaty (*1493, item 11). Since the addition took place in 1506, in which King Hans issued his letter of treaty first (p. 63), it was likely incorporated in the Russian text of that year, although by mistake not in item 11, but in item 10 where it will have remained through the treaty of 1516 – even though Christian II apparently dropped it when he revised the 1506 treaty in 1514. The name of the governor was probably deemed unimportant by the Russian side.

    The syntagm *na vsju zemlju sveiskuju* (against the whole Swedish land) is most likely the Russian interpretation of *alios occupatores regni Suecie* in *1506, item 11, but influenced by item 15: *i sveiskie zemli dostavati nam* (and we shall appropriate the Swedish lands). "The whole Swedish land" is probably not a spatial, but a socio-political term; in a mandate issued by Maximilian in 1492 for an envoy to Sweden, the latter was to negotiate with "the prelates, nobility and towns of the Kingdom of Sweden" (Lichnowski, p. DCC, 1747).

Items 11, 13 and 14

    The reconstructions are based on *1516, but with Svante Nilsson, not his son Sten Svantesson, as regent and "occupier" in that year. I have only been able to find a reference to Svante Nilsson in Russian in one source which spells his name Швант.[55] Since however his son is addressed here as *[на] свантова сына* (against the son of Svante) I tentatively spell his name with an initial S. For the appearance of "the whole Swedish land," see the previous comment.

Item 16

    For the purposes of reconstruction, I use the Russian text of *1516. I include the name Sigismund in analogy not only with *1516, but also *1490, items 10, 11, 13 and 14, despite it being absent in item 16 of the Danish text.

Item 36

    The item repeats the title of item 05, but in the dative.

---

[55] Swedish-Russian treaty of 1513 confirming the 60-year truce of 1510 in SGGD V, 60, and ST III, 581.

3. Vasilij III to Christian II, 1514

The annulled original Russian letter of 1514 will have been identical to the one that was finally issued two years later, i.e. *1516. Only the titles of the signatories and the date would have been slightly different.

02 & 33	Мы великий господарь Василей божиею милостию царь и господарь всея Русии и великий князь владимерский московский новгородцкий псковский тферский югорский пермьский вятцкий болгарский и иныхъ господарь и великий князь новагороданизовские земли и черниговский и рязанский и волотцкий и ржевский и белский и ростовский и ярославский и белозерский и удорский и обдорский и кондинский и иных	We the great lord Vasilij, by the grace of God Emperor and Sovereign of all Russia and Grand Prince of Vladimir, Moscow, Novgorod, Pskov, Tver', Jugra, Perm', Vjatka, Bulgar and others, Sovereign and Grand Prince of Nižnij Novgorod and Černigov and Rjazan' and Volokolamsk and Ržev and Bel'sk and Rostov and Jaroslav and Beloozero and Udora and Obdora and Konda and others
05	С Крестерном нареченным королем датцким и свеиским и истинным наследником норвеиским и князем слезвитским и олшатскимъ и сторманским и дитмерским и комит алдемборским и дельменгорским и иныхъ	with Christian, Elected King of Denmark and Sweden and Rightful Heir to Norway and Duke of Schleswig and Holstein and Stormarn and Ditmerschen and Count in Oldenburg and Delmenhorst and others
36	Крестерну нареченному королю датцкому и свеискому и истинному наследнику норвеискому и князю слезвитскому и олшатскому и сторманскому и дитмерскиому и комит алдемборскому и дельменгорскому и иныхъ	Christian, Elected King of Denmark and Sweden and Rightful Heir to Norway and Duke of Schleswig and Holstein and Stormarn and Ditmerschen and Count in Oldenburg and Delmenhorst and others
40	Писанъ в нашемъ государстве в нашем граде Москве о созданьи мира лета 7022 апреля въ [??] день.	Written in our realm in our city Moscow in the year 7022 since the creation of the world, on the [??] day of April.

Comments

Items 02 and 33

> The designation *smolenskij* which appears in the title of 1516 should be deleted here as Vasilij III did not conquer Smolensk until after the issuing of his letter of treaty in the spring of 1514 (p. 144).

Item 05

> Christian II's title should accord with the fact that he had not yet been crowned in any of his realms when Vasilij III issued his letter of 1514. Fortunately, the Russian version appears in the letter of credence for his envoys to Copenhagen in that year (p. 174).[56] It leaves out "the Slavs and the Goths", perhaps because they would have been positioned after "rightful heir" which would not apply to them.

Item 36

> The item repeats the title of item 05, but in the dative.

Item 40

> Vasilij III's letter was presumably issued on April 9 or 10, 1514, for which reason the year will be 7022 AM. The exact date is unknown.

---

56   Russkie akty, 1.

Epilogue

With this book and my previously published catalogue of Danish and Muscovite diplomatic missions 1493-1523,[1] I hope to have laid a solid foundation for a deeper, more comprehensive study of the Danish-Muscovite alliance than what has been written so far. With more than fifty registered missions over thirty years, all of which cannot possibly have been empty gestures, the relationship clearly warrants attention in its own right and for what it can tell us about early East-West relations, Danish and Muscovite foreign policy, power politics in the Baltic region, Moscow's incipient diplomacy with the Catholic world and the minutiae of cross-confessional diplomatic exchanges in the late Middle Ages.

Not that Denmark should all of a sudden be perceived as Moscow's paramount ally or the alliance considered the pre-eminent force in Baltic politics of the age. This would be taking the analysis too far. Rather, historians should approach the Danish-Muscovite *confoederatio* as a practical, down-to-earth working relationship in which the parties mutually pressed both their own and their common advantage by communicating their desires, needs, grievances, claims and ideas for joint action in an ongoing diplomatic process. Much came to naught – a perfectly normal feature in medieval diplomacy – but some objectives were attained and some benefits gained, while certain projects would have stood a fair chance of success had it not been for the warfare that repeatedly absorbed the attention of the treaty partners.

Historians have yet to determine whether or not the Russian invasion of Finland in 1495-6 or the Danish invasion of Sweden in 1497, by which King Hans acquired the Swedish crown, were agreed in advance and intended to have been joint ventures and, if so, why they failed this aim. Nor are we certain about the prize demanded by Ivan III for joining the alliance proposed by King

---

[1] Pape, Comprehensive Register.

Hans. In 1498-1501, the grand prince claimed parts of Finland in return for his services, stating in a drawn-out process involving multiple embassies that King Hans had acceded to the claim in the treaty of 1493. This was most certainly not true, but the question remains what Ivan *had* been promised and in what form. I cite these issues because they demonstrate both that the Danish-Muscovite relationship was far from void of real content and that a significant amount of research into the politics of the alliance remains to be undertaken.

While the controversy just mentioned serves as an example of strained yet continuing relations, the commercial policy of Christian II and Vasilij III provides a stellar example of a joint venture that *could* have come to fruition had it not been for the king's unfortunate war with Sweden in 1517-1520 and his deposal from the Danish throne in 1523. Not only did the Muscovite grand prince agree to hosting a group of young Danes for Russian language training. In 1517 he granted Christian II a major commercial privilege (p. 82) which, as a minimum, signalled the shared political ambition of the two rulers to challenge the Hanse dominance of the Baltic trade. Again, the Danish-Muscovite concord mattered and again more research is warranted.

There are many more examples in the sources illustrating the importance the rulers of both countries placed on their relationship. To them, the alliance was a potential vehicle for achieving a constant string of greater or lesser political benefits. Vasilij III asked for and was given Western arms and master artisans by King Hans (p. 66); Ivan III suggested that his son, the future Vasilij III, marry King Hans' daughter to strengthen the alliance and bolster his claim to Finnish teritory. (The king refused, but the proposal confirms his high standing at the Muscovite court);[2] Vasilij III dispatched an increasing number of embassies to Emperor Maximilian via Copenhagen instead of the traditional entry point, Lübeck, presumably because he trusted Christian II to facilitate the journey and guarantee the safety of the route; King Hans successfully asked Ivan III to free the Swedish prisoners of war taken by the Russians during the 1495 invasion of Finland. And so on and on.

Perhaps most significantly it was seen as important by rulers of the Middle Ages to be *in amicitia*, in a mutual bond of friendship with other sovereigns irrespective of the practical gains. As stated in the Introduction, Ivan III in-

---

2   The counterfactual consequences of the proposal are quite breathtaking. Had the marriage taken place, Ivan the Terrible would never have been born!

creased his political prestige by being allied and thereby ranking on a par with sovereign monarchs of the Catholic West. So did King Hans, oddly enough, by allying himself with a schismatic, Orthodox ruler. The Vatican bought the spin – which may actually have been sincere – that his aim with the alliance was to convert the Russians to Catholicism and gave him *post mortem* credit for it. In one of the first treatises on Muscovy written in Europe Albert van Kampen, arguing the pressing need to involve the Russians in the common fight against the Turk, opined that not only was Vasilij III ready to convert to Catholicism, but he had also, "as everyone knows," actively pursued the idea: when news of the upcoming Fifth Lateran Council (1512-17) spread around the world, wrote Kampen, "he [Vasilij], through King Hans of Denmark, with whom he had a close friendship, requested permission from [Pope] Julius [II] to participate in the aforesaid council through his ambassadors."[3] The argument was repeated in a similar treatise written in the same year by Paolo Iovio.[4] In both examples, King Hans was lauded for his foresight in allying himself with the Muscovite convert-to-be.[5]

The fact that the treatises were written in 1525, twelve years after the death of the king and two years after the demise of the Danish-Muscovite alliance, aptly testifies to the perceived importance of that bond by contemporaries. With the risk of repeating myself, modern historians should follow the lead and take a more focused interest in this than has hitherto been the case.

---

3   "His [Vasilij] per Ioannem Danorum Regem quo cum illi auctior amicitia intercesserat petebat sibi a Iulio impetrari, ut dicto consilio per oratores suos sibi interesse liceret." The treatise in question is Albert van Kampen's "De Moscovia ad Clementem VII. Pont. Max. Albertus Campensis" which was written in 1525 and published in 1543. It is published, with a translation into Russian and substantial comments, in Kudrjavcev, Rossija v pervoj polovine, pp. 63-134. The quote is on p. 86.

4   "Paucis enim ante annis Basilius ardente cum Polonis bello, cuum Lateranensis conuentus haberetur, per Ioannem Daciae Regem [...] postularat, ut iter tutum legatis Moschouitis ad urbem Romam praeberetur" (A few years earlier, while waging an ardent war with the Poles, Vasilij during the Lateran Council asked through King Hans of Denmark [...] that Muscovite envoys be given a safe journey to the city of Rome). See Paolo Iovio's "De legatione Moschovitarum libellvs ad Ioannem Rufum archiepiscopum consentinum," written *and* published in 1525, in Kudrjavcev, Rossija v pervoj polovine, pp. 217-306. The quote is on pp. 231-32.

5   The naiveté of these notions was a psychological response to the imminent threat posed by the Osmannic advance in Europe and the desire to strengthen the Western cause by involving the Russians in the crusade against the Turk.

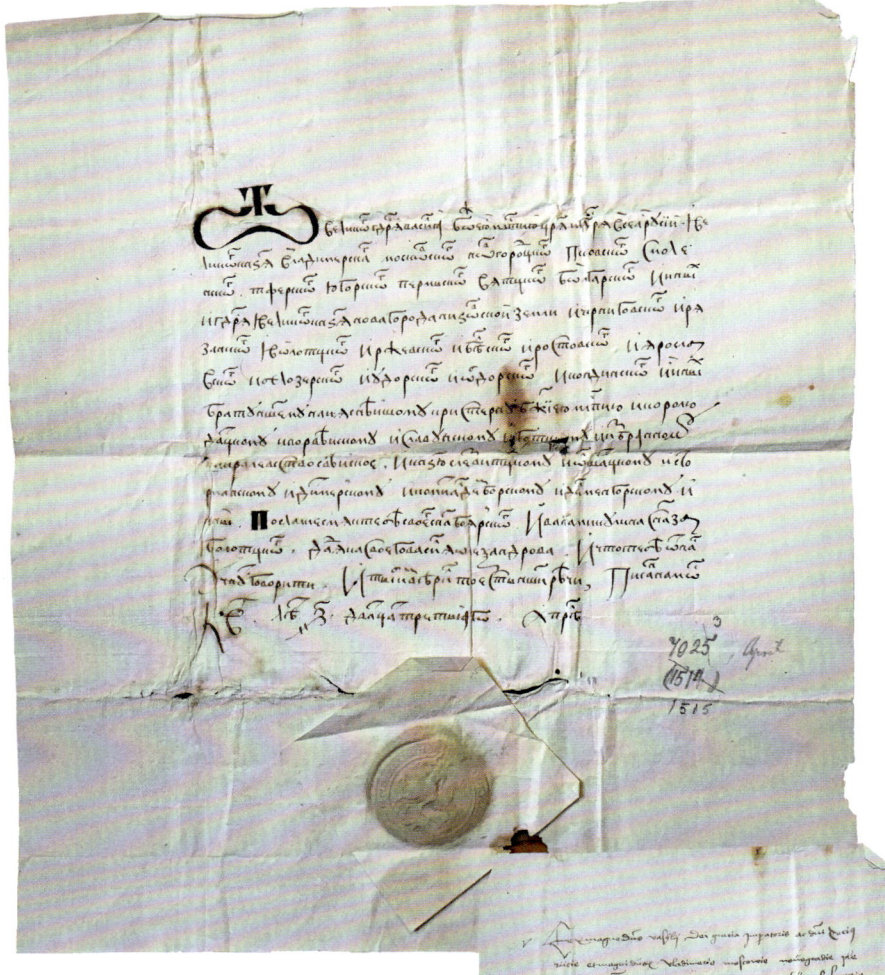

Muscovite letter of credence

The images show Vasilij III's letter of credence for his envoys to Copenhagen in 1515. The original (top) is written in Russian and sealed with the grand prince's wax seal with orig. protective slip. Sometime in the late 1490s, the Muscovite chancery began attaching Latin translations of the diplomatic instruments its envoys handed over to the foreign rulers during their audiences (right). The translations were not sealed.
Danish National Archives. Photos: Carsten Pape

Appendix: Text Matrix

The matrix that follows displays the surviving texts, including the Russian text of 1490 (only excerpts matching items in the other texts), in four columns, with the texts aligned horizontally by item for easy comparative surveying.

I have added interpunctuation and capital letters to the texts to facilitate reading. Further, in the Danish documents (columns 3 and 4) I have eliminated the copyists' revisions if they have no relevance for their interpretation.

There are a few notes to the Russian text at the end of the Matrix. They are marked by [++] in the text.

Russian Texts

	1. *Extant Copy, Ivan III to Maximilian,* *1490 [*1490]*	*2.* *Original, Vasilij III to Christian II, 1516* *[*1516]*
01	По божиеи воле и по нашеи любви.	По божией воле и по нашей любви.
02	Мы Иоанъ, божиею милостию господарь всеа Русии, володимерскии, и московскии, и новогородскии, и пъсковскии, и тферскии, и югорскии, и вятскии, и пермьскии, и болгарскии, и иных,	Мы великий господарь Василей, божиею милостию царь и господарь всея Русии и великий князь владимерский, московский, новгородцкий, псковский, смоленский, тферский, югорский, пермьский, вятцкий, болгарский, и иныхъ [++]
03	взяли есмя любовь и вечное докончание	взяли есмя любовь и вечное докончанье
04	съ своим братом	съ своим братом
05	с Максимианом, кралем римским и князем авъстрьским, и князем бертонским и лургинским, и стырским, и карантенским, и иных.	с Кристерном, королем датцким и свеиским и норвеиским и словунским и готцким и князем слезвитским и олшатскимъ и сторманским и дитмерским и комит алдемболским и дельменгорским и иныхъ.
06	Быти нам с ним въ братстве и в любви и въ единачстве	Быти нам с нимъ в братстве и в любви и во единачстве
07	по сеи грамоте.	по сей грамоте
08	Где будет тобе, нашему брату Максимиану кралю, надобе наша помочь на твоих недругов, и нам тебе помагати где будет намъ мочно.	Где будет тебе, брату нашему Кристерну королю, надобе наша помочь на твоих неприятелей, и нам тебе помогати где будеть нам мочно.
09	А где будет нам надобе твоя помочь на наших недругов, и тебе нам помагати где будет тебе мочно.	А где будет нам надобе твоя помоч на наших неприятелей, и тебе нам помогати где будет тебе мочно.
10	А быти нам с тобою на Казимера	А на твоих неприятелей, на свеиского

Danish Texts

		3. *Extant Copy, Hans to Ivan III, 1493* [*1493]	4. *Extant Copy, Hans to Vasilij III, 1506* [*1506]
00		Jn nomine sancte trinitatis.	
01		Ex voluntate dei et nostro amore.	Ex voluntate dei et nostro amore.
02		Nos Johannes, Dei gracia Dacie, Suecie, Noruegie, slauorum gottorumque rex, dux slesuicensis, ac Holsacie, Stormarie et Ditmercie dux, comes in Oldenborg et Delmenhorst,	Nos Cristiernus, Dei gracia Dacie, slauorum, et gotorum rex, et electus in regem Suecie et Noruegie etc, dux slesuicensis etc,
03		facimus amiciciam et perpetuam confederacionem	facimus amiciciam et perpetuam confederacionem
05	▲ ⋮ ▼	cum illustrissimo et potenti domino Johanne, tocius Rutzsie imperatore, magno duce Volodimerie, Muscouie, Nouogardie, Plescouie, Otpherie, Vngarie, Vetolsy, Permie, Bolgardie, etc,	cum jllustrissimo et potentissimo principe [et] domino Basilio, totius Rutzie imperatore, magno duce Wolodimerie, Muscouie, Nouogardie, Plescouie, Muscouie, Nouogardie, Plescouie, Otpherie, Jugorie, Wetkie, Permie, Bulgardie, etc,
04		ffratre et confederato nostro carissimo.	ffratre et confederato nostro charissimo.
06		Nos esse vnum cum eo in fraternitate amicicia et confederacione	Nos esse vnum cum eo in fraternitate et amicitia et confederacione
07		per presentes nostras literas,	per presentes literas nostras,
08		ita ut vbi ipse habuerit opus nostro auxilio contra suos hostes et inimicos, erimus sibi in auxilium quantum possibile nobis est.	jta ut vbj ipse habuerit opus auxilio nostro contra suos hostes et inimicos, erimus sibi in auxilium quantum possibile nobis est.
09		Et vbi nos sui indigemus auxilio contra nostros hostes et inimicos, erit nobis in auxilium iuxta suum posse.	Et vbi nos sui indigemus auxilio contra nostros hostes et inimicos, erit nobis in auxilium iuxta suum posse.
10		Et nos esse vnum cum fratre nostro	Et nos esse vnum cum fratre nostro

	- 1 -	- 2 -
	на короля и на его дети заодин и до живота. А тебе с нами быти на Казимера на короля заодин и до живота. [+]	обдержателя на свантова сына на Стенстура и на выборского наместника и на всю землю свеискую быти нам с тобою съ своим братом заодинъ.[+++]
11	[А будет нам валка с Казимером с королем и с его детми]	А как нам будеть валка почати с свеиским обдержателем с свантовым сыномъ Стенстуром и со всею землею свеискою,
12	[и тебе нам весть послати]	и нам межь себя сослатися,
13	[и тебе нам на Казимера короля и на его дети помагати въ правду без хитрости]	и мне тебе на свантова сына на Стенстура и на всю землю свеискую помогати в правду без хитрости.
14	[и тебе нам на Казимера короля и на его дети помагати въ правду без хитрости]	А тебе нам на свантова сына на Стенстура и на всю землю свеискую помогати в правду без хитрости,
15		и свеиские земли доставати нам с одного.[+++]
16		Также и на нашего неприятеля на Жигимонта, короля полского и великого князя литовского, тебе, нашему брату, быти со мною заодинъ и помогати тебе на Жигимонта, короля полского и великого князя литовского, в правду без хитрости. [++++]
17		А которые наши земли сошлись с твоими землями, ино рубежь ведати на обе стороны по старине.
18		Которые земли и воды и ухожаи и ловища и всякие угодья издавна

	- 3 -	- 4 -
	contra suum inimicum et hostem, ~~Stenonem Stwre, regnj Suecie gubernatorem~~ *Swantonem regni Suecie occupatorem.*	contra suum inimicum et hostem, ~~Swantonem~~ *Stenonem*, regni Suecie occupatorem.
11	Et qum aliquis nostrum incipiet lites contra ~~Stenonem Stwre,~~ *~~inimicum nostrum,~~ et aduersus Swantonem, qui nunc gerit se pro gubernatore regnj, Suecie Ericum Stwre, capitaneum in Wiburgh, aliosque occupatores regnj nostri Suecie, infideles subditos atque rebelles,*	Et qum aliquis *nostrum* incipiet lites aduersus ~~Swantonem~~ *Stenonem* Swantesson, qui se nunc gerit gubernatorem regni, et alios occupatores regni Suecie,
12	tunc prius inter nos alterutrj significabimus.	tunc prius inter nos alter alteri significabit.
13	Et nos erimus fratri nostro in auxilium, quantum nobis possibile est, in veritate absque dolo.	Et nos erimus fratri nostro in auxilium, quantum nobis possibile est, et in *veritate* absque dolo.
14	Et ipse nobis erit in auxilium, in veritate absque dolo, quantum sibi possibile est, contra ~~Stenonem Stwre~~ *Swantonem et alios predictos,*	Et ipse nobis erit in auxilium, in veritate absque dolo, quantum sibi possibile est, contra Stenonem et alios predictos,
15	ut possimus recuperare et obtinere regnum Suecie.	vt possumus recuperare et optinere regnum Suecie.
16	Erimus vnum cum fratre nostro contra hostem et inimicum suum, magnum ducem Litwanie, quantum nobis possibile est, in veritate absque dolo.	Erimus vnum cum fratre nostro contra hostem et inimicum suum, regem Polonie et ducem Letuonie, quantum nobis possibile est, in veritate absque dolo.
17	Et vbi nostra regna se contingunt mutuo, distinctio siue diuisio erit sicut ab antiquo continuata fuerit.	Et vbi nostra regna se contingunt mutuo, distinctio siue diuisio erit sicut ab antiquo continuata fuerit.
18	Et piscatorie, venaciones et alij vsus, quj sunt in illis aquis et terris et ex antiquo	Et piscatorie, venaciones et alii vsus, qui sunt in illis aquis et terris et ex antiquo

	- 1 -	- 2 -
		потягли к нашим землям, и в те земли и в воды и в ухожаи и в ловища и во всякие угодья тебе и твоим людем у нас и у наших людей не вступатись.
19		А которые земли и воды и ухожаи и ловища и всякие угодья издавна потягли к вашимъ землям, и в те земли и в воды и в ухожаи и в ловища и во всякие угодья нам и нашим людемъ у тебя и у твоих людей не вступатись.
20		А что будет учинилось межи нашими людми, наперед сего до сего нашего докончанья, наезды и войнами и татбами и розбои, того всего не искати ни поминати на обе стороны по се наше докончанье.
21		А вперед что учинится межи нашими людми, каково дело, в сей нашей любви, тому всему судъ и изправа без перевода.
22		А блюсти тебе наших людей и управа им давати с своими людми во всяких делех в своих землях и твоим наместником и всем твоим приказчиком, какъ и своим людем, по вашему обычею в правду без хитрости.
23		А нам блюсти твоих людей и управа им давати с своими людми во всяких делех в своих землях и нашим наместником и всем нашим приказчиком, какъ и своим людем, по нашему обычею в правду без хитрости.
24	А твоим послом и гостем по нашим землям путь чистъ, без всяких зацепок.	А посломъ нашимъ по твоим землям землею и водою путь чистъ без всяких зацепок.

	- 3 -	- 4 -
	nostro attinent regno, nobis et nostris libere cedant absque eiusdem fratris nostri aut suorum impedimento.	nostro attinent regno, nobis et nostris libere cedant absque eiusdem fratris nostri aut suorum impedimento.
19	Et piscarie, venaciones et alij vsus, qui sunt in terris aut aquis ex antiquo ad suum spectant regnum, libere sibi et suis cedant absque nostrj aut nostrorum impedimento.	Et piscatorie, venaciones et alij vsus, qui sunt in terris aut aquis ex antiquo ad suum spectant regnum, libere sibi et suis cedant absque nostri et nostrorum impedimento.
20	Et que hactenus hucusque ad istud nostrum pactum inter ambo regna nostra et nostrorum subditos facta sunt per spolia, rapinas et lites, de cetero non accusentur nec menti tradentur.	Et que hactenus hucusque ad istud nostrum pactum inter ambo regna nostra et nostros subditos facte sunt per spolia rapinas et lites, de cetero non accusentur nec menti tradentur.
21	Et que postmodum ex vtraque parte inter nostros subditos contingunt, iudicium et expedicionem absque temporis longa prolongatione habebunt.	Et que postmodum ex vtraque parte inter nostros subditos contingunt, iudicium et expedicionem absque temporis longa prolongacione habebunt.
22	Et isdem frater noster, suj officiales et procuratores, secundum suam consuetudinem nostros homines foueant et expediant sicut suos proprios, in veritate absque dolo.	Et idem frater noster, sui officiales et procuratores, secundum suam consuetudinem nostros homines foueant et expediant sicut suos proprios, in veritate absque dolo.
23	Et nos, nostrique officiales et procuratores, suos homines quemadmodum nostros nostra consuetudine foueamus et expediamus, in veritate et absque dolo.	Et nostri officiales et procuratores suos homines quemadmodum nostros nostra consuetudine foueamus et expediamus, in veritate absque dolo.
24	Et nostri nuncij et ambasiatores in suo regno viam mundam in terris et aquis absque impedimento habebunt.	Et nostri nuncii et ambasiatores in suo regno viam mundam in terris et aquis absque impedimento habebunt.

	- 1 -	- 2 -
25	А нашим послом и гостем по твоим землям путь чистъ без всяких зацепок.	Также и твоим послом по нашим землям землею и водою путь чистъ без всяких зацепок.
26		А гостем нашим и купцом и иным всяким делным людем ездити по нашимъ землям, землею и водою, торговати и всякое дело делати доброволно, на обе стороны, без всякие боязни.
27		А пошлины и мыта им пълатити как есть обычай в которой земле.
28		А управляти их и обороняти, на обе стороны, в правду без хитрости.
29		Также которых наших людей занесет ветром неволею по морю в твои земли, или твоих людей занесет в наши земли, и нашим наместником и всем нашим приказчиком товару у тех людей ничем не двинути, а пособляти им безпосулно, на обе стороны, без всякие задержки.
30		А где прилучится им котороя пошлина дати, и им та пошлина платити.
31		А холопа, робу, должника, поручника, татя, беглеца, розбоиника, рубежника по исправе выдавати, на обе стороны.
32	А на том на всем	А на том на всемъ
33	Мы Иоанъ, божею милостью господарь всея Русии, володимерскии, и московскии, и новогородскии, и псковскии, и тферскии, и югорскии, и вятскии, и пермьскии, и болгарскии и иных,	мы великий господарь Василей, божьею милостию царь и господарь всеа русии и великий князь володимерский, московский, новгородцький, псковский, смоленский, тферский, югорский,

166   The Early Danish-Muscovite Treaties, 1493-1523

	- 3 -	- 4 -
25	Et sui ambasiatores et nuncij in nostro regno viam mundam in terris et aquis absque impedimento habebunt.	Et sui ambasiatores et nuntii in nostro regno viam mundam in terris et aquis absque impedimento habebunt.
26	Mercatores et institores et alij negotiatores regnorum vtrorumque in vtrisque nostris regnis ex alterutro, in terris et aquis, ambulare, equitare et libere negocianda tractare possint absque timore et perturbacione	Mercatores ceterique negociatores regnorum vtrorumque in vtrisque regnis, in terris et aquis, ambulare, equitare et libere negocianda tractare possint absque timore et perturbacione,
27	consuetis solutis theoloneis iuxta morem terre,	solutis consuetis theoloniis iuxta morem terre,
28	eosque ex vtraque parte fouere et expedire debemus, in veritate absque dolo.	eosque ex vtraque parte fouere et expedire debemus, in veritate et absque dolo.
29	Et si casu aliqui de nostris vento agitati in et ad regna sua deuenerint, vel aliqui de suis in nostro, tunc nos aut ipse, nostri uel sui officiales et procuratores, ex vtraque parte, eorum bona uel mercancias nullatenus impediamus, sed eos iuuare absque precio et impedimento debemus,	Et si casu aliqui de nostris vento agitati in et ad regna sua deuenerint, vel aliqui de suis in regno nostro peruenerint, tunc nos aut ipse, nostri vel sui officiales et procuratores, ex vtraque parte, eorum bona et mercancias nullatenus impediamus, sed eos iuuare absque pretio et impedimento debemus,
30	et quod soluere tenentur nostre terre, soluant consuetum.	et quod soluere tenentur more terre, soluant consuetum.
31	Sclaui et sclaue, debitores et fideiussores, fures, fugitiuj, raptores et ceteri malefactores, qui veniunt de vno regno in alterum, cum expedicione restituantur, ex vtraque parte.	Sclaui et sclaue, debitores, fures, *fugitiui*, raptores, fideiussores et ceteri malefactores, qui veniunt de vno regno in alterum, cum expedicione restituantur, ex vtraque parte.
32	jn et per omnia ista	jn et per omnia
33	nos Johannes, Dei gracia Dacie, *Suecie*, Noruegie, slauorum, gottorumque rex, ~~electus in regem Suecie~~, dux slesuicensis, ac Holsacie, Stormarie et Ditmercie dux, comes in Oldenborg et Delmenhorst,	nos Cristiernus, Dei gracia Dacie, slauorum et gotorum rex, electus in regem Suecie et Noruegie etc

	- 1 -	- 2 -
		пермьский, вятцкий, болгарский, и иных[++]
34	целовали есмя крестъ	целовали есмя крестъ
35	к тебе къ своему брату	к брату своему
36	к Максимиану, кралю римскому, и князю авъстрьскому, и князю бергонскому, и лургинскому, и стырскому, и каратенскому, и иных,	х Кристерну, королю датцкому и свеискому и норвеискому и словунскому и готцкому и князю слезвитцкому и олшатцкому и сторманскому и дитмерскому и комить алдемборскому и делменгорскому и иных,
37	по любви въ правду.	по любви в правду.
38	А по сеи нам грамоте правити.	А по сей нам грамоте и правити.
39	А к сеи нашеи утвержнои грамоте и печать нашу привесили есмя.	А к сей нашей утверженной грамоте и печать нашу привесили есмя.
40	А писан на Москве, от созданиа миру в лето шесть тысячь девятсотъ девятдесять осмое, месяца августа 16.	Писанъ в нашемъ государстве, в нашем граде Москве, о созданьи мира лета 7024, августа въ 9 день.

Notes to the Russian Texts

[+]   At this point the 1490 text continues by specifying the mutual alliance obligations of the two rulers. It includes, *inter alia*, the following stipulations, which I have added in square brackets in column 1, items 11-14 for comparison with the corresponding items in *1516:

и тебе нам весть послати / и намъ тебе на Казимера на короля, и на его дети помагати въ правду без хитрости / и тебе нам на Казимера короля, и на его дети помагати въ правду без хитрости / А будет нам валка с Казимером с королем, и съ его детми

[++] At this point the title of Vasilij III continues as follows:

господарь и великий князь новагороданизовские земли и черниговский и рязанский и волотцкий и ржевский и белский и ростовский и ярославский и белозерский и удорский и обдорский и кондинский и иных.

As the expansion of the title was first used in the treaty with Maximilian of February 1514, it is not relevant for the reconstruction of the previous Danish-Muscovite agreements.

	- 3 -	- 4 -
34	osculatj sumus crucem	osculatj sumus crucem
35	fratri nostro carissimo,	fratri nostro charissimo,
36	domino ~~Johanne~~ *Basilio*, imperatori tocius Russie, magno duci Voledimorie, Muscouie, Nouegardie, Plescouie, Otpherie, Vngarie, Vethelsie, Permie, Bulgarie, etc,	domino Basilio, imperatori totius Rutzie etc,
37	ad tenendum amiciciam et veritatem	ad tenendum amiciciam et veritatem
38	cum nostris presentibus literis patentibus,	cum hiis nostris patentibus literis.
39	appendens hiis nostris fortibus literis sigillum nostrum.	Et ad fortificationem harum nostrarum litterarum, sigillum nostrum apposuimus.
40	Datum in castro nostro haffnense, anno diuine incarnacionis millesimo quadringentesimo nonagesimo tercio, octaua die menssis nouembris.	Datum in castro nostro hafnense etc. 3[a] die mensis Julii, anno xiiij.

[+++] Item 10: In the original, the final word *zaodin* is followed immediately by the phrase *i sveiskie zemli dostavati nam s odnogo*. I have arbitrarily moved the phrase to item 15 to facilitate comparison with the corresponding clause in the Danish texts.
Item 15: See the preceding sentence.

[++++] At this point the text is followed by the anti-Polish clause added to the treaty by Vasilij III in 1514-6 (p. 109, item 16[b]). As it is not relevant for the reconstruction of the previous treaties, it is left out here.

Bibliography

Unpublished Sources

1: Danish National Archives

Udenrigsministeriet, Forholdet til udlandet (traktater): E 1 Forholdet til udlandet. Pergamentsbreve (1454-1751) a-83: Rusland 1516 8 2.

Udenrigsministeriet, Forholdet til udlandet (traktater): E 1 Forholdet til udlandet. Pergamentsbreve (1454-1751) b-425: Rusland 1517 7 2a

Udenrigsministeriet, Forholdet til udlandet (traktater): E 1 Forholdet til udlandet. Pergamentsbreve. Polen.

TKUA, Rusland: Akter og dokumenter vedrørende det politiske forhold til Rusland, l.nr. 73-13, 1493-1578.

TKUA, Rusland: Breve fra russiske kejsere og kejserinder til danske konger, l.nr. 73-1 – 73-2, Storfyrst Vasili III Ivanovitsch af Moskva 1516 – Storfyrst Vasili III Ivanovitsch af Moskva 1528.

2: RGADA (Russian State Archive of Ancient Acts)

Rossijskij gosudarstvennyj archiv drevnich aktov (RGADA), Ф. 32. Оп. 1. Ед. хр. 1: *Книга Посольского приказа по дипломатическим сношениям с Австрией и Германской империей 1488-1517 гг*. Online access: http://rgada.info/kueh/index.php?T1=&Sk=30&B1. Accessed March 23, 2020. Published as PDS I (see Published Sources below).

Handbooks

Allgemeine Deutsche Biographie, Vol. III. Leipzig, 1876 (reprint Berlin, 1967-71).

Ausführliches lateinisch-deutsches Handwörterbuch, edited by Karl Ernst Georges, 8th ed. Hanover-Leipzig, 1913.

Bauer, Richardt W. *Calender for Aarene fra 601 til 2200 efter Christi Fødsel.* Copenhagen, 1868 (reprint 1974).

Čerepnin, Lev V. *Russkaja chronologija.* Moscow, 1944.

Dictionary of Medieval Latin from British Sources. London-Oxford: British Academy, 1975-2013.

Ordbog over dansk middelalderlatin, edited by Franz Blatt. Aarhus, 1987.

Slovar' drevnerusskogo jazyka (XI–XIV vv.). Moscow: Akademija Nauk SSSR, 1988 ff.

Slovar' russkogo jazyka XI–XVII vv. Moscow: Akademija Nauk SSSR, 1975 ff.

Published Sources

Aarsberetninger: *Aarsberetninger fra Det kongelige Gehejmearkiv*, edited by Caspar F. Wegener, Vols. I and IV. Copenhagen, 1852-55, 1866-70.

Acta Pontificum: *Acta Pontificum Danica. Pavelige aktstykker vedrørende Danmark 1316-1536*, edited by Alfred Krarup and Johannes Lindbæk, Vols. IV (1471-92) and VI (1513-36). Copenhagen, 1910, 1915.

ÆDA: *De ældste danske arkivregistraturer*, edited by William Christensen, Vols. IV and V, Part 1. Copenhagen, 1885, 1910.

Bantyš-Kamenskij, Obzor: Bantyš-Kamenskij, Nikolaj N. *Obzor vnešnich snošenij Rossii (po 1800 god),* Vol. I. Moscow 1894.

Breve og aktstykker: *Breve og aktstykker til oplysning af Christiern den Andens og Frederik den Førstes historie*, edited by Carl F. Allen, Vol. 1. Copenhagen, 1854.

BSH IV: *Bidrag till Skandinaviens historia ur utländska arkiver*, edited by Carl G. Styffe, Vol. IV. Stockholm, 1875.

Büschings Magazin: *Magazin für die neue Historie und Geographie*, edited by Anton F. Büsching, Part 3. Hamburg, 1769.

Codex Diplomaticus: *Codex Diplomaticus Regni Poloniæ et Magnus Ducatus Litvaniæ*, edited by Matthias Dogiel, Vols. I and IV. Vilnius 1758, 1764.

Corps Universel: *Corps Universel Diplomatique du Droit des Gens* [etc.], edited by Jean Dumont, Vols. III and IV. Amsterdam-The Hague, 1726 (each volume is subdivided in sections with individual pagination).

Danmarks gilde- og lavsskraaer: *Danmarks gilde- og lavsskraaer fra middelalderen*, edited by Camillus Nyrop, Vol. I. Copenhagen, 1899-1900.

Datskij archiv: *Datskij archiv. Materialy po istorii drevnej Rossii, chranjaščiesja v Kopengagene*, edited by Jurij N. Ščerbačev. Moscow, 1893 (Čtenija Moskovskogo obščestva istorii i drevnostej rossijskich, 1893, Book 1).

DDG: *Duchovnye i dogovornye gramoty velikich i udel'nych knjazej XIV–XVI vv.*, edited by Lev V. Čerepnin. Moscow, 1950.

DN: *Diplomatarium Norvegicum*, Vols. III, edited by Christian C. A. Lange and Carl R. Unger, and VI, edited by Carl R. Unger and Henrik J. Huitfeldt. Oslo, 1855, 1864.

Epistolæ Jacobi Quarti: *Epistolae Jacobi Quarti, Jacobi Quinti, Et Mariae, Regum Scotorum, Eorumq; Tutorum & Regni Gubernatorum; Ad Imperatores, Reges, Pontifices, Principes, Civitates, & alios, ab Anno 1505, ad Annum 1545*, Vol. I. Edinburgh, 1722.

FMU: *Finlands Medeltidsurkunder*, edited by Reinhold Hausen, Vols. V (1481-95), VI (1496-1508) and VII (1509-18). Helsingfors 1928, 1930, 1933. Online version: *Diplomatarium Fennicum* (df.narc.fi).

Grönblad, Nya källor: *Nya källor till Finlands medeltidshistoria*, edited by Edvard Grönblad, Vol. I. Copenhagen, 1857.

GVNP: *Gramoty Velikogo Novgoroda i Pskova*, edited by Sigizmund N. Valk. Moscow-Leningrad, 1949.

Hanserecesse: *Hanserecesse*, edited by Dietrich Schäfer, Section 3, Vols. V and VI. Leipzig, 1894, 1899.

Herberstein, Synoptische: von Herberstein, Sigismund. *Rerum Moscoviticarum Commentarii. Synoptische Edition der lateinischen und der deutschen Fassung letzter Hand, Basel 1556 und Wien 1557*, edited by Hermann Beyer-Thoma. Munich 2007. (https://www.dokumente.ios-regensburg.de/publikationen/Herberstein_gesamt.pdf).

Historiske Aktstykker: *Historiske Aktstykker til Danmarks og Christian II's Historie, fornemmelig fra Aarene 1523 til 1532, af bayerske og nederlandske Arkiver*, edited by Holger C. Reedtz. s. l., 1831.

Huitfeldt, Kong Hans: Huitfeldt, Arild. *Danmarks Riges Krønike. Kong Hans' Historie*. 1599, reprint Copenhagen, 1977.

Huitfeldt, Christian II: Huitfeldt, Arild. *Danmarks Riges Krønike. Kong Christian II's Historie*. 1596, reprint Copenhagen, 1976.

Ideja Rima v Moskve: *Ideja Rima v Moskve XV–XVI veka. Istočniki po istorii russkoj obščestvennoj mysli = L'idea di Roma a Mosca secoli XV–XVI. Fonti per la storia del pensiero sociale russo*, edited by Pierangelo Catalano, Vladimir T. Pašuto. Rome-Moscow, 1989.

Kopengagenskie akty: *Kopengagenskie akty otnosjaščiesja k russkoj istorii*, edited by Jurij N. Ščerbačev, Part 1, 1326-1569. Moscow, 1915 (Čtenija Moskovskogo obščestva istorii i drevnostej rossijskich, 1915, Book 4).

Lichnowsky: Lichnowsky, Eduard M. *Geschichte des Hauses Habsburg*, Vol. 8: Kaiser Friedrich III. und sein Sohn Maximilian, 1477-1493. Vienna, 1844.

Lietuvos metrika: *Lietuvos Metrika (1427-1506)*, edited by Egidijus Banionis. Vilnius, 1993.

Lindbæk, Christiern: Lindbæk, Johannes. "Christiern den andens Ægteskabskontrakt." *Danske Magazin*, Series 5, Vol. VI. (1909): 186-92.

LUB II: *Liv-, est- und kurländisches Urkundenbuch*, edited by Leonid Arbusow, Section 2, Vols. 1-3. Riga-Moscow, 1900, 1905, 1914.

Løffler: Løffler, Julius B. *Gravstenene i Roskilde købstad*. Copenhagen, 1895.

Missiver: *Missiver fra kongerne Christiern I's og Hans's tid*, edited by William Christensen, Vols. I and II. Copenhagen, 1912-14.

München-Samlingen: *München-Samlingen. Kong Christiern II's, dronning Elisabeth med fleres arkiver*, edited by Emilie Andersen. Copenhagen, 1969 (Vejledende Arkivregistraturer XV).

Neizdannye akty: "Neizdannye akty XV–XVI vv. Revel'skogo gorodskogo archiva." *Čtenija v Imperatorskom obščestve istorii n drevnostej rossijskich pri Moskovskom universitete*, edited by Elpidifor V. Barsov, Book 2, Section IV/1. Moscow, 1897.

Olaus Petri: *Olaus Petri Svenska Krönika*, edited by Gustaf E. Klemming. Stockholm, 1860.

Opis': *Opis' arkhiva Posol'skogo prikaza 1626 goda*, edited by Sigurd O. Šmidt, Vol. I. Moscow, 1977.

Opisi: *Opisi Carskogo archiva XVI veka i archiva Posol'skogo prikaza 1614 goda*, edited by Sigurd O. Šmidt. Moscow, 1960.

PDS I: *Pamjatniki diplomatičeskich snošenij s imperieju rimskoju*, Vol. I (1488-1594). Saint Petersburg, 1851 (Pamjatniki diplomatičeskich snošenij drevnej Rossii s deržavami inostrannymi, čast' pervaja: Snošenija s gosudarstvami evropejskimi).

PSRL: *Polnoe sobranie russkich letopisej*, Vols. VI/2, VIII, XII, XIII, XX and XXIV. Moscow, 2001, 2001, 2000, 2000, 2005, 2000.

Regesta diplomatica: *Regesta diplomatica historiæ Danicæ*, Vol. I and 2nd Series, Vol. I/2. Copenhagen, 1847, 1889.

Repertorium diplomaticum: *Repertorium Diplomaticum Regni Danici Mediævalis*, edited by William Christensen, 2nd Series, Vols. IV–VII. Copenhagen, 1932-5.

RK 1977: *Razrjadnaja kniga 1475-1605*, edited by Viktor I. Buganov, Vol. I, Part 1. Moscow, 1977.

Russisch-Livländische Urkunden: *Russisch-Livländische Urkunden*, edited by Karl E. Napiersky. Saint Petersburg, 1868 (Russian title: *Russko-Livonskie akty*).

Russkie akty: *Russkie akty Kopengagenskogo gosudarstvennogo archiva*, edited by Jurij N. Ščerbačev. Saint Petersburg, 1897 (Russkaja istoričeskaja biblioteka, Vol. XVI).

Russkie akty Revel'skogo archiva: "Russkie akty Revel'skogo gorodskogo archiva", *Russkaja istoričeskaja biblioteka*, Vol. 15, Section 1. Saint Petersburg, 1894.

Rymer XII: *Foedera, Conventiones, Literæ, et Cujuscunque Generis Acta Publica inter Reges Angliæ et alios quosvis Imperatores, Reges, Pontifices, Principes, vel Communitates ab Ineunte Sæculo Duodecimo, viz. ab Anno 1101, ad nostra usque Tempora, Habita aut Tractata*, edited by Thomas Rymer, Vol. XII. London, 1711.

SGGD V: *Sobranie gosudarstvennych gramot i dogovorov, chranjaščichsja v gosudarstvennoj kollegii inostrannych del*, Vol. V. Moscow, 1894.

SIRIO 35: *Pamjatniki diplomatičeskich snošenij Moskovskogo gosudarstva s Pol'sko-Litovskim*, Vol. I (1487-1533) = Sbornik Imperatorskogo russkogo istoričeskogo obščestva, Vol. XXXV. Saint Petersburg, 1882 (Pamjatniki diplomatičeskich snošenij drevnej Rossii s deržavami inostrannymi).

SIRIO 41: *Pamjatniki diplomatičeskich snošenij Moskovskogo gosudarstva s Krymskoju i Nagajskoju ordami i s Turciej*, Vol. I (1474-1505) = Sbornik Imperatorskogo russkogo istoričeskogo obščestva, Vol. XLI. Saint Petersburg, 1884.

SIRIO 53: *Pamjatniki diplomatičeskich snošenij Moskovskogo gosudarstva s Nemeckim ordenom v Prussii, 1516-1520 g.* = Sbornik Imperatorskogo russkogo istoričeskogo obščestva, Vol. 53. Saint Petersburg, 1887 (Pamjatniki diplomatičeskich snošenij drevnej Rossii s deržavami inostrannami).

ST III: *Sverges traktater med främmande magter jemte andra dit hörande handlingar*, edited by Olof S. Rydberg, Vol. III. Stockholm, 1895.

Sturekrönikan: *Svenske medeltidens rim-krönikor*, edited by Gustaf E. Klemming, Vol. III. Stockholm, 1867-8. [See Hagnell under "Literature" below].

ULS: *Ustjužskij letopisnyj svod (Archangelogorodskij letopisec)*, edited by Ksenija N. Serbina. Moscow, 1950.

Vertrag Vasilijs III: Stöckl, Günther. "Vertrag Vasilijs III. mit Kaiser Maximilian vom Februar 1514." In *1100 Jahre österreichische und europäische Geschichte. In Urkunden und Dokumenten des Haus-, Hof- und Staatsarchivs*, edited by Leo Santifaller, no. 34. Vienna, 1949.

Weisskunig: *Kaiser Maximilians I. Weisskunig*, edited by Heinrich T. Musper et al., Vols. I and II. Stuttgart, 1956.

Literature

Agošton, Magdolna. "Titul moskovskogo gosudarja i informacija o nem Sigismunda Gerberštejna." *Vestnik Volgogradskogo gosudarstvennogo universiteta*, Series 4, Issue 12 (2007): 127-37.

Agošton, Magdolna. "Titul pravitelja Moskovskogo gosudarstva (1474-1533 gg.)." *Vestnik Volgogradskogo gosudarstvennogo universiteta*, Series 4, Issue 9 (2004): 6-15.

Albrechtsen, Esben. *Danmark-Norge 1380-1814*, Vol. 1. Copenhagen, 1997.

Alef, Gustave. "Diaspora Greeks in Moscow." *Byzantine Studies/Études Byzantines* 6 (1979): 26-34.

Alef, Gustave. *The Origins of Muscovite Autocracy. The Age of Ivan III* (Forschungen zur osteuropäischen Geschichte, Vol. 39). Berlin, 1986.

Alekseev, Jurij G. *Istorija Rossii v èpochu velikogo knjazja Ivana III*, Saint Petersburg 2018. The book is a collective reprint, with new pagination, of the author's previously published works *Osvoboždenie Rusi ot ordynskogo iga* (Leningrad, 1989), *Gosudar' vseja Rusi* (Novosibirsk, 1991) and *Pod znamenami Moskvy: Bor'ba za edinstvo Rusi* (Moscow, 1992).

Allen, Carl F. *De tre nordiske rigers historie under Hans, Christiern den Anden, Frederik den Første, Gustav Vasa, Grevefeiden, 1497-1536*, Vols. I and II. Copenhagen, 1864, 1865.

Andersen, Niels K. and Poul G. Lindhardt. *Den danske kirkes historie*, Vol. III. Copenhagen, 1965.

Arup, Erik. *Danmarks Historie*, Vol. II. Copenhagen, 1932.

Bazilevič, Konstantin V. *Vnešnjaja politika russkogo centralizovannogo gosudarstva. Vtoraja polovina XV veka.* Moscow, 2001 (orig. 1952). Note that the two editions have different paginations; I refer to the 2001 edition throughout.

Bedos-Rezak, Brigitte M. *When Ego Was Imago. Signs of Identity in the Middle Ages*. Leiden-Boston, 2011 (Visualising the Middle Ages, Vol. 3).

Bessudnova, Marina B. "Prevratnost' sud'by (Velikij Novgorod v sisteme russko-livonskich otnošenij konca XV veka)." *Novgorodskij istoričeskij sbornik* (2013): 171-83.

Bisgaard, Lars. *Christian 2. En biografi*. Copenhagen, 2019.

Biskup, Marian. "Rivalität zwischen Jagiellonen und Habsburgern um die böhmische und die ungarische Krone im 15. und Anfang des 16. Jahrhunderts." *Österreichische Osthefte* 32, no. 2 (1990): 269-85.

Bittner, Ludwig. *Die Lehre von den völkerrechtlichen Vertragsurkunden*. Berlin-Leipzig, 1924.

Bojcov, Mikhail A. "Kakim moskovskie posly uvideli dvor Maksimiliana I v 1517 g., da i uvideli li oni ego?" In *Ot teksta k real'nosti: (Ne)vozmoznosti istoričeskich rekonstrukcij*, edited by Ol'ga I. Togoeva and Igor' N. Danilevskij, 162-98. Moscow, 2012.

Borisov, Nikolaj S. *Ivan III. Otec russkogo samoderžavija*, 3rd ed. Moscow 2018.

Bresslau, Harry. *Handbuch der Urkundenlehre für Deutschland und Italien*, 2nd Ed., Vols. 1 and 2/1. Leipzig, 1912-5.

Bruun, Henry. *Poul Laxmand og Birger Gunnersen. Studier over dansk politik i årene omkring 1500*. Copenhagen, 1959, reprint 1975.

Carlsson, Gottfrid. *Kalmar recess 1483*. Stockholm, 1955 (Historiskt arkiv 3).

Čerepnin, Lev V. *Russkie feodal'nye archivy XIV–XV vekov*, Vol. 1. Moscow, 1948.

Černaja, Ljudmila A. "Evropa kak 'Zapad' v russkom srednevekovom vozprijatii." In *Evropejskoe vozroždenie i russkaja kul'tura XV-serediny XVII v.*, edited by Oleg F. Kudrjavcev, 5 ff. Moscow, 2013.

Choroškevič, Anna L. *Russkoe gosudarstvo v sisteme meždunarodnych otnošenij konca XV–načala XVI v.* Moscow, 1980.

Christensen, Svend Aa. and Henning Gottlieb, eds. *Danija i Rossija – 500 let*. Moscow, 1996.

Christensen, Svend Aa. and Henning Gottlieb, eds. *Danmark og Rusland i 500 år*. Copenhagen, 1993.

Christensen, Svend Aa. and Knud Rasmussen. *Politikens Ruslandshistorie*, 2nd ed., Vol. I. Copenhagen, 1992.

Croskey, Robert M. "Byzantine Greeks in Late Fifteenth- and Early Sixteenth Century Russia." In *The Byzantine Legacy in Eastern Europe*, edited by Lowell Clucas, 33-56. Boulder-New York, 1988 (East European Monographs, No. CCXXX).

Croskey, Robert M. *Muscovite Diplomatic Practice in the Reign of Ivan III*. New York and London, 1987.

Crummey, Robert O. *The Formation of Muscovy 1304-1613*. London-New York, 1987.

Daldrup, Oliver. *Zwischen König und Reich. Träger, Formen und Funktionen von Gesandtschaften zur Zeit Sigmunds von Luxemburg (1410-1437)*. Westfälische Wilhelms-Universität Münster, 2009 (doctoral diss.).

Danstrup, John and Hal Koch, eds. *Politikens Danmarkshistorie*, Vol. 5. Copenhagen, 1970.

Duranti, Luciana. *Diplomatics. New Uses for an Old Science*. Lanham, MD and London, 1998.

Enemark, Poul. *Fra Kalmarbrev til Stockholms blodbad. Den nordiske trestatsunions epoke 1397-1521*. Nordisk Ministerråd, 1979.

Feldbrugge, Ferdinand J. M. "The Treaties of Medieval Russia – A Survey." In *International and National Law in Russia and Eastern Europe. Essays in Honor of George Ginsburgs*, edited by Roger Clark, Ferdinand Feldbrugge, and Stanislaw Pomorskij, 157-205. Haag-Boston-London, 2001 (Law in Eastern Europe, No. 49).

Fennell, John L. I. *Ivan the Great of Moscow*. London, 1961.

Fiedler, Joseph. "Die Allianz zwischen Kaiser Maximilian I. und Vasilji [sic] Ivanovič, Grossfürsten von Russland, von dem Jahre 1514." *Sitzungsberichte der Kaiserlichen Akademie der Wissenschaften*, Philosophisch-Historische Classe 13, no. 2 (1863): 183-289.

Filjuškin, Aleksandr I., *Tituly russkich gosudarej*. Moscow-Saint Petersburg, 2006.

Filjuškin, Aleksandr I., *Vasilij III*. Moscow, 2010.

Fisch, Jörg. *Krieg und Frieden im Friedensvertrag. Eine universalgeschichtliche Studie über Grundlagen und Formelelemente des Friedensschlusses*. Stuttgart, 1979 (Sprache und Geschichte, Vol. 3).

Forsten, Georgij V. *Bor'ba iz-za gospodstva na Baltijskom more v XV i XVI stoletijach*. Saint Petersburg, 1884.

Forstreuter, Kurt. *Preussen und Russland von den Anfängen des Deutschen Ordens bis zu Peter dem Grossen*. Göttingen, 1955 (Göttinger Bausteine zur Geschichtswissenschaft, 23).

Gallén, Jarl. *Nöteborgsfreden och Finlands medeltida östgräns*. Helsingfors, 1968 (Skrifter utgivna av Svenska Litteratursällskapet i Finland, no. 427:1).

Gallén, Jarl and John Lind. *Nöteborgsfreden och Finlands medeltida östgräns*. Andra delen + del III: Kortbilag. Helsingfors, 1991 (Skrifter utgivna av Svenska Litteratursällskapet i Finland, no. 427:2-3).

Gasiorowski, Antoni. "Friedensvertragsurkunden zwischen Polen und dem Deutschen Orden im 15. Jhdt." *Folia Diplomatica* II. (1976): 159-71.

Gleixner, Sebastian. *Sprachrohr kaiserlichen Willens: Die Kanzlei Kaiser Friedrichs II, 1226-1236*. Cologne, 2006.

Gorskij, Anton A. *Russkie zemli v XIII–XIV vekach. Puti političeskogo razvitija*. Moscow, 1996.

Grey, Ian. *Ivan III and the Unification of Russia*. London, 1964.

Grischmanova, Marija. "Sprachkontakt und Textstruktur am Beispiel der zwischen der Hanse und Russland ausgetauschten Urkunden aus dem 13.–14. Jh." *Deutsche Grammatik im europäischen Dialog*, edited by Norbert Fries, 1-5. Krakow, 2006,

Grosjean, Alexia N. L. "A time when fools and dwarfs were highly esteemed? Seeking the late medieval Scandinavian herald." In *The Herald in Late Medieval Europe*, edited by Katie Stevenson, 165-98. Woodbridge, UK, 2009.

Hagnell, Karin. *Sturekrönikan 1452-1496. Studier över en rimkrönikas tillkomst och sanningsvärde*. Lund, 1941.

Halecki, Oscar. *From Florence to Brest (1439-1596)*, 2nd edition. Hamden, Connecticut, 1968.

Harris, Jonathan. *Greek Emigres in the West 1400-1520*. Camberley, 1995.

Heise, Carl Arnold Leopold. *Danmarks Riges Historie*, Vol. III/1. Copenhagen, 1905.

Hösch, Edgar. "Die Stellung Moskoviens in den Kreuzzugsplänen des Abendlandes." *Jahrbücher für Geschichte Osteuropas* 15 (1967): 321-40.

Ignat'ev, Anatolij V. et al., ed. *Istorija vnešnej politiki Rossii. Konec XV–XVII vek (ot sverženija ordynskogo iga do Severnoj vojny)*. Moscow, 1999.

Jablonowski, Horst. *Westrussland zwischen Wilna und Moskau. Die politische Stellung und die politischen Tendenzen der russischen Bevölkerung des Grossfürstentums Litauen im 15. Jahrhundert*. Leiden, 1955, reprint 1961 (Studien zur Geschichte Osteuropas, II).

Jahn, Ferdinand H. *Danmarks politisk-militære historie under unionskongerne*. Copenhagen, 1835.

Juzefovič, Leonid A. "*Kak v posol'skich obyčajach vedetsja…*" Moscow, 1988.

Jørgensen, Ellen. "Danske og norske Studerende ved Universitetet i Cølln i Tidsrummet 1476-1559." *Personalhistorisk tidsskrift* 44, Series 8, Vol. 2 (1923): 91-98.

Jørgensen, J. C. *Traktatformalia (Traktatteknik)*. Copenhagen: Udenrigsministeriet, 1964 (unpublished, typed version available at the Royal Library, Copenhagen).

Kämpfer, Frank. "Die Ratifizierung des ersten deutsch-russischen Vertrages von 1514." *Studia philologica slavica. Festschrift für Gerhard Birkfellner*, Vol. I (2006): 237-43.

Karamzin, Nikolaj M. *Istorija gosudarstva rossijskago*. 2nd. ed., Vol. VI. Saint Petersburg, 1819.

Karge, Paul. "Die Ungarisch-Russische Allianz von 1482-1490." *Deutsche Zeitschrift für Geschichtswissenschaft* 7 (1892): 326-33.

Karge, Paul. "Kaiser Friedrich's III. und Maximilian's I. Ungarische Politik und ihre Beziehungen zu Moskau, 1486-1506." *Deutsche Zeitschrift für Geschichtswissenschaft* 9, no. 1 (1893): 259-87.

Kaštanov, Sergej M. *Očerki russkoj diplomatiki*. Moscow, 1970.

Katajala, Kimmo. "Drawing Borders or Dividing Lands? The Peace Treaty of 1323 Between Sweden and Novgorod in a European Context." *Scandinavian Journal of History* 37, no. 1 (2012): 23-48.

Katajala, Kimmo. "The Origin of the Border." In *Vid gränsen. Integration och identitet i det förnationella Norden*, edited by Harald Gustafsson and Hanne Sanders, 86-106. Gothenburg, 2006.

Kazakova, Natalija A. "Danija, Rossija i Livonija na rubeže XV i XVI stoletij." *Skandinavskij sbornik* 25 (1980): 107-17.

Kazakova, Natalija A. "Russko-datskie torgovye otnošenija v konce XV-načale XVI v." In *Istoričeskie svjazi Skandinavii i Rossii IX–XX vv. Sbornik statej*, edited by Nikolaj E. Nosov and Igor' P. Šaskoľskij, 89-104. Leningrad 1970.

Kellerman, Gösta. *Jakob Ulvsson och den svenska kyrkan*, Vol. 1: Under äldra Sturetiden 1470-1497. Uppsala, 1935.

Klose, Dietmar. *Dänemark und der Moskauer Staat bis ins 17. Jahrhundert*. Darmstadt, s. d. [post-1964, M. A. dissertation].

Korpela, Jukka. "Finland's Eastern Border After the Treaty of Nöteborg: An ecclesiastical, political or cultural border?" *Journal of Baltic Studies* 33, no. 4 (2002): 384-97.

Kraft, Salomon. *Sveriges Historia till våra dagar*. Vol. 3: Senare medeltiden, II. Tidsskedet 1448-1520. Stockholm, 1944.

Krom, Michail M. *Roždenie gosudarstva. Moskovskaja Rus' XV–XVI vekov*. Moscow, 2018.

Kudrjavcev, Oleg F. "'Kayser vnnd herscher aller Rewssen': Obraščenie k russkomu gosudarju kak k imperatoru v gabsburgskich dokumentach pervoj treti XVI v." *Drevnjaja Rus'* 63, no. 1 (2016): 41-55.

Kudrjavcev, Oleg F. *Rossija v pervoj polovine XVI v.: vzgljad iz Evropy*. Moscow, 1997.

Leist, Friedrich. *Urkundenlehre*. 2nd ed. Leipzig, 1893.

Lesaffer, Randall. "Amicitia in Renaissance Treaties." *Journal of the History of International Law* 4 (2002): 77-99.

Lesaffer, Randall. "Medieval Canon Law and Early Modern Treaty Law." *Journal of the History of International Law* 2, no. 2 (2000): 178-98.

Lesaffer, Randall. "Peace Treaties and the Formation of International Law." In *The Oxford Handbook of the History of International Law*, edited by Bardo Fassbender and Anne Peters, 71 ff. Oxford, 2012.

Lesaffer, Randall. "Peace Treaties from Lodi to Westphalia." In *Peace Treaties and International Law in European History from the Late Middle Ages to World War One*, edited by Randall Lesaffer, 9-44. Cambridge, 2004.

Lesaffer, Randall. "The Three Peace Treaties of 1492-1493." In *Kalkül-Transfer-Symbol: Europäische Friedensverträge der Vormoderne*, edited by Heinz Duchhardt and Martin Peters, 41-52. Mainz, 2006.

Lind, John. "Den dansk-russiske traktat 1302. Erik Menveds østpolitik og omvæltningen i de nordiske alliance." *Historisk Tidsskrift* 96, no. 1 (1996): 1-31 (with an English summary).

Lind, John. "De russiske ægteskaber. Dynasti- og alliancepolitik i 1130'ernes danske borgerkrig." *Historisk Tidsskrift* 92, no. 2 (1992): 225-63 (with an English summary).

Lind, John. "The Russian-Swedish Border according to the Peace Treaty of Nöteborg (Orekhovets-Pähkinälinna) and the Political Status of the Northern Part of Fennoscandia." *Medieval Scandinavia* 13 (2000): 100-17.

Lind, John. "Scandinavian Nemtsy and Repaganized Russians. The Expansion of the Latin West During the Baltic Crusades and Its Confessional Repercussions." In *The Crusades and the Military Orders. Expanding the Frontiers of Medieval Latin Christianity*, edited by Zsolt Hunyadi and József Laszlovszky, 481-97. Budapest, 2001.

Ljubavskij, Matvej K. *Očerk istorii Litovsko-russkogo gosudarstva do Ljublinskoj unii vključiteľno*. Moscow, 1910.

Lobin, Aleksej N. "Poslanie gosudarja Vasilija III Ivanoviča imperatoru Karlu V ot 26 ijunja 1522 g.: Opyt rekonstrukcii teksta." *Studia Slavica et Balcanica Petropolitana*, no. 1 (2013): 130-41.

Lobin, Aleksej N. "Poslanija Vasilija III velikomu magistru Aľbrechtu 1515 g. iz sobranija istoričeskogo Kenigsbergskogo sekretnogo archiva." *Studia Slavica et Balcanica Petropolitana*, no. 1 (2012): 141-52.

Lundholm, Kjell-Gunnar. *Sten Sture den Äldre och stormännen*. Lund, 1956.

Maasing, Madis. "Infidel Turks and Schismatic Russians in Late Medieval Livonia." In *Fear and Loathing in the North. Jews and Muslims in Medieval Scandinavia and the Baltic Region*, edited by Cornelia Hess and Jonathan Adams, 347-88. De Gruyter Online, 2015.

Martin, Janet. *Medieval Russia, 980-1584*. Cambridge, 1996.

Mattingly, Garrett. *Renaissance Diplomacy*. Harmondsworth, 1965.

Meron, Theodor. "The Authority to Make Treaties in the Late Middle Ages." *American Journal of International Law* 89 (1995): 1-20.

Metzig, Gregor M. *Kommunikation und Konfrontation: Diplomatie und Gesandtschaftswesen Kaiser Maximilians I. (1486-1519)*. Berlin-Boston, 2016 (Bibliothek des Deutschen Historischen Instituts in Rom, Vol. 130).

Mikhailova, Yulia and David K. Prestel. "Cross Kissing: Keeping One's Word in Twelfth-Century Rus." *Slavic Review* 70, no. 1 (2011): 1-22.

Mitteis, Heinrich. "Politische Verträge im Mittelater." In *Die Rechtsidee in der Geschichte. Gesammelte Abhandlungen und Vorträge*, edited by Heinrich Mitteis, 567-612. Weimar, 1957.

Neitmann, Klaus. *Die Staatsverträge des Deutschen Ordens in Preussen 1230-1449. Studien zur Diplomatie eines spätmittelalterlichen deutschen Territorialstaates*. Cologne-Vienna, 1986 (Neue Forschungen zur Brandenburg-Preussischen Geschichte, Vol. 6).

Nicolson, Harold. *The Evolution of Diplomatic Method*. London, 1954.

Nitsche, Peter. "Die Mongolenzeit und der Aufstieg Moskaus (1240-1538)." In *Handbuch der Geschichte Russlands* I, no. 1, edited by Manfred Hellmann, 534-715. Stuttgart, 1981.

Palme, Sven U. *Sten Sture den äldre*. 2nd ed. Halmstad, 1968.

Paludan-Müller, Caspar. *De første Konger af den Oldenborgske Slægt*. Copenhagen, 1874.

Pape, Carsten. *Comprehensive Register of Danish-Muscovite Diplomatic Missions 1493-1523*. https://www.academia.edu/48965631/Comprehensive_Register_of_Danish_Muscovite_Diplomatic_Missions_1493_1523_final_version_.

Pape, Carsten. "Fælles front." *Skalk*, no. 3 (1999): 20-27.

Pape, Carsten. "In fraternitate, amicicia et confederacione: Det dansk-russiske forbund af 1493 og striden om Kalmarunionen ca. 1490-1506." In *Dansk-russiske forbindelser gennem 500 år*, edited by Michael Jensen et al., 11-22. Aarhus, 1993 = *Svantevit: Danish Journal of Slavistics* XVI, 1993, 1.

Pape, Carsten. "Rethinking the Medieval Russian-Norwegian Border." *Jahrbücher für Geschichte Osteuropas* 52, no. 2 (2004): 161-87.

Pape, Carsten. "Three Forgotten Border Treaties: Implications for Our Understanding of the Medieval Russian-Norwegian Frontier." In *Russia-Norway. Physical and Symbolic Borders*, edited by Tatjana Jackson and Jens P. Nielsen, 29-39. Moscow, 2005.

Pape, Carsten. "Titul Ivana III po datskim istočnikam pozdnego srednevekov'ja." *Studia Slavica et Balcanica Petropolitana*, no. 2 (2016): 65-75.

Petersson, Erik. *Furste av Norden: Kristian Tyrann*. Stockholm, 2017. Danish translation: *Fyrste af Norden. En biografi om Christian 2.* Copenhagen, 2018.

Picard, Bertold. *Das Gesandtschaftswesen Ostmitteleuropas in der frühen Neuzeit. Beiträge zur Geschichte der Diplomatie in der ersten Hälfte des sechzehnten Jahrhunderts nach den Aufzeichnungen des Freiherrn Sigmund von Herberstein*. Graz-Vienna-Cologne, 1967 (Wiener Archiv für Geschichte des Slawentums und Osteuropas, Vol. IV).

Pierling [Pirling], Paul. *Rossija i papskij prestol*, Vol. I. Moscow, 1912 (translated from the French original, *La Russie et le Saint-Siège: Études diplomatiques*, Vol. I. Paris, 1896).

Pinborg, Jan. "Danish Students 1450-1535 and the University of Copenhagen." *Cahiers de l'Institut du Moyen-Âge Grec et Latin* 37 (1981): 70-122.

Pisarevskij, Grigorij G. "K istorii snošenij Rossii s Germaniej v načale XVI veka." *Čtenija v Imperatorskom obščestve istorii i drevnostej rossijskich pri Moskovskom universitete*, Vol 2., chapter 3: Materialy inostrannye: 1-21. Moscow, 1895.

Pochlebkin, Vil'jam V. *Vnešnjaja politika Rusi, Rossii i SSSR za 1000 let v imenach, datach i faktach*. Issue 1: Vedomstva vnešnej politiki i ich rukovoditeli. Moscow, 1992.

Queller, Donald E. *The Office of Ambassador in the Middle Ages*. Princeton, N.J., 1967.

Rasmussen, Knud. "Historie og diplomati." In *Dansk-russiske forbindelser gennem 500 år*, edited by Erik Dal, 11-45. Copenhagen, 1964.

Riis, Thomas. *Kongen og hans mænd. Danmarks politiske rigsinstitutioner ca. 1100-1332*. Copenhagen, 2018.

Rogožin, Nikolaj M. *Posol'skie knigi Rossii konca XV-načala XVII vv.* Moscow, 1994.

Roshchin, Evgeny. *Friendship in International Relations: A History of the Concept*. Jyväskylä, 2009.

Roshchin, Evgeny. "Supplanting Love, Accepting Friendship: A History of Russian Diplomatic Concepts." In *Redescriptions. Yearbook of Political Thought, Conceptual History and Feminist Theory*, Vol. 13, edited by Kari Palonen and Tuija Pulkkinen, 125-46. Manchester, 2009.

Sach, Maike. *Hochmeister und Grossfürst. Die Beziehungen zwischen dem Deutschen Orden in Preussen und dem Moskauer Staat um die Wende zur Neuzeit*. Stuttgart, 2002.

Šaskol'skij, Igor' P. *Bor'ba Rusi za sochranenie vychoda k Baltijskomu morju v XIV veke*. Leningrad, 1987.

Šaskol'skij, Igor' P. "Ob odnom plavanii drevnerusskich morechodov vokrug Skandinavii (Putešestvie Grigorija Istomy)." In *Putešestvija i geografičeskie otkrytija XV–XIX vv.*, edited by Mikhail I. Belov, 7-30. Leningrad, 1965.

Šaskol'skij, Igor' P. "Sud'ba gosudarstvennogo arkhiva Velikogo Novgoroda." *Vspomogatel'nye istoričeskie discipliny* 4 (1972): 213-28.

Šaskol'skij, Igor' P. "Èkonomičeskie svjazi Rossii s Daniej i Norvegiej v IX–XVII vv." In *Istoričeskie svjazi Skandinavii i Rossii IX–XX vekov*, edited by Nikolaj E. Nosov and Igor' P. Šaskol'skij, 9-42. Leningrad, 1970.

Schleinert, Dirk. *Pommerns Herzöge. Die Greifen im Porträt*. Rostock, 2012.

Schreiner, Klaus. "'Gerechtigkeit und Frieden haben sich geküsst' (Ps. 84, 11). Friedensstiftung durch symbolisches Handeln." In *Träger und Instrumentarien des Friedens im hohen und späten Mittelalter*, edited by Johannes Fried, 37-86. Sigmaringen, 1996.

Schultz Danmarkshistorie: Vort folks historie gennem tiderne, Vol. II, edited by Aage Friis, Axel Linvald and Mouritz Mackeprang. Copenhagen, 1941.

Selnes, Kåre. "König Christiern II und Russland." *Scando-Slavica* 7 (1961): 306-11.

Skržinskaja, Elena Č. "Kto byli Ralevy, posly Ivana III v Italiju (k istorii russko-ital'janskich svjazej v XV veke)." In *Rus', Italija i Vizantija v srednevekov'e*, edited by Elena Č. Skržinskaja, 153-79. Saint Petersburg, 2000.

Šmidt, Sigurd O. "Carskij archiv serediny XVI v. i archivy praviteľstvennych učreždenij (Opyt izučenija Opisi Carskogo archiva)." *Trudy Moskovskogo gosudarstvennogo istoriko-archivnogo instituta* 8 (1957): 260-78.

Solov'ev, Sergej M. *Istorija Rossii s drevnejsich vremen*, Vol. I. 2nd Ed. Saint Petersburg, s.d.

Steiger, Heinhard. "Vorsprüche zu und in Friedensverträgen der Vormoderne." In *Kalkül—Transfer—Symbol: Europäische Friedensverträge der Vormoderne*, edited by Heinz Duchhardt and Martin Peters, 6-40. Mainz, 2006.

Tiberg, Erik. *Moscow, Livonia and the Hanseatic League 1487-1550*. Stockholm, 1995 (Studia Baltica Stockholmiensia 15).

Tolstikov, Alexander. "From *Mezha* and *Rån* to *Rubezh* and *Gränsen*: Conceptualizing the Russo-Swedish Border in the Late Middle Ages and Early Modern Period." *Revue d'Histoire Nordique/Nordic Historical Review* 19 (2015): 31-55.

Uebersberger, Hans. *Österreich und Russland seit dem Ende des 15. Jahrhunderts*, Vol. 1: Von 1488-1605. Vienna-Leipzig, 1906 (Veröffentlichungen der Kommission für Neuere Geschichte Österreichs).

Ullmann, Walter. *Law and politics in the Middle Ages. An Introduction to the Sources of Medieval Political Ideas*. Cambridge, 1976.

Venge, Mikael. "Københavner-traktaten 1493 og de dansk-russiske forbindelser i 1500-tallet." In *Danmark og Rusland i 500 år*, edited by Svend Aa. Christensen and Henning Gottlieb, 10-33. Copenhagen, 1993.

Venge, Mikaêľ. "Kopengagenskij traktat 1493 goda i datsko-russkie svjazi v XVI veke." In *Danija i Rossija – 500 let*, edited by Svend Aa. Christensen and Henning Gottlieb, 10-33. Moscow, 1996.

Vozgrin, Valerij E. and Aleksandr I. Terjukov. "Ešče raz o naznačenii Ivangoroda." *Vestnik Sankt-Peterburgskogo universiteta*. Istorija, 64, no. 1 (2019): 311-22.

Verwohlt, Ernst. "Kongelige danske herolder." *Heraldisk Tidsskrift* 3 (1970-4): 201-29 (also as separate offprint with the same title, Copenhagen, 1972).

Westergaard, Waldemar. "Denmark, Russia, and the Swedish Revolution, 1480-1503." *Slavonic and East European Review* 16, no. 46 (1937): 129-40.

Wielers, Margret. *Zwischenstaatliche Beziehungsformen im frühen Mittelalter (Pax, Foedus, amicitia, Fraternitas)*. Munich, 1959.

Wiesflecker, Hermann. "Das älteste russische Originaldokument in Österreich?" *Mitteilungen des österreichischen Staatsarchivs* 25 (1972): 141-50.

Wiesflecker, Hermann. *Kaiser Maximilian I. Das Reich, Österreich und Europa an der Wende zur Neuzeit*, Vols. 1 and 4. München, 1971, 1981.

Wimmer, Elke. "Livland – ein Problem der habsburgisch-russischen Beziehungen zur Zeit Maximilians I.?" In *Deutschland-Livland-Russland. Ihre Beziehungen vom 15. bis zum 17. Jahrhundert*, edited by Norbert Angermann, 53-110. Lüneburg, 1988.

Ylimaunu, Timo et al. "Borderlands as Spaces: Creating Third Spaces and Fractured Landscapes in Medieval Northern Finland." *Journal of Social Archaeology* 14, no. 2 (May 2014): 244-67.

Zernack, Klaus. "Handelsbeziehungen und Gesandtschaftsverkehr im Ostseeraum." In *Aus Natur und Geschichte Mittel- und Osteuropas*, edited by W. Schmitz, 116-38. Giessen, 1957 (Giessener Abhandlungen zur Agrar- und Wirtschaftsforschung des europäischen Ostens, Vol. 3).

Zimin, Aleksandr A. *Gosudarstvennyj archiv Rossii XVI stoletija. Opyt rekonstrukcii*, Vol. 1. Moscow, 1978.

Zimin, Aleksandr A. *Rossija na poroge novogo vremeni*. Moscow, 1972.

Zimin, Aleksandr A. *Rossija na rubeže XV–XVI stoletij*. Moscow, 1982.

Zoltan, Andraš. "K predystorii russk. 'gosudar'." *Studia Slavica Hungarica* 29 (1983): 71-110.

Index

Aleksandrov, Vasilij, Muscovite envoy 74

Alexander, Grand Prince of Lithuania, King of Poland 10, 19, 24, 26-8, 34, 43, 54, 57-8, 61, 68, 83, 89, 100, 106, 119, 141, 146-7

Ambassadorial oration, 1514 (Vasilij III to Christian II) 26, 28, 73-4, 78-81, 113-4, 148

Ambassadorial oration, 1515 (Vasilij III to Christian II) 73-4, 76, 78, 80

Archival Inventories, Russian 10, 28, 32, 34-5, 54, 67, 74

Archival Inventories, Danish 33, 52, 64, 71

Baltic, Baltic Area, Baltic Space 12, 14, 39, 46, 49, 147, 155-6

Baltic Sea 45, 56

Bay of Bothnia 44-5

Bille, Ove, Danish Chancellor 33, 64

Bogislaw X, Duke of Pomerania 51-2

Bohemia 33, 45, 49, 86

Boyars, Muscovite 27, 53, 62, 89

Brandenburg, ruling house 45, 69

Byzantium 17, 41, 52, 54, 66

Calendars 17, 149

Catholicism, Catholic World 9-10, 22, 24, 39-43, 49, 65, 82, 155, 157

Chancery Copy 21, 32-4, 36, 91, 102, 130, 131, 132-4, 136

Charlamov, Nekras, Muscovite envoy 85, 123

Charles V, German-Roman Emperor 72, 115-6

Christendom 39, 61, 70, 140

Christian I, King of Denmark and Norway, King of Sweden 47

Christian II, King of Denmark and Norway, King of Sweden 11, 13, 26, 28-9, 31-3, 36, 48, 55, 67, 69-86, 102, 106-8, 113-5, 118-20, 123, 129-30, 132, 134, 141-4, 148, 151-3, 156, 160, Appendix

Christian II, Habsburg marriage 71-3, 76, 120

Claussen, Hans, Danish envoy Inside front cover, 39, 49, 50-54, 96, 126, 128, 138, 147-8

Cochran, David, Danish envoy and herald 39, 56-8, 62-6, 68-9, 73-83, 85, 123, 144

Congress of Vienna, 1515 86

Corresponding Letter of Treaty 19, 22-4, 27-9, 35, 54-5, 66, 68, 75-8, 81, 85, 133, 136, 142, 147

Council of the Realm, Denmark 50, 58, 59

Council of the Realm, Norway 50, 58, 59

Council of the Realm, Sweden 47, 58, 61
Cross–Kissing, see Kissing of the Cross

Danish Letter of Treaty, 1493 31, 35, 36, 39, 54, 57, 63, 76, 91, 101, 123, 127, 136-8, 140-1, 152, Appendix
Danish Letter of Treaty, 1506 31, 35, 36, 62-4, 66, 80, 91, 102, 123, 131-2, 140-2, 148, 151-2, Appendix
Danish Letter of Treaty, 1514 (annulled) 36, 75, 78, 81, 83, 102, 143-4
Danish Letter of Treaty, 1516 76-7, 80-1, 85, 142-3
Danzig (Gdansk) 45, 71, 120
Denmark 12, 16-7, 35, 42, 45-7, 49, 55, 59, 66, 69, 71-3, 114, 129, 155, 157
Dokončal'naja gramota, see Letter of Treaty

Elena Ivanovna, daughter of Ivan III, wife of Alexander of Lithuania 34, 58, 100
Elisabeth of Habsburg, see Isabella of Burgundy
Embassy Book 25-7, 53, 132-4
England, King of 22, 65, 96

Finland 44-5, 49, 51, 60, 66, 101, 140, 155-6
Florentine Union of 1439 42
France, King of 65
Frederik I, King of Denmark and Norway 33, 49
Frederik II, King of Denmark and Norway 11, 34, 120
Friedrich III, German–Roman Emperor 120

German-Roman Empire 42, 69, 82, 86, 132
Gotland 45, 51, 65
Gulf of Finland 44, 45, 60

Habsburg, House of 9, 43, 49, 69, 76, 86, 113, 119-20
Hans, King of Denmark and Norway, King of Sweden Inside front cover, 7, 9-11, 22, 31-6, 39, 46-9, 51-67, 71, 78-80, 83, 91, 97, 99-102, 106, 112, 115, 128-29, 131-2, 135-8, 141-2, 145-8, 150-2, 155-7, Appendix
Hanse, Hanseatic League, the 40, 44, 46-7, 52, 58, 65, 70, 82-3, 99, 151, 156
Herberstein, Sigismund von, Imperial envoy 25, 41, 56, 64, 86
Hungary 9-11, 42-3, 45, 49, 69, 86, 119

Imperial Ban (*Reichsacht*) 59
Imperial Chamber Court (*Reichskammergericht*) 59
Isabella of Burgundy (Elisabeth of Habsburg), wife of Christian II 71-2
Istoma, Grigorij, Muscovite envoy 56, 64-6
Istoma Malyj, see Istoma, Grigorij
Italy, Italian States 41-2
Ivan III, Grand Prince of Moscow Inside front cover, 9-11, 15-6, 19, 22, 24-7, 31-2, 34-6, 39-44, 46-7, 49-54, 57-62, 75, 83, 89, 91, 97, 99-100, 106, 112-13, 117, 119, 127-9, 132-3, 135-7, 140, 145-8, 151-2, 155-7, Appendix
Ivan IV, Tsar of Russia 11, 34, 46, 120, 156
Ivangorod 44-5, 58, 60, 82-3, 85

Jagiellonian Dynasty 9, 11, 41, 43, 49, 52, 68, 86, 100, 106
James III, King of Scotland 65
James IV, King of Scotland 65, 97
Julius II, Pope 65, 157

Kalmar 45, 50, 58

Kalmar recess 47

Kalmar Union 46-7, 58-9

Kalmar Verdict 58-9

Karelia 44, 46, 149

Kazimir IV, Grand Duke of Lithuania and King of Poland 43, 52, 119

Kiev, Kiev State, Kiev Rus' 41, 43, 83

Kissing of the Cross 19, 24, 26-8, 31, 39, 53-4, 63, 66, 73, 75, 78, 85, 89, 95, 105, 112

Kola Peninsula, the 45, 56, 64, 98

Konrad, Duke of Mazovia 53, 147

Lascaris, Antonis, Polish envoy 51-2

Laskirev, Dmitrij, Muscovite envoy 55, 66

Letter of Treaty 22-4, 26-7, 29

Linz 72, 76

Lithuania 9-10, 19, 21, 24-27, 34, 41-3, 45, 49, 52-4, 56-8, 60-1, 68-9, 73, 83, 86, 89-90, 100, 106, 116, 118-20, 141, 144, 147, 149

Livonia 43-6, 51, 60, 69-70, 120

Lübeck 45, 51-2, 83, 85, 147, 156

Mandate 11, 20-1, 28, 30, 50, 62, 71, 73, 96, 126, 152

Margaret, sister of King Hans, Queen of Scotland 65

Matthias Corvinus, King of Hungary 9-10, 34, 42, 119

Maximilian I, German-Roman Emperor (effectively) 9-11, 15, 23, 31, 34, 43, 49, 51-3, 55, 59, 66, 69-74, 76, 81-84, 86, 98, 114-5, 119-20, 127-9, 132-3, 136, 147-8, 152, 156, 168, Appendix

Mecklenburg, Dukes of 51-2, 147

Mengli-girej, Khan of the Crimean Tatars 75

Metropolitanate of Moscow 41

Milan 41

Moldavia 42, 45

Moscow Inside front cover, 9-11, 16, 19, 23-8, 31-2, 34-5, 39-42, 44-7, 49-53, 56-60, 62-72, 74-5, 78, 80-3, 85-6, 89, 91, 97-100, 102, 106, 115, 120, 128-9, 131, 140, 143-4, 147-9, 151, 155

Muscovy 10-3, 16, 19, 21-3, 25, 35, 41-43, 45, 47, 49, 56, 60, 67, 69-70, 83, 89, 98-9, 118, 124, 132, 157

Naples 41

Narva 44-5, 51, 65-6, 68, 70, 72, 74, 147

Nilsson, Svante, see Svante Nilsson

Norway 9, 11, 45, 47, 50, 56, 59, 64, 80-1, 98-9, 106, 143

Nöteborg Treaty, see Treaty of 1323

Novgorod 40-1, 43-6, 51, 60, 65-6, 82, 98-9, 128, 140

Nykøbing 64

Oldenborg, Danish royal dynasty 80

Orthodoxy, Orthodox Faith 9-10, 39-41, 49, 157

Orthodox Church, Russian 42

Ottoman Turks 39-40, 42, 61, 70, 86, 157

Papacy, see Vatican

Philip of Burgundy, son of Emperor Maximilian, father of Isabella of Burgundy 49, 72

Plena Potestas, see Mandate

Poland 26-7, 34, 41, 43, 45, 49, 51-3, 61, 65, 68-71, 73, 81-2, 86, 89, 95, 100, 106, 120, 141, 144, 149
"Polish Clause" (Treaty of 1514-1516) 73, 76-7, 107, 127-8, 169
Polish-Lithuanian Union of 1385 41, 43
Posol'skaja kniga, see Embassy Book
Powers, see Mandate
Preliminary Letter of Treaty 24, 26-8, 32-4, 53, 71, 73, 78, 81, 131
Privilege of 1517 (Vasilij III to Christian II) 82, 156
Prussia 27, 45, 69, 116
Pskov 40, 43, 45, 60

Ralev, Dmitrij, Muscovite envoy 54, 56
Ratification 20-2, 28-30, 71, 82
Rerum Moscovitarum Commentarii 25, 56, 64
Reval (Tallinn) 44-5, 51, 54, 65-6, 74-5, 85, 147
Russia 9, 10, 12, 16-7, 34-5, 40-1, 43-4, 45, 47, 49, 56-7, 65-6, 68, 72, 82-3, 85-6, 100, 107, 116-7, 146, 151
Russian Letter of Treaty, 1490 53, 119, 127-9, 132-3, 136-7, 141, 145-9, 151-2, 159-60, 168
Russian Letter of Treaty, 1493 35, 53, 129, 147
Russian Letter of Treaty, 1506 32, 34, 66, 73, 151
Russian Letter of Treaty, 1514 (cancelled) 68, 76, 78-9, 81, 98, 129, 144, 154
Russian Letter of Treaty, 1516 14, 31, 36, 73, 84-6, 90, 108, 112, 113, 120, 123, 129-30, Appendix

Russian-Lithuanian-Livonian War 60
Ruthenians 41

Saxony, ruling house 69, 147
Seals, Sealing 20, 23-4, 26-8, 34-5, 53-5, 63, 66, 72-3, 75, 77-8, 84-5, 89, 112-3, 141-2
Sestroretsk 44
Sigismund I, King of Poland and Grand Prince of Lithuania 34, 43, 68-72, 74, 76-7, 82, 86-7, 106, 120, 141, 144, 152
Smolensk 60, 69, 83, 154
Stockholm 45, 60-1, 67, 69, 140
Sture the Elder, Sten, Regent of Sweden 47, 57-8, 60-1, 67, 99, 106, 137
Sture the Younger, Sten, Regent of Sweden 67, 99, 106, 119, 140-1, 144, 148
Sukov, Elizar, Muscovite envoy 55, 66, 97
Svante Nilsson, Regent of Sweden 60, 67, 69, 106, 131, 140, 152
Sweden 9, 12, 44-7, 49, 51, 58-62, 67-71, 74, 76, 78-81, 83, 86, 90, 99, 106, 128, 136-8, 140-1, 143-4, 147, 149, 152, 155-6

Tatars 40, 42, 70, 75
Teutonic Order, the 27, 44-6, 64, 69-70, 86, 98, 144, 115-6
Titles, Danish 80-1, 95, 99, 117, 136, 140, 147-8, 151, Appendix
Titles, English 97, 116, 118
Titles, French 117-8
Titles, Imperial 116, 119-20, Appendix
Titles, Polish 116
Titles, Russian 10, 83, 112, 114, 116-20, 138, 140-1, 143-4, 146-7, 151, 154, 168, Appendix
Titles, Scottish 97, 118
Titles, Venetian 116

Trachaniot, Jurij, Muscovite envoy 52
Treaty Form (material) 19-29
Treaty Form (intellectual) 29-31
Treaty-making 19-29
Treaty of 1323 (Nöteborg Treaty) 44-6
Treaty of 1482 (Ivan III–Matthias Corvinus) 9, 10, 34, 42-3, 119
Treaty of 1490 (Ivan III–Maximilian I) 9-10, 15, 42, 49, 53, 119, 127-9, 132-3, 136-7, 141, 145-9, 151-2, 159-60, 168, Appendix
Treaty of 1490 (Hans–Henry VII) 22, 96
Treaty of 1493 (Ivan III–Hans) 9, 11-2, 14-5, 26, 31-3, 35-6, 39, 42, 46-7, 49-58, 61, 63-4, 73, 76, 81, 91-7, 101, 106, 117, 123-5, 127-32, 134-8, 140-2, 144-9, 151-2, 156, Appendix
Treaty of 1494 (Ivan III–Alexander of Lithuania) 21, 24-27, 34, 53-4, 56, 100, 118-9
Treaty of 1503 (Ivan III–Alexander of Poland–Lithuania) 25-7, 42, 60, 89
Treaty of 1506 (Vasilij III–Hans) 11, 14-5, 31-2, 34-6, 58, 73, 75-7, 79-81, 91-2, 95-6, 98-9, 101-7, 117, 123, 127-9, 131-2, 134, 136-42, 144-5, 148-52, Appendix
Treaty of 1509 (Vasilij III–Sigismund I) 82
Treaty of 1510 (Hans–Sigismund I) 69, 71, 86, 97
Treaty of 1514 (Vasilij III–Christian II, annulled) 13, 26, 32, 34, 36, 67-83, 102, 123, 127, 129, 134, 142-5, 153-4
Treaty of 1514 (Vasilij III–Maximilian I) 11, 55, 66, 70, 81, 83, 98, 114-5, 144, 168
Treaty of 1516 (Vasilij III–Christian II) 13-4, 31-3, 36, 55, 67-85, 90, 96, 98, 102, 107-14, 123-4, 127-30, 134, 136-8, 141-5, 148-9, 151-4, Appendix
Treaty of 1516 (Christian II–Sigismund I) 71, 86
Treaty of 1517 (Vasilij III–Teutonic Order) 27, 64, 98, 115
Treaty of 1523 (Vasilij III–Sigismund I) 82
Treaty of 1527 (Vasilij III–Sigismund I) 82
Treaty of Nöteborg, see Treaty of 1323
Turesson, Erik (Bielke), Swedish governor at Viborg 61, 67, 99, 131, 140-4, 152
Turks, see Ottoman Turks
Tver' 34, 119, 128, 137

Ulvsson, Jakob, Archbishop of Uppsala 72
Ustjug 45, 56

Vasilij III, Grand Prince of Moscow 11, 23, 25-6, 28, 31-6, 55, 58-9, 61-4, 66-86, 91, 98, 100-2, 106, 108, 112-9, 123, 128-30, 132, 137-8, 140-4, 146-8, 150-1, 153-4, 156-7, Appemdix
Vatican, the 41-2, 86, 157
Venice 41, 69, 116
Viborg (Vyborg) 45, 65-6
Vilnius 9, 24, 27, 45
Visby, Gotland 45, 65-6
Vladislav, King of Bohemia and Hungary 43, 86

Wallachia 69
West, the (as political space) 9-10, 17, 22-3, 25-31, 39-44, 70, 99, 118, 126, 128, 138, 147, 149, 155-7
White Sea, the 44-5, 56

Zabolockij, Ivan, Muscovite envoy 74
Zajcev, Dmitrij, Muscovite envoy 54, 56